Rehabilitating Inerrancy
in a Culture of Fear

Rehabilitating Inerrancy
in a Culture of Fear

CARLOS R. BOVELL

WIPF & STOCK · Eugene, Oregon

REHABILITATING INERRANCY IN A CULTURE OF FEAR

Wipf & Stock
An Imprint of Wipf and Stock Publishers
199 W. 8th Ave., Suite 3
Eugene, OR 97401
www.wipfandstock.com

ISBN 13: 978-1-60899-884-5
Manufactured in the U.S.A.

For Babe

"To make light of philosophy is to be a true philosopher."

—Pascal

Contents

Foreword

THE EVANGELICAL DOCTRINE OF biblical inerrancy was developed in response to perceived attacks on the Bible over the last 300 years, particularly in the nineteenth century in response to European higher criticism. Inerrancy was once the unquestioned epistemological foundation for evangelical faith. In recent generations, it has become *within evangelicalism* a theological problem needing to be addressed.

Many evangelical thinkers over the last several generations, more so in the current post-evangelical environment, have raised their voices to say that we can no longer marginalize or explain away broadly agreed upon developments in theology, philosophy, and biblical studies that happen to rest uncomfortably with long-standing evangelical thinking. Such a call has created considerable tensions for evangelicals, for evangelicalism's theological identity is rooted in pre-critical European assumptions about the nature of Scripture. Evangelicalism has built its theological identity around a protective mechanism, its intent being not to reconsider core theological commitments of evangelicalism but to find ways of definitively protecting them.

But now, many younger evangelicals are saying openly that inerrancy does not have the explanatory power that its defenders once claimed for it. New paradigms are needed and have been for some time. Evangelicals across the world are eager to engage in conversations that will respect their evangelical heritage but not simply leave things there for the sake of convenience or cause them to fear ostracism should they step outside of well-defended boundaries. The question before us is how post-inerrantist evangelicals can remain in dialogue with their inherited inerrantist evangelical culture while at the same time looking for theological language to move beyond those categories, honoring God and building up the people of God in the process.

Toward that end, these newer evangelicals are sensing the need to create an evangelical culture that not only accepts but is also oriented toward such discussions, where critical doctrinal self-reflection is the norm, not the pariah. These are fresh, young thinkers who, in the true spirit of the Protestant Reformation, want to transform evangelicalism rather than leave it behind.

Over the last several decades, we have seen a recurring pattern, where promising evangelical thinkers leave their evangelical seminaries to pursue further study in biblical studies, theology, and philosophy in secular research universities. In time, they begin to see that an inerrantist paradigm does not explain well certain pressing biblical and historical issues (such as the authorship of biblical books and the historicity of many biblical narratives). In response, this younger generation wants to name the problem for what it is and have a constructive dialogue, becoming primarily interested in proposing better intellectual models of Scripture, ideally ones still conversant with their evangelical culture.

This scenario is common to anyone participating in evangelical academic culture, but it is too often caricatured by inerrantists as a failure on the part of these impressionable youth to hold firm the faith of the fathers. Rather than defend the faith as they should, this new, foolhardy generation has become enamored of the thought of academic fame and fortune and so forsaken their first love. Either that, or they are simply judged as being too incompetent to address the issues at hand, proceeding unaware of the subtleties contained in various tomes written by guiding lights of centuries past.

But surely this caricature is more propaganda than truth; it can hardly explain the current willingness on the part of younger evangelicals to examine critically core elements of their evangelical heritage. The reason that the same issues keep coming up is not some spiritual, moral, or intellectual failure on the part of younger evangelicals. The inerrantist paradigm is being called into question because the paradigm does not have explanatory power and new ones are needed.

The true failure lies with the evangelical culture and how it does not recognize the despondency of the cycle. Younger evangelical leaders are basically left with three choices: They can speak up (and suffer the consequences), keep silent (and so suffer tremendous cognitive dissonance, not to mention a wasting of their gifts for future generations), or leave evangelicalism altogether. Failure to name the cycle for what it is will only perpetuate it.

Evangelical conversations over inerrancy are happening and will continue to happen. The only question is whether they will be conducted openly or on the side, whether gatekeepers will loosen their grip on the control they have over their churches and institutions and join the conversation willingly or have it come upon them through the back door. At the heart of the problem is a question: will we continue to approach these issues in fear, that our faith needs to be protected like a dried and brittle flower, or will we trust God rather than our own intellectual certainty?

There is no more deliberate and persuasive conversation partner in the evangelical world concerning the problems with inerrancy than Carlos Bovell. I know of no one who is both so fully conversant with the evangelical paradigm and also willing to engage openly in an honest and constructive criticism of inerrancy. Any defender of inerrancy who does not address squarely and persuasively the arguments Bovell has laid out here and in his other writings will simply be perpetuating the very problem Bovell exposes. Bovell is not an iconoclast, but a constructive theological voice for post-inerrantist evangelicals. He is an intellectual and spiritual journeyman who is seeking a way forward.

Those who are also looking for a way forward will find here a compelling and knowledgeable conversation partner. Those who resist Bovell's probing questions will nevertheless have to respond and offer an alternate, more convincing paradigm, or rest content with winning minor victories here and there while losing in the long run the very heritage they wish to defend.

Peter Enns
Eastern University
Christmas 2011

Preface

IN *BIBLICAL INSPIRATION*, I. H. Marshall asks the following questions: "If historical statements in the Bible appear to be mistaken, do we not have the ability to question them? If we detect contradictions between different theological statements, have we not the right—and the duty—to choose between them? If we come across moral principles which conflict with our own principles (which may themselves be biblically based), are we not at liberty to question them?" In another place, Marshall observes: "To raise questions like these is probably in itself to pass outside fundamentalism."[1] Fundamentalist or not, these questions and others like them continue to play on my conscience as a believer.

Where does the Bible make truth-claims? What *kinds* of "truth-claims" would be appropriate for a book like the Bible to make? What rationale does a Bible reader have for concluding the Bible makes propositional truth-claims? What indications are there that the Bible is making truth-claims *in specific passages*? How is it that a book can make a truth-claim at all? Is it not usually *authors* who make truth-claims? How can a character in a narrative make a truth-claim? Does a character in a narrative even exist? Is it conceivable that characters in a narrative (if they exist and can make truth-claims) might make some claim that the authors themselves never intend to make? Conversely, is it conceivable that an author might make a truth-claim that a character in a narrative (or the historical figure whom the character represents) never actually makes? Could an author make a claim that "the Bible" is not making? What *is* the Bible anyway? What genre is the Bible that we should expect it to make truth-claims? What does "truth" mean in the phrase "*truth-claim*"? Is truth as "correspondence" the most fruitful way to frame truth when dealing with such a diversity of biblical genres?

1. Marshall, *Biblical Inspiration*, 122; Marshall, "Are Evangelicals Fundamentalist?," 21–22.

If authors are the ones who make truth-claims, do we have an appropriate model of "authorship" for the type of literature the Bible is or for the type of literature the Bible contains or for the way biblical literatures were diachronically compiled? Is the compilation we call the Bible more than the sum of its parts? How do each of the scriptural parts relate to a canonical whole? Is it unavoidable that we adopt a "canon within the canon"? What traditions are responsible for the traditions in the Bible? Is it necessary that the Bible must act as its own tradition? Can the Bible really close itself off from the variety of traditions that formed it? How about from traditions that use it or from traditions that transmit it? What would it mean for bibliology that the Bible has a messy history, a history that scholars can more or less reconstruct to their satisfaction?

When it comes to reading the Bible should I not expect to proceed as I do when reading other literature? Is it not strange that I should be expected to selectively cast aside pertinent data and information that cause problems for inerrancy? Why have I been advised to disarm my critical capacities while reading scripture? Is it telling that I do not tend to do so when reading other kinds of literature? If I think I am reading history in a given book of the Bible and the biblical "historian" includes an account where animals are talking, is this a guiding suggestion that what I initially thought was reporting history is not reporting history after all? Why should I refuse to listen to specialists and accept their disciplinary findings (as I normally would) simply because their findings conflict with inerrantist tradition? Should not the findings of secular disciplines help readers more competently assign genre to the variety of biblical literature?

What would it mean for God to "write" a book? Or a *collection* of books composed and compiled over the course of a millennium? Can God write (or inspire) a myth? Can he write (or inspire) a legend about kings and prophets or perhaps a nationalistic saga? Can he mix and match genres and weave in "history" with "fiction" or can he inspire the biblical tradents to do so on his behalf? What principle might readers use to help identify the difference between history and story in the Bible? What fallout would there be if only small portions of biblical literature turned out to be "historical" in the modern sense of the term?

B. Ramm once declared that scripture is "a record of all that this Triune God has done for the salvation of man."[2] He explained: "Scripture

---

2. Ramm, *Special Revelation*, 185.

is not the whole story; it never was intended to be the whole story; and the people of God do not need the whole story." Ramm considered the book of Acts to be biblically paradigmatic: "*It is a few acts of a few apostles at a few places during a few years* [italics in original]." He clarifies that the years described in the book of Acts serve as "the hinges of history."[3] What rationale can we provide for agreeing with Ramm? What reason is there to extrapolate from the hinges of an ancient story to the hinges of history? I have already tried in print to address some of these questions. In this book, I try my hand at discussing several more.

Inerrancy is a position in bibliology, a locus of evangelical theology treating the doctrine of scripture. Inerrantists hold that the Bible makes propositional truth-claims and that wherever these truth-claims are made in the Bible, the claims must turn out to be true. What effect has inerrancy had on our regard for one another? What effect has inerrancy had on our regard for *outsiders*? To what extent has inerrantist doctrine become shorthand for the whole Christian faith? Why do faculty and staff have to watch what they say with reference to inerrancy in order to keep their jobs? Are students being asked to fight the fight of a bygone evangelical era? If students were minded to join the conversation, do they have an obligation to rehabilitate inerrancy? How are students supposed to go about doing their work as students in an inerrantist culture that is so wracked with fear? Questions like these, of course, are easier to ask than answer and I make no pretense of offering definitive answers. I can only hope to make a small contribution.

I would like to take an opportunity to express my gratitude to family and friends who have been supporting me both in my growth as a believer and as a student of bibliological theory. Special thanks to Peter Enns for taking time to write a foreword for this book. I would like also to acknowledge the work of the ILL staff at Rutgers University libraries as well as the editorial staff at Wipf and Stock Publishers. But most of all, I am thankful for my wife, Jen, who has embarked on this adventuresome life with me, a journey we take together with four magnificent blessings in tow: Jamie, Elena, Mateo and Luisa. May the Lord never cease to bless you and keep you and to make his face shine upon you. Amen.

---

3. Ramm, *Special Revelation*, 169–70.

Introduction

I HAVE WRITTEN THIS book for students of the Bible, mainly students who identify as evangelicals. But not every evangelical student will be helped by it. The chapters that follow are intended for a small, growing segment of evangelical students, one socially rooted in inerrantism but not necessarily academically committed to it. Some may even be convinced that inerrancy is untenable. Either way, an important concession they will grant is that critical scholars understand what the Bible is in ways that inerrantists programmatically cannot. The principal reason for this is that inerrancy works on an ideological level to effectively shield inerrantists from seeing the kind of Bible God has given. The present book does not argue for a "post-inerrantist" perspective but rather assumes students are on the way to acquiring one or perhaps have already managed to come to one.

For such students, inerrantist scholars add insult to injury when they argue that inerrantist scholarship accounts better for historical and biblical data than does non-inerrantist scholarship.[1] When students read inerrantist biblical scholarship, they engage the material with vested interest, yet they often do so in generally unguarded ways. The assumption is that inerrantist scholars are "safe" to read. Although inerrantist authors may be wrong, they will never fundamentally lead astray, i.e., never undermine a student's faith (in the Bible). Not without irony, while reading inerrantist scholarship students are constantly positioned to experience firsthand inerrancy's functional inadequacy. For by exposure to inerrantist literature, students are enabled to see for themselves how inerrancy lacks the methodological versatility required for getting a handle on historical-critical data. In other words, how inerrantists respond to advances in critical scholarship can do more to drive students

---

1. See, for example, Young, "Inerrantist Scholarship."

i

away from inerrantism than what critics themselves propose.[2] My main concern regards how inerrancy can stultify a student's progress along Fowler's "stages of faith."[3] Presumably, students pursue biblical studies to learn more about the God they worship. If God reveals something about himself through the *kind* of scripture he has given, inerrancy may get in the way of students learning more about God. Not only this, but students also have to make a conscious decision regarding whether they are willing to constantly challenge the findings of entire disciplines in order to perpetuate the theoretical viability of inerrancy.[4] The students who will most likely benefit from this book, then, are the ones now wondering, what are we to make of the scriptures? And what role should they play in a "Bible-based" faith? Is inerrancy even worth rehabilitating? Or is it time to move on? These questions need to be asked—with candor—even if they elicit severe censure.[5]

Notwithstanding a recent spate of defenses, inerrancy remains a paradigm in crisis.[6] In this book, I deliberately suspend judgment on inerrancy, expecting readers will be willing to do the same.[7] The aim is to work toward creating a space where more discussions like the present one can be had. I will be the first to admit I have no "answers," only

2. Compare K. Sparks: "Paradoxically, it was Kitchen himself—not Van Seters—who convinced me that the critics were right." Sparks had access to an old set of study notes while taking a class with Van Seters. The notes were from K. Kitchen, an accomplished evangelical Egyptologist. See Sparks, *God's Word*, 11.

3. See Fowler, *Stages of Faith*.

4. For more on these points, see Bovell, *Inerrancy*. See also Harlow, "After Adam."

5. Peter Enns' resignation from Westminster Theological Seminary (over the publication of *Inspiration and Incarnation*) and Bruce Waltke's resignation from Reformed Theological Seminary (in the aftermath of criticisms he made of evangelical anti-evolutionism [for the story, see <http://blog.christianitytoday.com/ctliveblog/archives/2010/04/ot_scholar_bruc.html>]) give an idea of what is at stake for both inerrantist faculty and institutions. (A moot point is that Waltke argued *against* Enns' approach to scripture in the pages of *Westminster Theological Journal*.) Also worth mentioning is a situation involving mathematician-philosopher William Dembski. After giving his honest scientific opinion regarding Gen 4–11, he was pressured into retracting what he had written: "Before I write on this topic again, I have much exegetical, historical, and theological work to do." See Dembski, *End of Christianity*; Roach, "How Old?"

6. Bovell, "Inerrancy." Compare Fitch, *End of Evangelicalism?*.

7. For the students I have in mind, embracing Wilkens and Thorsen's conciliatory gesture will not suffice: "[Inerrancy] is a viable doctrine, one held by many Christians. However, it does not define evangelicalism." See Wilkens and Thorsen, *Everything You Know*, 105.

questions. I am searching for different ways to develop and spiritually nourish what might be called a post-inerrantist mindset. There is an overwhelming peace that comes with realizing how faith lies not in whatever answers one happens to chance upon. On the contrary, trusting Jesus while still searching out the options *is* a life of faith! Salvation entails an enduring personal journey, one filled both with mystery and due diligence (Phil 2:12).

Somewhere on the periphery of evangelicalism, beyond the designations *inerrancy* and *infallibility*, there is a need for a book like this to become available to students, for what is happening in the broader world of inerrantist evangelicalism is that practitioners of faith are losing their bearings. The publication of a collection of essays by D. A. Carson defending and elaborating an inerrantist doctrine of scripture can be interpreted as evidence of this.[8] The essays have all already appeared in print. Yet proponents still think it prudent to reissue them, this time as a "classic" under a conservative publisher's imprint.[9] Also pertinent is J. Ligon Duncan's enthusiastic endorsement of the very idea, explaining that Carson "is for this generation what B. B. Warfield was for his."[10] Incidentally, Carson is also coordinating "The Scripture Project" to "address contemporary discussion on the nature of the Bible," helping inerrantists work together toward articulating "a robust confessionalism" on scripture.[11] This indicates at the very least an inerrantist reaction to cultural forces that are operating from within evangelicalism itself, posing formidable challenges to inerrantism and calling for authoritative responses from an inerrantist standpoint.

Perhaps another example is a recent book by J. P. Moreland entitled, *Kingdom Triangle*. In the closing chapter, Moreland writes:

> Dear fellow sojourner in the Way of Jesus, these are unprecedented times for the church to fill the huge void in our culture that has resulted from decades of secularization. We actually

8. Carson, *Collected Writings*.

9. According to J. Woodbridge, Carson's book "will become a classic." Carson, *Collected Writings*, back cover. Compare also the collection of articles by G. Beale by the same publisher which critiques a recent book by P. Enns. In this case, the title of the book gives no indication it is a "collection." See Beale, *Erosion of Inerrancy*.

10. Carson, *Collected Writings*, back cover.

11. See <http://www.henrycenter.org/programs/faculty-initiatives/> announcing a two-volume work that Eerdmans will release some time in 2012 (last accessed May 18, 2011). "Robust confessionalism" is Carson's phrase. See Carson, *Collected Writings*, 11.

have "the way, and the truth, and the life" (John 14:6). There is however a problem. Pollster George Barna warns that there is a growing sense of boredom with playing church, with the encrusted practices of the traditional church whose only rationale is that they are the way we have always done things.[12]

For Moreland, the remedy involves a "kingdom triangle," which is comprised in three parts: "acquiring a thoughtful Christian worldview," "developing emotional intimacy with God," and "developing a supernatural lifestyle."[13] For Moreland, secularism is the chief culprit and supernaturalism the ultimate cure.

For the students I have in mind, however, the present moment's narrative will read quite differently. For them, it is not naturalism but *super*naturalism that is the problem—a hyper-supernaturalism—that accompanies believing inerrancy. Over time, insistence upon inerrancy as the sine qua non for orthodoxy has bred emotional, spiritual and intellectual dysfunction into evangelical churches and institutions, particularly among students. D. Milavec saw this coming a generation ago:

> [Emerging] from two centuries of vigorous battles with scientists, philosophers, and historians who attempted to reduce the Bible to their own disciplines . . . Christians have fashioned the weapon of an unassailable supernaturalism which attested to the divine origins of the Sacred Scriptures and to the divine assistance necessary for infallibly interpreting them . . . The successes of supernaturalism, however, have so blocked our access to (and distorted our sense of) the natural origins of the Scriptures and the natural skills necessary to interpret them, that the Christian's best weapon is rapidly working for his own self-destruction. In swinging it so mightily, he has lost his balance. And, while he has saved his own life, his unbalanced position is unwittingly calculated to injure his children—those who were to be the future generation of Christians.[14]

Causes for the dysfunction are complex, while the search for its cure is still incipient.[15] My suggestion is that publications like Carson's and Moreland's are indicative that conservative evangelicalism is undergo-

12. Moreland, *Kingdom Triangle*, 195.

13. Moreland, *Kingdom Triangle*, 196.

14. Milavec, "Bible," 215.

15. Among the definitive histories include Sandeen, *Roots*, and Marsden, *Fundamentalism*. See also Barr, *Fundamentalism*; Harris, *Fundamentalism*; Dorrien, *Remaking*; and Wuthnow and Lawson, "Sources."

ing profound changes, dovetailing N. Ammerman's observation that "fundamentalist movements seem to arise at times when the definitions of good and evil are in the process of being renegotiated, when long-standing implicit polarities have been called into question."[16] D. Fitch identifies evangelicalism as "an unraveling ideology losing its hold on its people." Appropriating the philosophy of S. Žižek, Fitch observes that within evangelicalism "the Inerrant Bible" serves as a master-signifier characterized by "irruptions of over-identification," giving every indication that the ideology in question is "in crisis."[17]

It should be clear by now that this book seeks to reach those who authors like Carson and Moreland cannot.[18] Many American evangelical students are in the throes of spiritual disorientation. Inerrantist evangelicalism is still deciding how to respond to postmodern and post-Christian cultural revolutions. In the meantime, parts of its subculture are coalescing and producing an ideational culture of fear. As a result, an ideological repressiveness aimed at archaizing doctrine is artificially restricting students' options. I understand better than most why many inerrantists believe their fears are well-founded. Nevertheless, there are students who are already past the point of no return and with whom dialogue is very much still needed. Beyond the eager audiences of senior inerrantists and those no longer interested in bibliological debate, some students are still wondering what to make of the Bible but in the interim are becoming spiritually emaciated. They require nourishment from the Father, the Son, and the Spirit; in a word, they are hungering for God. Without inerrancy, they feel as though God has died, which partially substantiates the associating of inerrancy with bibliolatry. It is for such students that this book has been written. My hope is that it will encourage them to keep their conversations going.

In a sense, it is unfortunate that the time-frame for publishing books and journal articles is so drawn out. It is not uncommon for an author to experience a year or two of delay between completion of a manuscript and the time it appears in print. In some cases, books and articles that students are reading give snapshots only of what authors were thinking *several years before*. In my case, over the course of producing this book,

16. Ammerman, "Accounting," 155.

17. Fitch, *End of Evangelicalism?*, 58–61. Moreland sees something similar happening but is not minded to find fault with inerrancy. See Moreland, "How Evangelicals."

18. For my own independent effort to try to give voice to the many perspectives, see the collection of essays in Bovell, *Interdisciplinary*.

a growing preoccupation with how inerrancy functions in practice has brought me to question whether the "baseline consideration" of inerrantist interpretation was ever really the scriptural texts in the first place. To my chagrin, I have come to understand that in his analysis of meaning-construction Wimbush has gained considerable insight into the cultural architecture of American inerrantism:

> Such a claim is a ruse: it has more often than not been the dominant culture's interpretation of itself masked or certainly projected as (culture-sanctioned) interpretation of "sacred" text that has been the agenda. It is only when the culture is so taken for granted as reflection or reification of truth and realty and power that the text is foregrounded.[19]

Put another way, if one does not come to scripture from within a high-powered culture already armed with inerrancy along with traditional interpretations, the possibility of a twenty-first century believer inferring scriptural inerrancy from biblical data "alone" greatly diminishes. As a result of my college and seminary education, I had come to a place where I needed to re-formulate the doctrine from scratch, "from the Bible," as it were. I was astonished to find I could not credibly do so. In fact, without the supports of the inerrantist culture taken for granted, the doctrine lost all plausibility.[20] By insisting that the Bible is the Word of God, the inerrantist mindset seems to me to engender collective projections upon God of culturally sanctioned interpretations.

In my experience, how Christians understand biblical authority is very much a product of the subculture in which they participate. Had it not been for the social and cultural supports afforded inerrancy by American, evangelical community, inerrancy would never have suggested itself to me as a viable theory of bibliology. It is simply not the case that twenty-first century Christians can deduce inerrancy from scripture by reading "scripture alone." I came to this conclusion as I brought my research in the history and philosophy of mathematics to bear on the

---

19. Wimbush, "And the Students," 6.

20. Making matters worse, the very fact I was trying to do this at all made others immediately suspicious of me. While some remained tacit, others were more confrontational: "You are not really a believer." "You never were a believer." "His wife is spiritually single." "Your kids need to be saved." "Your presence is sending thousands of people to hell." "You are on the way to perdition." "The schools have gotten to you too, eh?" "We'll pray the Lord might help you see the light." Hence, the title of this book.

historical and cultural development of "biblicist foundationalism."[21] In a recent book, C. Smith corroborates the point with cumulative findings drawn from the social sciences. He explains: "[E]mpirical research shows that evangelicals tend to live in more religiously homogeneous worlds than most (though not all) other religious Americans. For biblicists these relatively small worlds function as effective 'plausibility structures' to sustain the 'reality' and believability of their particular assumptions and convictions."[22] His conclusion resonates with mine: "Biblicism is impossible. It literally does not work as it claims that it does and should."[23]

Even so, calling into question what one has been taught all one's life is not an easy thing to do, particularly when inerrancy continues as a shibboleth of fellowship within conservative evangelicalism. Not too long ago—and knowing better—I still felt compelled to go back to re-read the writings of key evangelical authors who, through their books, were formative influences on me insofar as helping me understand what a respectable, evangelical faith is supposed to look like. One author has already been mentioned, philosopher J. P. Moreland, whose three books, *Scaling the Secular City*, *Love Your God with All Your Mind*, and *Creation Hypothesis*, I had read at important points along my journey. Out of curiosity I went back specifically to examine how big a part inerrancy played in these books, particularly with respect to how integral inerrancy is for formulating a thoughtful approach to orthodox Christianity. To my surprise, I found no explicit discussion about inerrancy other than a footnote in the back matter of *Love Your God with All Your Mind* suggesting how one might defend the doctrine without reasoning in a circle:

> One can start by taking the Bible as merely a set of historical documents and not an inspired book, argue for its general historical trustworthiness, use its general trustworthiness to argue for both Christ's divinity (which would imply that as God, Christ would speak the truth since, for most forms of monotheistic belief, the Deity speaks all and only truths) and the fact that the New Testament contains enough history to know Christ's view of Scripture, and then show that Christ held to the full inerrancy of Holy Writ. Therefore, the Bible is inerrant.[24]

21. See Bovell, *By Good and Necessary*.

22. See Smith, *Bible Made Impossible*, 60–61.

23. Smith, *Bible Made Impossible*, 173.

24. Moreland, *Love Your God*, 242, n. 14. In chapter 5 of *Scaling the Secular City*, Moreland presents a case for the "substantial historicity" of the NT.

Even if confined to a footnote, the argument is not straightforward. Not by any means. Inerrancy, I began to realize—even if it occupies a central place for Moreland personally—could be fruitfully relegated to playing little to no role in an evangelical's theoretical explorations of faith.[25]

Also informing my understanding of evangelicalism were D. A. Carson's *The Gagging of God*, *Exegetical Fallacies*, and *Scripture and Truth*. As I did with Moreland's books, I read through these again with the intent of discerning what place inerrancy should occupy in evangelical biblical studies, and particularly *why* it was important that believers should agree that it should. In *The Gagging of God*, I came across a letter by Carson written to an unnamed senior scholar. In it, Carson actually executes something like Moreland's argument above on behalf of a "high" view of scripture. Carson writes:

> I think you would agree that the first Christians' convictions, represented in the New Testament documents, include the conviction that antecedent Scripture is truthful . . . For many reasons, I think that the most plausible explanation of this conviction is that the early Christians were right, and that their convictions in this area also prepared the way for the conceptualization of what became the NT Scriptures.[26]

During the course of the letter, Carson invokes Jesus' view of the Old Testament along with those of New Testament writers, explaining: "But I would nonetheless argue that the evidence for the existence of such a 'high' view of Scripture in the first century is very strong . . . ." and it behooves believers today to maintain that same view. Carson's aim in writing the letter was to convince the unnamed scholar to subscribe to inerrancy.

What I took away from the exchange was that the emotional certainty correlative to belief in inerrancy is not commensurate with the strength of the evidence marshaled in support of it. S. Hackett's analysis is sober: the Bible's inerrancy "is certainly not logically inevitable or inescapable. . . . What we have here instead is an extended fabric of developing plausibility, through the whole of which there runs an unbroken thread of reasonableness characterized by a degree of probability high enough to justify rational commitment on the part of any serious reflec-

---

25. Compare Malley, "Biblical Authority."
26. Carson, *Gagging of God*, 159.

tive person."[27] While for many inerrantists this may be enough, for others it will not pass muster.[28] Inerrantist apologists make it difficult, however, for dissident students to articulate their concerns. To take an extreme example, Moreland challenges naysayers to posit a problem-free theory of rationality before criticizing the rationality of inerrancy.[29]

Of course, the student audience I am targeting has no concern for inerrancy's rationality. They were already convinced that inerrancy was true. It was over time through the course of study that they came to *experience* how inerrancy does not work in practice: inerrancy cannot deliver what its proponents promise, at least not without a prohibitively high cost. For them, it seems more a matter of exercising wisdom, is it wise to continue as inerrantists given what they have learned about the Bible (or about faith)? If inerrancy is proving a hindrance to Bible study, piety, evangelism, integrating theology with other disciplines, etc., is it wise to continue to insist upon it? In their minds, inerrancy leads to what R. Webb calls a "static hermeneutic within the text." According to Webb, "The static alternative ultimately leads to a hollow or empty fulfillment of Scripture within our generation, for it leaves behind the spirit of the text. It produces a generation of gridlocked Christians."[30] Inerrantists themselves are aware of this danger. They concede as much in their various attempts to constantly contextualize scripture. At this point, two observations can be made: 1) the way inerrantists contextualize identical parts of scripture will vary from in-group to in-group, and 2) the way inerrantists contextualize parts of scripture is not markedly different from how "liberals" support circumventing orthodoxy.

Consider, for example, I. H. Marshall's account of how "liberals" argue from scripture that Christians are free to dispense with Christ's virgin birth:

> Much argument proceeds by relativisation of Scriptural teaching. If some doctrine belongs to only a part of the NT, it can be argued either that it is "primitive" and was superseded, or that it is "late" and represents a declension from the central teaching, or again that it is local to a particular community and not universally held, or again simply that it is one of several different and even

27. Hackett, *Reconstruction*, 280.
28. Compare Knuuttilla, "Biblical Authority," 125.
29. See Moreland, "Rationality."
30. Webb, *Slaves*, 254–55.

contradictory expressions of Christian faith and therefore cannot be made normative.[31]

Do not these same considerations confront every formulation of doctrine? Is not every application of scriptural texts involved with precisely these questions? Webb suggests that any culturally sensitive hermeneutic will make conscientious attempts to delineate between "cultural and transcultural aspects within Scripture." The process is multi-faceted but typically involves three main hermeneutical phases:

1. Develop various rationale that *appear* [italics in original] to indicate that a component of a text/teaching is culturally relative.
2. Develop various rationale that *appear* [italics in original] to indicate that a component of a text/teaching is transculturally binding.
3. Weigh the relative strengths of these two streams of data.[32]

Practically speaking, inerrantists accomplish little when they declare the Bible inerrant. Inerrancy does nothing to help navigate the convoluted and complex hermeneutical processes implicit in all scripture reading. In fact, inerrancy qua doctrine must actually *wait to see* what exegesis and hermeneutics tentatively deliver. It seems to follow that if hermeneutical engagement with scripture is an open and ongoing procedure (what inerrantists like to call, "hermeneutical spiral") then every formulation of inerrancy, by its very nature, must remain provisional, which means its implications are not only uncertain but also always open to revision. Inerrancy cannot predict what the Bible will or will not say. If inerrancy is strictly a post-hermeneutical commitment it should have no right whatever either to inform or restrict hermeneutical activity.

On all counts, our students are evangelicalism's most creative resource. If they find inerrancy is crimping their imagination, they should be free to dispense with its existential burden. Inerrancy is routinely suspended for the sake of doing hermeneutics anyway. Therefore, students should be encouraged to explore. Accordingly, this book is not intended to cause unnecessary offense, at least not by way of "flippantly" challenging inerrancy. To the contrary, its express aim is to help students

31. Marshall, "Are Evangelicals Fundamentalist?," 21.
32. Webb, *Slaves*, 67–68.

test the practical limits of the doctrine and remark on the prospect of its contemporary rehabilitation within the context of American inerrantist evangelicalism, keeping its ideational culture of fear specifically in mind.

1

Outsiders from the Standpoint
of Inerrantist Bibliology

B EFORE GETTING TO ISSUES that have to do with philosophy, theology and biblical studies, I would like to make some connection between fundamentalism's and conservative evangelicalism's psychological attachment to the doctrine of inerrancy and inerrantist believers' understated disinterest in social charity. In this opening chapter, I reflect upon two main themes. First, I observe that *reconciliation* appears to be the primary religious value of those who devote their lives to the establishment and maintenance of peace and social justice. Second, I observe that the quintessential theological habits of fundamentalist and evangelical inerrantism are fundamentally at odds with a spirit of reconciliation. In fact, conscious efforts to sustain an inerrantist mindset often involve perpetuating an overly defensive stance against outsiders—even when those outsiders pose no real threat. For various reasons, fundamentalist and evangelical inerrantism foster an almost indomitable impulse to recast outsiders—whether threatening or not—*as* threatening in order to sustain the vitality and viability of their own religious and social identities.

Imagine what it might take for wolves to live with lambs and for leopards to lie down with young goats as depicted in Is 11:6. One component would include achieving a minimal threshold of peace and social understanding. In such a context, some names that come to mind include Ghandi, Mother Theresa and Martin Luther King, Jr., among other individuals who have devoted their lives to championing the religious values of love, mercy, peace and long-suffering. In *Living Faith*, C. DeYoung offers character profiles of Dietrich Bonhoeffer, Malcolm X, and Aung San Suu Kyi and wonders, what is it about their faith that inspired in them an all-consuming passion for social justice? He observes that social activists of this caliber often interpret their faiths according to the maxim: "Some see things as they are and say why; I dream of things that never were and say why not." In DeYoung's view, these social activists understand their faith in intriguing ways that provide something more than a general hope that societal conditions will improve. Rather, theirs is a faith comprised of a visionary mysticism that emphasizes vital interpersonal and social dimensions of religiosity.

"I use *mysticism*," explains DeYoung, "to speak of a faith experienced through a direct relationship with the divine in contrast to a religion mediated through rituals or rules. The activists in this study testify of a vibrant, alive and engaged faith."[1] The individuals DeYoung writes about are portrayed as more than mere mystics, they are *mystic-activists*. Citing Dennis, Gold and Wright, DeYoung observes that "few who climb the mystical mountain of Carmel reach the great heights of mystery without walking back down to embrace the rag-tag people pushing history toward blessing or curse." Interestingly enough, the fundamental value that makes this possible with any sort of consistency is *reconciliation*.

To illustrate, DeYoung considers how in the final year of his life Malcolm X became so concerned for reconciliation that he had finally come to the point where he found it necessary to set aside the black separatism that had earlier influenced his teaching. Malcolm X came to realize that "[w]e must approach the problem as humans first, and whatever else we are second. . . . It is a situation that involves humans not nationalities. It is in this frame of reference that we must work."[2] Bonhoeffer, in a similar way, concerned himself with achieving reconciliation by overcoming the limitations that beleaguer the privileged social classes. Bonhoeffer envisioned a way for people of privilege to gradually arrive at a position where they could come face to face with human suffering. He recounts: "There remains an experience of incomparable value. We have for once learnt to see the great events of world history from below, from the perspective of the outcasts, the suspects, the maltreated, the powerless, the oppressed, the reviled—in short from the perspective of those who suffer."

DeYoung remarks: "a worldview blessed by marginality 'makes it possible to hold several different perspectives and so gain a more complex

1. DeYoung, *Living Faith*, 8.
2. DeYoung, *Living Faith*, 88.

and sensible way of seeing, unavailable to those with only one point of view."[3] Along these lines, sociologist C. Willie identifies marginal people as those "who live in, between, and beyond" racial, social, and cultural boundaries.[4] Those who have an interest in social charity are existentially able to identify a common humanity that binds the human race. They are willing to risk their sense of social and spiritual *individual* identity for the sake of broader social and societal reconciliation. DeYoung also emphasizes the importance of risk: "Mystic-activists never dismiss the consequences of taking risks, but as their lives become wedded to their vision, the risks seem less optional. The extent to which they no longer choose their risks reflects how much they have become one with the life of the oppressed."[5] The Dalai Lama has made the same point: "When we enhance our sensitivity toward others' suffering through deliberately opening ourselves up to it, it is believed that we can gradually extend our compassion to the point where the individual feels so moved by even the subtlest suffering of others that they come to have an overwhelming sense of responsibility toward those others."[6]

While DeYoung goes on to consider how diverse religious scriptural traditions contribute to mystic-activists' emphasis on reconciliation, Katongole and Rice restrict their focus to Christianity, specifically to how the Bible can (and should) be read with an eye toward reconciliation. According to these two authors, scripture should play a major part in the spiritual conditioning of Christian believers for reconciliation. In order for this to happen, scripture must be received as a gift from God that enables believers to begin on a life journey of reconciliation. When read in appropriate ways, scripture can predispose believers toward a more profound spiritual grasp of biblical reconciliatory values. As this gradually occurs, believers begin to appreciate that "Scripture is neither a catalogue of spiritual insights nor a collection of moral guidelines and principles. It is a story. As a story, Scripture can be read through the central plot of Creation, Fall, Promise and Restoration—a plot that is in essence the movement from old creation to new creation."[7]

---

3. DeYoung, *Living Faith*, 52.

4. DeYoung, *Living Faith*, 53.

5. DeYoung, *Living Faith*, 59.

6. DeYoung, *Living Faith*, 60.

7. Katongole and Rice, *Reconciling All Things*, 63.

Katongole and Rice insist that "reconciliation is not in the first place an activity or set of attitudes but an invitation into a story. Reconciliation names God's story of creation, which is at the same time a promise of restoration. . . . To be drawn into the story of Scripture is to join this journey toward new creation."[8] Their tenth thesis for recovering reconciliation as the mission of God observes

> . . . the work of reconciliation is sustained more through storytelling and apprenticeship than by training in techniques and how-tos. Through friendship with God, the stories of Scripture and faithful lives, and learning the virtues and daily practices those stories communicate, reconciliation becomes an ordinary, everyday pattern of life for Christians.[9]

It is interesting to note that when Katongole and Rice exegete scriptural passages, they introduce their analysis of each pericope with the phrase, "According to the story . . . " In this and other ways, the authors draw attention to the narratival presentation of biblical values. Scripture functions on a mythic level of discourse informing believers on issues of peace and social justice: they are invited to become authentic participants in its narrative of cosmic redemption. The journey is risky and uncertain, and "the challenge is to keep fresh and continue growing along the way."[10]

How well does the conservative evangelical preoccupation with safeguarding inerrancy help foster the value of reconciliation both in inerrantists individually and among inerrantist communities generally? My hypothesis is that it cannot contribute much and may very well preclude it. To see why, consider how fundamentalism's and conservative evangelicalism's sense of social and spiritual identity is existentially rooted in and deliberately constructed upon a basic, core commitment to specific doctrinal tenets. Although it is true that historic Christianity has used confessions and creeds to help clarify what churches believe, fundamentalists and conservative evangelicals are prone to use these idiosyncratically, that is, in peculiarly authoritarian ways. In my view, Protestant inerrantism has become the main culprit or at the very least has come to play a more significant role. This is because, for all intents and purposes, Protestant inerrantism emasculates the spiritual awaken-

---

8. Katongole and Rice, *Reconciling All Things*, 74.

9. Katongole and Rice, *Reconciling All Things*, 151.

10. Katongole and Rice, *Reconciling All Things*, 124.

ing new converts initially experience upon conversion, which surreptitiously effects a full cognitive reversal of the *ordo salutis*.

In *By Good and Necessary Consequence*, I sought to describe how in my experience this reversal is accomplished:

> Inerrantist propaganda, in its apologetic fervor to justify, promote and defend the faith, fails to recognize the spiritual trajectory set by conversions that progress from faith to understanding. Instead, inerrantists set out to unnaturally integrate inerrancy into the existential equation. In others words, the inerrantist message practically amounts to an inversion of the experiential progression to the effect that faith comes first, *inerrancy second*, and then seeking third, a seeking, we should point out, that must never show itself to be in contradiction with the inerrantist foundation.[11]

Many times, doctrinal fidelity, expressed in terms of doctrinal purity—particularly when it comes to bibliology—is implicitly expressed in soteriological terms. Make no mistake. It is no mere literalism that typifies fundamentalism or conservative evangelicalism. Much rather, it is a constellation of three basic attitudes: (1) "'a very strong emphasis on the inerrancy of the Bible,' (2) 'a strong hostility to modern theology' and 'the modern critical study of the Bible,' and (3) a sharp distinction between 'nominal' and 'true' Christians (i.e., fundamentalists)."[12] The net effect is one that R. Alves recounts from his firsthand involvement in the Presbyterian Church of Brazil:

> In our case one proceeds by denying to the original emotional experience any cognitive significance. And this is obtained by means of a reversal: the new convert "learns" that his or her experience, far from being the origin of knowledge, is rather based on an absolute knowledge which antecedes it. *And this is done by means of the doctrine of the divine origin and character of the Scriptures* [my italics].[13]

Compare how G. Sheppard observed a similar dynamic at work amongst the changes of faculty at Fuller Theological Seminary during the mid twentieth century:

---

11. Bovell, *By Good and Necessary*, 131.
12. Dayton, "Evangelicalism without Fundamentalism."
13. Alves, *Protestantism*, 56.

In no instance in Fuller's history did this controversy in bibliology have at stake a departure in the confession of the deity of Christ, the resurrection, virgin birth, Second Coming, or any other major orthodox doctrine. Indeed, the centrality of the hermeneutical theme in ponderous works on biblical apologetics produced by evangelicals in this same period almost leaves the impression that after one's Christian conversion the real scandal of faith is no longer the resurrection but obtaining and defending a correct theory of biblical hermeneutics. A minimal conclusion is that within establishment evangelicalism after World War II, the language of biblical fidelity provided the most common rhetorical means by which nuances were officially distinguished in the evangelical identity.[14]

The doctrine of inerrancy is taken to be a banner of identification for the integrity of "true" Christianity. Whatever spiritual certainties the faithful happen to enjoy are thought to ultimately depend upon the inerrancy of scripture. Understandably, inerrantists take it upon themselves to foster an explicitly apologetic stance against any real or perceived challenges to inerrantist doctrine. If inerrancy is not tenaciously defended, other foundational doctrines (and these differ by tradition) are put into immediate jeopardy. In very important ways—both methodologically and psychologically—the doctrine of scripture is existentially construed as preceding all others. Inerrancy acts as a rhetorical metonymy for the entire faith. In essence, inerrancy is made to stand or fall for "true" Christianity.[15]

Socially, too, a similar pattern is seen in the way inerrantists like to distinguish themselves not only from non-believing non-Christians but also from other "nominal" Christians. C. Allert observes that conserva-

---

14. Sheppard, "Biblical Hermeneutics," 88.

15. Compare Harris, "Fundamentalism," 14–15. Although fundamentalists and other conservatives extol Warfield for his seminal work in bibliology, I think he is the one responsible for popularizing this methodological predicament among inerrantists today. To my knowledge, Warfield was among the first to cleverly loop inerrancy back in to the theological circle in such a way that he could say inerrancy is the "capstone" of Reformed theology and not its foundation. However, inerrancy still becomes a virtual and practical foundation because all Protestants seek to draw their doctrinal constructs from scripture. So if inerrancy falls as a doctrine, then any doctrine based on scripture will fall with it. I engage Warfield's apologetic strategy below in chapter six where I also briefly remark on J. Woodbridge's repeated attempts to reduce the variety of inerrancies held throughout church history to the version presented in the Chicago Statement of Biblical Inerrancy, for example.

tive evangelicals like to speak adamantly about conserving the faith even though they cannot agree upon the aspects of faith they are supposed to be conserving. Surprisingly, the profound disagreements that arise in this context have somehow managed to cumulatively perpetuate a recalcitrant solidarity around a religious ethos of protest.[16] According to Allert, fundamentalists and conservative evangelicals have not yet sought to put what they wish to conserve into proper historical perspective.[17] Nevertheless, a barebones, sure-fire way to affirm fundamentalist and conservative evangelical identity today is to continue to identify, locate and decry ideological opposition to inerrancy wherever it might be found, whether within broader ecclesial contexts or without the wider non-ecclesial culture. S. Hunt explains:

> For fundamentalism it is imperative to sustain a world view that embraces a superior form of the "truth" . . . Where such a world view designates itself as the elect of the powers of good, there must be room for the powers of darkness. In particular, evidence of the powers of evil brings as much confirmation of a world view as does that of the powers of good.[18]

M. Percy further elucidates the idea: "[Fundamentalism] feeds off what it fights—without opposition it dies."[19]

An illustration of this can be found in the doctrinal agreement of the Evangelical Theological and Philosophical Societies. Until recently the only theological tenet contained in their doctrinal affirmation was: "The Bible alone, and the Bible in its entirety, is the Word of God written and therefore inerrant in the originals." Prospective members of both societies have to affirm this doctrinal statement in order to become members. After becoming members, they have to reaffirm the statement when it is time to renew in order to remain members. The practice of publicly affirming inerrancy to be accepted into community is not restricted to the ETS/EPS. Inerrantist seminaries, universities and schools, along with a host of other church and parachurch ministries, all have similar expectations. There is a connection to be made between this kind of inerrantist identity formation and J. Barr's description of inerrantists'

16. Compare Allert, *High View*, 26–27.
17. See Allert, "What Are We Trying to Conserve?"
18. Hunt, "Devil's Advocates," 74.
19. "Fundamentalism," 186.

understanding of outsiders: "A psychological necessity of membership in the fundamentalist organizations is that one should be convinced that everyone outside is completely 'liberal' in theology, or at least that he has no stable defences against the adoption of a totally liberal position."[20] One reason for this is, as B. Malley observes, that "Biblical authority—as manifest in the discursive practice of framing one's speech in relation to the Bible—is one of the foundational assumptions of evangelical communities, one of the practices in which community members, in order to *be* [italics in original] community members, participate."[21] Fundamentalist and conservative evangelical community is, for better or worse, deliberately structured so that the inordinate emphasis given to an inerrant set of scriptures becomes the very criteria by which believers understand themselves to be submitting to God (since they accept inerrancy) and also by which believers can know what constitutes rebellion to God (anything resembling "autonomy," i.e., anything genuinely critical of an inerrantist mindset). Inerrancy easily becomes the social and spiritual mechanism by which insider status is minimally defined and achieved. According to C. Mercer, an otherwise paralyzing fear lies at the heart of inerrantism's "cognitive schema": "If I don't get it right, I am not a Christian, and I will go to hell."[22]

As high-stakes as this may be for believers, this is not their only concern. As inerrantist apologists readily acknowledge, contemporary inerrantism comes built-in with a fully equipped, guilt-driven slippery slope dynamic that believers are quick to use and often to full advantage. C. Sullivan recounts:

> [B]y adopting the inerrancy postulate, by arguing that the Bible is completely void of problematic passages, by insisting that others agree with them, inerrantists have trapped non-inerrantists into a corner not of their choosing . . . Many inerrantists, I've observed, have bully mentalities which compel them to impose their views on others. Thus non-inerrantists have no choice but to respond to inerrantists' aggressive tactics. Our behavior is motivated by a desire to deliver fellow believers from the ideological cul-de-sac down which inerrantists want everyone to travel.[23]

20. Barr, *Fundamentalism*, 165. British writers tend to refer to evangelicals as fundamentalists.

21. *How the Bible Works*, 140.

22. Mercer, *Slaves to Faith*, 144.

23. Sullivan, *Toward a Mature Faith*, 56.

Slippery slopes are commonly invoked to help facilitate the entrenchment of an absolutist mindset: what is not "in" (anything other than inerrancy) is not merely "not in" on a local, religio-social level, but also, and more importantly, on a universal, cosmic level—the level that has to do with eternal and spiritual redemption. In other words, an all-or-nothing approach toward piety overwhelmingly appeals to inerrantist soteriological sensibilities, which has the added benefit of decisively uprooting believers' emotional anxieties. In fact, sometimes the appeal can prove so extensive that an almost smug sense of certainty and security sets in which cannot help but carry over to interactions with outsiders. Some, however—regrettably mainly outsiders—have become increasingly aware of inerrancy's manipulative dynamic. An interesting example is found in one psychotherapist's paraphrase of an inerrantist theologian's claim.

When writing on fundamentalism, S. Schimmel paraphrases W. Grudem as follows: "Anyone who believes that even one word of Scripture is not from God, does not believe in God."[24] However, Grudem himself would certainly have never put things so starkly.[25] What Grudem actually writes is this: "The authority of Scripture means that all the words in Scripture are God's words in such a way that to disbelieve or disobey any word of Scripture is to disbelieve or disobey God."[26] On the face of it—at least to an evangelical—there is a world of difference between Schimmel's statement and Grudem's. Nevertheless, it is telling that Professor Schimmel, a specialist in the psychology of fundamentalism, decides *not* to quote Grudem verbatim but rather writes the only thing (in his view) that Grudem could possibly mean by what he wrote.[27] Reflecting on the matter, let us consider a question, "What practical difference is there between what Schimmel writes and what Grudem means?" For insight, let us consider Nichols' recounting of a sermon where a preacher at a pastors' conference

> held up a bottle of Tylenol. [In the early 1980s Tylenol pills had been tampered with leading to seven people dying from taking them]. "If I knew there was one capsule in this bottle that was

24. Schimmel, *Tenacity*, 101.

25. Grudem, in email correspondence with me, explained that he disagreed with Schimmel's paraphrase of what he wrote.

26. Grudem, *Bible Doctrine*, 33.

27. So Schimmel, personal communication.

laced with cyanide, I would throw the whole bottle out," he thundered. Then he picked up his Bible. "If I knew of one error in this book"—everyone saw this coming—"I'd throw the whole thing out."

Nichols draws the obvious moral: "Inerrancy, in other words, either is or it isn't. And that was and continues to be the line of demarcation."[28]

I suggest that Schimmel nevertheless makes a keen observation in his (mis-)quoting of Grudem. Fundamentalists and conservative evangelicals maintain a functional, triple dichotomy—in/not in; inerrant/errant; belief/unbelief—that mounts sufficient psychological pressure upon believers to adapt an absolutist mindset toward their faith, predisposing them to spiritual nonchalance toward issues of peace and social charity to outsiders. Recall how DeYoung identifies reconciliation as the most important value among the exemplars of social justice. It seems to me—at least on the face of it—that a value like reconciliation is in diametrical tension with the absolutist mindset inerrantism seems to foster.[29] Furthermore, the defensive postures that come with accepting inerrantism are at least partially motivated by the existential demands of wanting to guarantee and maintain that the gospel is not only "true" but also genuinely accessible to the average believer. In Protestant America, this involves social patterns where "the propagation of Christian faith [needs] neither establishment nor hierarchy, but only the proclamation of the biblical word to the believing individual in the free marketplace of ideas." R. Harrisville and W. Sundberg describe the dynamic at play: "Truth is presented objectively in the biblical world. The common man of common sense, empowered in faith by the Holy Spirit is capable of understanding this objective word or 'plain fact' that the Bible delivers."[30] Inerrantists go out of their way to stress the existential import of special revelation: scripture must be duly recognized as a vital part of the economy of faith. R. Jensen, a non-inerrantist, is only being honest when he remarks the "old Lutheran . . . analyses of the grounds and nature of scriptural authority are convincing."[31] In inerrantist circles, however, inerrancy is seen as a Maginot Line, a minimal standard of doctrinal

---

28. Nichols and Brandt, *Ancient Word*, 64.

29. Nichols candidly admits that "[t]hose more prone to peace than pugilism may question all of this controversy." See Nichols and Brandt, *Ancient Word*, 64.

30. Harrisville and Sundberg, *Bible in Modern Culture*, 199–200.

31. See Jensen, "Authorities of Scripture," 57.

purity. M. Volf calls such tendencies, "militant exclusivism," which raises a question of "whether it is possible to talk about ultimate reality and its claims on the world in a non-fundamentalist way."[32]

One thing seems sure. So long as institutions and denominations identify and advertise inerrancy as a component essential to evangelicalism (by listing it, for example, as a first or second tenet in their statements of faith), the popular perception will be that inerrancy is central to Christianity. The reasoning behind this is quite simple. Evangelicals have been known to only stress what is *fundamental* to Christianity. Since inerrancy is a doctrine stressed by evangelicals, inerrancy will continue to be promoted as fundamental for Christian faith. Is it any wonder that in conservative circles a believer's willingness to accept inerrantism is gratuitously accepted as implicitly correlate to one's willingness to submit to Christ? Conversely, it will come as no surprise that a believer who inveighs against inerrancy is judged also to be well on their way to apostasy.

An epistemological ideal is being tacitly promoted: one's belief *about* "the Rock" has to be just as solid *as* "the Rock," and this is only accomplished by believing inerrancy.[33] The inerrantist expectation is that if a Christian adherent is genuinely a member of the spiritually-privileged remnant that God has left for himself, then they will instinctually gravitate toward inerrantism. They will not be afraid to publicly defend it, particularly in the face of cultural ridicule. Some inerrantist claims go further. Some go on to suggest that the Spirit is actively guiding true believers to accept the inerrancy of scripture and that this is principally achieved through the "plain" reading of biblical texts.[34] Even if the expectation is only rarely put so bluntly, the soteriological grammar that drives inerrantist epistemology remains in full effect.[35] Furthermore, an impetus for biblicist foundationalism is deeply entrenched within conservative Protestantism as a culture, which may help explain, incidentally, why proponents of inerrancy tend to react as if every negative

32. Volf, "Challenge," 104.

33. Adapted from Volf, "Challenge," 104.

34. The cultural legacy of inerrantists writing a generation ago: "As the Patristic age faced a *christological* watershed, as the Medieval and Reformation churches confronted *soteriological* crises, so the contemporary Church finds itself grappling with the great *epistemological* [italics in original] question in Christian dogmatics." See Montgomery, "Inspiration," 45–46.

35. See N. M. de S. Cameron, "Logic."

spiritual consequence they can imagine—ones suggested to them by their "slippery slope arguments"—inexorably take effect the very moment inerrancy is doubted. When this happens, a believer's trusting an inerrant Bible is made out to somehow culturally supervene on their soul's salvation.[36] How often have I heard proponents say that anyone who disavows inerrancy is "grieving" the Holy Spirit or stubbornly rebelling against God.[37]

Fundamentalists and conservative evangelicals presume they have been set apart for redemption, that they therefore comprise an elite spiritual community. As such, they perceive themselves as being predisposed by Christ and the Spirit to (among other things) "take God at his word." If God's word (construed as an inerrant Bible) is impugned, the integrity of this faith construct is irreversibly compromised. With this mindset, scripture literally becomes one's life. The only way to understand the human life-world is through it: the only way to reach outsiders is through it; the only way to recognize insiders is through it; the only way to relate to God is through it; the only way to see the world for what it *really* is is through it—the only way to do anything at all is through scripture, a scripture inerrant without errors in anything it affirms.[38] Fundamentalism's and conservative evangelicalism's social identities have become so intertwined with this one doctrine that once it appears threatened—even if in healthy and constructive ways—preserving its truth takes on a grandiose significance. Inerrancy cannot be found wanting; everything literally depends on it.[39] Since scripture is the only way to Christ and Christ the only way to God, when inerrancy is criticized the entire Christian faith construct is faced with imminent imperilment.

36. Compare Packer, "*Fundamentalism*," 37. The "junction of the Holy One" is said to help believers intuit that something would be spiritually amiss if inerrancy were denied.

37. Packer, for example, would have us choose between "carry[ing] through our repentance on the intellectual level, or . . . cherish[ing] our sinful craving for a thought-life free from the rule of God." See Packer, "*Fundamentalism*," 170–71.

38. D. A. Carson can be found on Youtube answering the question: what is inerrancy? Anytime the Bible makes a truth-claim, what it says in that case is true. Online:< http://www.biblicalstudies.org.uk/inerrancy.php>. Accessed: May 23, 2011.

39. Cohen recalls that his life as a "Bible-believer" "resembled nothing so much as a bout of substance abuse." See Cohen, *Mind*, 3.

In many ways, the inerrantist mindset introduces something of a paradox to inter-subjectivity. For on the one hand, fundamentalists and evangelicals are warned about venturing too far "outside" the in-group. Casual engagements with "non-believing" influences are off-limits. On the other hand, the same believers are exhorted to fully engage the world for Christ. Engagement with others is ideally characterized by an interesting mix of both confidence and trepidation. Oft-warned of the dangers of "worldly" thinking, believers can remain assured the true Christian's inerrant Bible has every answer, it is only "the world" that needs to—by the grace of God—open itself up to receiving that answer.[40] Inerrancy, then, is a trustworthy source of ultimate comfort in a world that has nothing more to offer than anxiety and uncertainties. In this light, Volf makes a rather unexpected connection:

> There are many Christians who live with uncertainties that reach even to the very core of their faith. But it is still an open question whether they can be successful in transmitting a living Christian faith to successive generations and to non-believers. One thing is certain, however. If they fail in this task, the future of Protestant Christianity might lie with the fundamentalists—with hard-core fundamentalists and with former fundamentalists who have mellowed with time.[41]

The future of Christianity (as understood by Protestants) may socially depend on fundamentalists and evangelicals and their commitment to inerrancy. I. H. Marshall describes how easily "insiders" connect their commitment to inerrancy to their commitment to God:

> First, in principle there is no difference in kind between a faith that puts its trust in God and one that does so through his revelation in Scripture or in Christ. In both cases, we are dealing with a faith that cannot prove the truth or reliability or whatever of God or Scripture . . . Second, the trustworthiness of God or Scripture is indeed a matter of faith—but it is a faith which is confirmed by experience to the point where it becomes a trusty foundation. . . .

40. N. Geisler's 1998 ETS Presidential Address comes to mind. See Geisler, "Beware of Philosophy." Some have gone so far as to say that scripture teaches there is a perpetual antithesis between *worldly* philosophy and *Christian* philosophy. Others merely observe inerrantism has successfully sustained every criticism inveighed against it for several generations now—so much so that it is inconceivable that new criticisms should arise that have not already received satisfactory answers from inerrantists in the past.

41. Volf, "Challenge," 105.

> But there comes a point in any relationship when the element of
> risk becomes minimal, and the faith is tantamount to knowledge
> and leads to ventures of faith which are not foolhardy.[42]

For some inerrantists, a set of inerrant scriptures has become such an integral part of their conception of the Christian's relationship to God that
to problematize inerrancy is, for them, to problematize the very idea of
a divine-human relationship. Understandably, W. Abraham writes: "To
be sure, there are some Christians who cannot survive if they abandon
inerrancy; I would not hesitate to counsel such believers to hold to their
vision of inerrancy."[43]

Along the same lines, a former inerrantist recounts that a major
part of his being able to *dis*avow inerrantism involved an all-consuming
"quest for truth wherever it might take me, trusting that any truth I
learned was no less true for being unexpected or difficult to fit into the
pigeonholes provided by my evangelical background."[44] To an absolutist mindset, however, a dilemma arises of the most acute sort. For in
their minds, an ultimate choice needs to be made between assurance
and certainty on the one hand and despair and risk on the other. I
submit that open engagements with outsiders when broached with an
absolutist mindset can both make and break inerrantism. How it pans
out for an individual believer will largely depend on their psychological
temperament.[45]

In this chapter, my interest is primarily in how the overriding prospect of uncertainty and risk that *should* characterize the insider-outsider
interface actually has the opposite effect on inerrantism: it *forestalls*
insider-outsider reconciliation and *bolsters* the solidarity of inerrantist
communities. To help see this, I would like to compare the ground I have
covered so far with what other authors have had to say about inerrantism.
J. Barr once noted, "it is a rhetorical necessity for [fundamentalist and
evangelical inerrantists] to depict their views as if surrounded by numerous implacable enemies." S. Coleman relates similar observations among
Faith Christians in Sweden and also the U.S.: "the rhetoric and practice
of converting others is significant to the self-identity of believers even

---

42. Marshall, "Are Evangelicals Fundamentalist?," 17–18.

43. Abraham, "Foreword," xiii.

44. Ehrman, *Misquoting Jesus*, 8. Compare Avalos, *¿Se puede saber?*, 280–81.

45. Compare Pinnock, *Scripture*, 268.

when nobody appears to be saved."[46] Coleman mentions other studies that show that where converts do not come easily there is a pattern of interacting with outsiders in only superficial ways. Researchers observe mechanisms of self-affirmation built-in to the very process of relating to outsiders. In the words of S. Hill, "Genuine fundamentalism *requires* [my italics] enemies."[47] According to Coleman, for such groups outreach *must* occur irrespective of whether the outside is even listening.[48] These social dynamics are consistent with those found in inerrantist philosophy of religion. B. R. Tilghman observes: "Since it is committed ahead of time to its conclusions, Biblical inerrantism must refuse to allow any evidence to count against its views. Any facts about scripture that would tend to show the doctrine to be mistaken will be ignored, discounted, or explained away."[49] In every interaction with outsiders, the inerrantist has no other recourse but to continue to maintain that inerrantism is right under any and every circumstance. Irrespective of the problem, "God's people can approach difficult texts with confidence, knowing that they are not actual errors."[50]

Representatives of this approach can be found in almost every quarter of inerrantism. Payne offers one of the clearest explanations in the literature:

> Let us say, for example, that X = Matthew and Y = quoting (27:9-10) words from Zechariah 11:12-13 (with possible allusions to Jer. 18:2 and 19:2), ascribing them to Jeremiah the prophet. When the believer says he CANNOT deny this, he does so on the basis of a presupposition. As a starting point he holds that the claims of the book itself to be words of God are accepted as a working hypothesis and ultimately, that all Scripture is inerrant (see Christ's statement in John 10:35 again).

46. See Coleman, "Global Consciousness," 100. Barr, *Fundamentalism*, 104 is cited by Coleman.

47. See Hill, "Spirit of Fundamentalism," 211. He writes: "Theirs is a black and white world . . . fundamentalism is *for* as well as *against*; indeed *against* because it is *for* [italics in original]."

48. See Coleman, "Global Consciousness," 100–101.

49. Tilghman, *Introduction*, 124.

50. Ankerberg and Burroughs, *Taking a Stand*, 43.

Therefore, no "real" error can ever arise:

> This presupposition does not destroy legitimate criticism. For rather than eliminating or even claiming to have answered the few seeming discrepancies that do occur, the evangelical simply transfers these to the supernaturalistic column. He places them where man is not to judge for himself, and where God (who is the only One in a position to know) denies him the privilege of saying, "It's not true," because God tells him that Scripture is inerrant.[51]

Another instructive example is given by K. Boone. According to Boone, fundamentalist inerrantism works toward insulating believers from the outside world for their own spiritual good. She explains: "The care taken to shield fundamentalist laypersons from non-fundamentalist discourse reflects the strong belief that the wrong words, the wrong combination of words, can subvert faith—an attitude traceable to the centrality of an inerrant text, without which fundamentalists claim that faith itself can be destroyed."[52] She observes further:

> The Word of God is not just primary in importance but singular. Physical poverty is merely God's way of "waking us" to the genuine need of the population. One cannot but respond viscerally to what is, in my opinion, a remarkable callousness here expressed. But if one understands the overriding concern with proper *belief* [emphasis in original] . . . one can appreciate the way in which the biblical message can be construed as primarily doctrinal rather than moral. Literalism and inerrantism tend to close off rather than creatively expand practical application.[53]

It would not be atypical for an inerrantist to count this as virtuous. Payne, for example, illustrates the case when he lambasts "liberal exegesis": "Whatever may have been said about 'the uneasy conscience of modern fundamentalism' regarding social ethics, the evangelical has an easy conscience, based upon a well integrated approach of logical con-

---

51. See Payne, "Higher Criticism," 92. More recently, T. Ward commends the same approach. For example, when it comes to historicity, inerrantists need only be patient: archaeology will eventually prove the Bible right. For there are no errors; there can never be. All errors are "apparent" only. Readers can be assured of this as they go back and read more carefully. See Ward, *Words of Life*, 138–40.

52. Boone, *Bible Tells Them*, 83.

53. Boone, *Bible Tells Them*, 95.

sistency, regarding Biblical historicity."[54] In a nutshell, one of the most important responsibilities an inerrantist Christian has before God in contemporary culture is to be faithful to inerrancy in the face of modern and postmodern pressures. Interestingly enough, in their reflections upon differences between fundamentalist Protestants and "originalist" Constitution interpreters Smith and Tuttle observe: "For literalism, interpretation is an act of faith in a God who is just and good. Accordingly, for the literalist, obedience to the biblical text—the Word of God—is the highest human good."[55] Or as S. Hill puts it: In every instance, "Being correct outranks being amiable."[56]

Inerrantism contributes to the isolation of fundamentalist and conservative evangelical believers from open engagement with the outside world by drawing and redrawing insider/outsider lines in a continual effort to underscore inerrantist, soteriological distinctions. V. Crapanzano points out, based on a typical inerrantist statement of faith, that "the basic hermeneutic assumptions of Fundamentalism [are] assumptions that do not divorce the ethical and the spiritual from the cognitive and intellectual."[57] In this way, believers are always identifying larger and larger segments of world-culture with the "outside" by putatively connecting the intellectual, the political, and the ethical to the spiritual. An image of concentric circles comes to mind depicting just how expansive the outside really is for inerrantists. Outsiders can be viewed as occupying as many of the outer circles as they please, so long as it is understood that the outside is "out there," posing ever-present ideological and spiritual threats to genuine faith.

Yet at the same time, inerrantists believe that the Bible is God's inerrant word. Since inerrantists are precisely the ones to whom God has revealed this fundamental truth, outsiders cannot ultimately pose a real threat to inerrancy: the Bible will always show itself to be right—and if this has not already been done, it will eventually be done once all the facts get in. As an insider, the inerrantist already knows what she believes *has to be right*. After all, what she believes is no mere human speculation, but rather what God has revealed, and not only that but what he has revealed he has revealed *inerrantly*. Practically speaking, then, outsiders

54. Payne, "Uneasy Conscience," 14.
55. Smith and Tuttle, "Biblical Literalism."
56. Hill, "Spirit of Fundamentalism," 211.
57. Crapanzano, *Serving the Word*, 59, compare 82.

become 1) entirely irrelevant to the more salient, existential demands of insider life, but also and more interestingly 2) the perfect vehicle for reassuring inerrantists that inerrancy is right. Consequently, it becomes natural for fundamentalists and conservative evangelicals to evince only minimal interest in peace and social charity. If inerrantists are primarily concerned with what is happening "inside" and they regard the outside as a practical means of re-establishing insider-identity, then engagement with the outside will hardly be "risky" enough to broker reconciliation.

C. Henry, a renowned inerrantist, remarked over half a century ago: "What concerns me more is that we have needlessly invited criticism and even ridicule, by a tendency in some quarters to parade secondary and sometimes even obscure aspects of our position as necessary frontal phases of our view." Some thirty years later, J. Dunn reiterated a similar concern, squarely placing the blame on the shoulders of inerrantism:

> In short, [inerrancy] seems to me to be a very dangerous kind of unselfcritical blinkeredness which makes it possible for some Christians to take an interpretation of scripture whose herme-neutical justification from within scripture is weaker than other interpretations, to exalt it above all other alternative views of scripture, and to use it to deny validity to those others, even when they have at least as strong an exegetical base.[58]

Twenty years later still, D. Dash, reflecting back on Henry's work, ob-serves that what Henry wrote back then remains valid today. He ex-plains his understanding of the contemporary landscape: "I have not read McLaren's new book, but I am seeing a trend. Some emphasize the social dimensions of biblical faith at the expense of the individual's need for salvation; others emphasize personal salvation at the expense of the social dimensions of biblical faith."[59]

Here, as before, there is something of a paradox inherent to iner-rantist approaches to inter-subjectivity. On the one hand, believers are taught that inerrantist faith is precious and easily corruptible. The faith must be handled with care, as it were, diligently protected from out-side, unbelieving influences. On the other hand, inerrantists are urged to heed contemporary calls for immediate cultural engagement: "This summons to develop a compelling Christian mind and broadcast its deliverances to the culture at large could not be more needed than it is

58. Dunn, *Living Word*, 104–5.

59. See Dash, "Evangelicalism's Uneasy Conscience."

today, when the very concept of objective, absolute, and universal truth is being corroded by the irrational acids of postmodernism."[60] The two admonitions seem to be in considerable tension. Perhaps the simplest way to simultaneously address both concerns is to find various strategies for making the "outside" look more like the "inside."[61] In other words, the only faithful way to engage outsiders at all—without putting the integrity of Christian faith at risk—is to always have "make outsiders become like insiders" as an ulterior motive for engagements with outsiders. But according to Katongole and Rice, *this is one of the worst approaches for achieving reconciliation.*

In various ways, the presumption of an inerrant text allows some inerrantists to foster and legitimate insular and uncritical lines of thinking. This can easily carry over into their overall attitude toward social engagement. Consider one popular view: "if the truth is there in the text and if no other text can add to the sacred text, then the truth is available to any individual who cares to look with faith and without evil intention."[62] Whenever *another* person does not look for truth in scripture in the same ways fundamentalists and conservative evangelicals are taught to do, this suggests to them that evil (i.e., unbelieving) intentions must ultimately be the reason. Unfortunately, peace and social charity—however commendable they may seem otherwise—are simply not up to the task of correcting the human condition because they do not address the underlying spiritual malady. Only conversion can do that, but (as I have already observed above and am now coming full circle) integral to the conversion process is an existential (pre-)commitment to inerrancy. Without the doctrine of inerrancy there is no "real" Christianity.[63] There are only differing degrees of unbelief.

Can there be a place for "unbelieving liberalism" among the doctrinally pure? The inerrantist consensus is emphatically, "No." As a result, believers who criticize inerrancy almost immediately find themselves ecclesial exiles, *personae non gratae.* They are spiritually discounted,

---

60. Groothius, "Review."

61. Take for example a church offering free classes to the public with the ulterior hope that they can ultimately convert the participants.

62. Lehmann, "Fundamentalism," 123.

63. However, interestingly enough, inerrancy by itself is not sufficient to establish true Christianity. A heretical group could also accept inerrancy, for example. "Old Princeton" famously tied the fate of "distinctive" Christianity to the fate of the doctrine of inerrancy. See chapter six below.

socially disconnected, psychologically disoriented and emotionally distressed. (There really is a need for psychologists of fundamentalism after all!) Before long, they become too scared to ask whatever questions they may genuinely have. Ironically, the prospect of actually finding an error in scripture can become the least of one's worries. *The social backlash that comes from seriously asking critical questions and entertaining critical answers becomes the main preoccupation.* A cost-benefit ratio would appear to suggest that even if peace and social charity should commend themselves to inerrantists as worthwhile pursuits, striving for them is simply *not worth the risk*—the risk of jeopardizing one's own evangelical identity and forfeiting all of the social and spiritual benefits that are associated with evangelical community. Dunn rightly decries this as a "spirit of slavery to fear," "that state of spiritual immaturity that Paul was delighted to have left behind."[64]

In my first book, *Inerrancy and the Spiritual Formation of Younger Evangelicals*, I observed that it is not generally conducive to students' spiritual formation for inerrancy to be presented to them as the default, orthodox, bibliological position. In this chapter, I am suggesting that a further case can be made that inerrantism tends to diminish the Christian inclination toward social reconciliation. In past generations, cultural analysts used to critique Protestant inerrantists for not having a social conscience, at least not one that extended beyond their limited ecclesial borders. For my part, I think inerrantist culture still has a long way to go toward extending a sense of peace and social charity *toward other Christian bibliologists.* "Sadly," D. Harlow observes, "American Evangelicalism still has a tendency to devour its young."[65]

If I am realistic about it, the prospect of changes happening soon given the present climate seems depressingly grim, not least because conservatives are the ones who financially give the most to evangelical institutions. Especially during a recession, this means they hold all the cards. Not only this, but there is a family of emotionally convincing slippery slope arguments that apologists have strategically placed around the stricter forms of inerrancy to prevent students from contemplating

64. See Dunn, *Living Word*, 107.

65. Harlow, "After Adam," 195, n. 54. He gives the "releases" of P. Enns from Westminster Theological Seminary and B. Waltke from Reformed Theological Seminary as examples. One can begin to better appreciate the far-reaching paranoia that typifies evangelical culture by considering the "resignations" of otherwise conservative faculty members at inerrantist institutions.

a disciplined exploration of less restrictive bibliologies. For if they do, they are constantly warned, they will be starting on an inexorable path that leads inerrantists right out of "believing" Christendom. By putting up so many hedges around Christian faith, inerrantists have gotten into the habit of overemphasizing ideological boundaries by continually finding reasons to distinguish their own belief systems from those of "unbelievers." The intent may have initially been to safeguard the doctrine of inerrancy—the certainty of which is what (in their view) makes faith possible[66]—but the practical effect is to distract believers from empathetically transcending the insider-outsider framework. In many ways, inerrantist culture denies believers the ordinary means by which they might engage the outside world to make reconciliation possible. Ironically, this outside world of theirs includes not only all unbelieving non-Christians, but it includes *other Christians* as well, most inexplicably those professing inerrantists and infallibilists who, for whatever reason, cannot bring themselves to agreement with a "full" inerrancy position.

For my part, I have written this book as part of an effort to help students explore what lies beyond the overly restrictive parameters that have been set for bibliology by contemporary inerrantists. I am sensitive to the fact that contemporary inerrantist evangelicalism is simply not capable of providing students with the requisite spiritual muster for venturing outside inerrantist confines in healthy ways (whether seeking reconciliation or not). In fact, so damaging have I come to deem inerrantism's popular, anti-reconciliatory ethos that acerbic remarks like those of R. Carroll no longer strike me as too sweeping:

> To hear different individuals talking about something called "biblical Christianity," and usually in a context of social action, is to be set to wondering about the social phenomenon behind such talk. In many cases the phrase is used in an authoritarian way by people who appear to want to force whatever they understand by it on other people. It is political talk. It is social engineering. It is political lobbying by religious factions within a modern democracy . . . But since pluralist societies cannot be shaped by one faction to the exclusion of all other groups, such pressure

66. Compare Antoun, *Understanding Fundamentalism*, 42: "Scripturalism meets this need for certainty and authority for many people and gives them confidence to continue their pursuits, often in situations where the odds are heavily against them. Scripturalism allows people to proceed in the face of adversity and often jeopardy when others without their faith do not."

groups may well constitute serious problems for the wellbeing of democratic society.[67]

Perhaps by rehabilitating the doctrine of inerrancy, evangelicals can begin credibly deflecting critiques like this one. To be fruitful, however, a truly progressive formulation of inerrancy will have to be the result, genuinely undertaken with generosity, good will and social confidence. The present climate within evangelicalism seems far too characterized by fear to support these kinds of efforts. Irrational fears persist of possibly getting things wrong. Irrational fears persist of possibly making mistakes. Yet this is exactly what students need to be able to do. We should expect that students will make mistakes. To wit, they *must* make mistakes and be encouraged to do so, to take risks in bibliology and be as imaginative as God would have them to be. Is this not how students learn in every over discipline?

Here is another thought: spiritually mature students are precisely the ones who can be trusted by evangelicalism-at-large to expose the archaic vestiges of inerrancy's reactionary traditionalism and take appropriate steps to call evangelical leaders to account for perpetuating them. In a word, I am suggesting that students must be free enough to truly *be* students, to genuinely explore the faith and get deliberately creative. My hope is that the present work might contribute in some small measure toward the promotion of this kind of environment for conservative evangelicalism's students.

67. Carroll, *Wolf*, 68.

2

Reestablishing Hermeneutical Distance between Believers and the Bible

D ESPITE BEING SUBJECT TO the oppressive dynamics of American inerrantist culture, students can still count themselves blessed for being able to participate in the larger cultural moment. In important respects, the old guard is changing, and a virtual evangelical renaissance is now emerging. Evangelical views of scripture are continuing to evolve despite conservative efforts toward stabilization.[1] An increasing number of evangelical scholars are actively considering what non-inerrantist views of scripture will have the best chance of sustaining the upcoming challenges of the twenty-first century. The search is on for bibliological outlooks that are, among other things, more hermeneutically-conscious and critically-informed than the ones 20th century inerrantists had to offer.[2] There is no reason for evangelical understandings of the Bible to get caught up in the unhealthy dynamics discussed in the last chapter. Yet in order to fully appreciate this, students must first learn to re-establish a healthy hermeneutical distance between themselves as believers and scripture.

1. I see now that I was wrong in *Inerrancy and the Spiritual Formation of Younger Evangelicals* to think that change could be a top-down procedure. The impetus for change is going to have to come from the young. They are going to have to create their own public theological space where they can dialogue and decide whether a workable bibliology for the twenty-first century should include inerrancy or not.

2. Although some would like to see evangelicalism more explicitly identify with the Chicago Statement of Biblical Inerrancy (1978), other evangelicals judge that "[contemporary statements of inerrancy] are not appropriate places to start." See Witherington, *Living Word*, xviii. For the audience I have in mind, I thought it might prove helpful to explicitly engage both the Chicago Statement and the Old Princetonians (see chapters three and six respectively).

Although initially it may seem threatening to attempt something like this, students still stand to benefit, particularly those for whom this book is written. More and more, hermeneutical considerations are convincing evangelical thinkers in the States that it is time to honestly incorporate what biblical scholars have learned about the Bible into their bibliology. To be sure, there is a certain amount of risk inherent to subjecting inerrancy to critical examination (not least the possibility of its eventual abandonment), but the risk, I contend, should never be construed as that of losing the faith once for all given to the saints. Much rather, what is being proposed is actually an opportunity: a very real prospect of producing legitimate bibliological results that are no longer "amenable to the populist politicking that looms so large for evangelicals in other intellectual spheres."[3]

An important hermeneutical point that has recently come to light is that followers of Christ are *already* involved in a relationship with God even before they begin to formulate their doctrines of scripture. In other words, the ontological status of the believer is one where she *already finds herself participating in a live, spiritual dynamic between herself and God*. It is from within this already established relationship that evangelical believers seek to gain a better communal understanding not only of what the scriptures are but how they might be revelatory. The relationship already thus established is not to be confused with one's theological belief system. Rather, the key insight to make is that the existential, participatory relationship of the believer to God is *historical* through and through. Only from within this historical, or better historically-conscious, vantage can any consideration of what scripture actually is be holistically undertaken.

As historically-situated subjects, evangelical believers conceive their faith in ways that are temporally and culturally constituted, giving rise to their fundamental, historical contingency. In other words, the believer who seeks to contemplate and express her relationship to God can only do so through the conceptual tools provided by her cultural world, that is, through the cultural artifacts produced over the course of its historical development. A. Thiselton describes the existential predicament this way: "the public domain of 'the world' in which persons are embedded as 'bodily' provides the conditions and necessary currency for inter-subjective agency and personal interaction, for the communi-

---

3. Noll, *Scandal*, 237. See also my concerns in Bovell, *Inerrancy*.

cation of meaning and understanding, and for the capacity to identify and to recognize other persons as they are."[4] Hermeneutics is not only spiritually inescapable; it ranks existentially *prior* to scripture.

In other words, evangelicals are intentional subjects who are always already engaged in complex hermeneutical processes. This indicates that evangelicals' relationship to God is constituted ontologically and existentially, not scripturally. Methodologically speaking, therefore, preference should be given to approaches to scripture that investigate it "from below."[5] After all, a believer's relationship to God is not symbolized by scripture, nor epitomized by scripture, *nor necessarily dependent upon scripture.*[6] The relation between God and evangelical believing communities is not even *made possible* by scripture. The relationship between the believer and God is a faith relation distinguishable from scripture and could just as easily have been established by God without the use of scripture. Unfortunately, within North American inerrantist evangelicalism, scripture has come to occupy an unnaturally central role in creating and sustaining a spiritual relationship between believers and God. Therefore, re-establishing a healthy, critical, hermeneutical distance between believers and scripture appears to be in order.

Some evangelicals seek to forestall such development by insisting that it was *necessary* for God to write down once and for all—for him to commit to writing—what he wanted to "say." Yet ecumenical creeds, confessional hymns, liturgical recitations, etc. have performed the same

---

4. Thiselton, *Hermeneutics of Doctrine*, 47. Thiselton has been one of the few voices to consistently and persistently teach that *hermeneutical* considerations should be at the heart of theological investigations of doctrine.

5. See Work, *Living and Active*, 33–34. Work advises that an approach "from above" would be better since "[d]ivine descent precedes and empowers human ascent, and so descent is where the bibliology begins." A more hermeneutical position might respond that a "-logy" of any kind begins with us, the believers, since we are the ones who are conducting the "study" or "description."

6. Many OT scholars have come to regard "covenant" as a central theme in Israelite religion, but recently conservatives have gone further and used covenant as a model for understanding the scriptural writings as a whole. J. Frame, for example, sees the covenant model as apt for describing scripture: "[E]ven if we have reservations about Kline's thesis that the Scripture historically developed from the original covenant document, we must admit that the five major elements of the covenant form each represent an important aspect of biblical revelation." See Frame, "Covenant." Evangelicals should take care not to obscure via their theology the fundamentally cultural and historical fabric within which the scriptures are intrinsically embedded. Compare Grenz and Franke, *Beyond Foundationalism*, 134–63.

historic, preserving function that scripture gradually helped play.[7] After all, there was an historic time when believers related to God as Christians *before* a scripture ever existed. These persons accepted the good news of Jesus Christ before any Gospel or epistle was written. Indeed, the hearing of the word that brings faith, although oftentimes making recourse to scripture, need not necessarily involve scripture. The message of the gospel that has spread through communities worldwide over the course of Christian history is not scripture per se, but rather a message that more basically belongs to the broader historic, cultural and traditional deposits of Christian churches. True, the revelation of Jesus Christ as Son of God may be communicated to faith communities via scripture, but this revelation belongs more fundamentally to the early churches' expression of their own existential commitments to God in light of the cultural concepts available to them. Although the message of the good news of Christ is bequeathed to later generations with the help of scripture, the message is more originally transmitted by communities of faith via their historic and cultural heritage with the aid of scripture. These traditions both receive and help construct the message of the gospel for contemporary and subsequent generations. From at least one perspective, then, hermeneutics is actually more necessary to faith than scripture. Scripture, as given by God, fully partakes in the cultural dialectic of believing communities in order to become scripture for them. Scripture comprises but one facet—a very important facet to be sure—of the faith communities' hermeneutical engagement with a more original gospel message, a message of salvation for those who come to believe. Or put more generally: "Scripture is both part of the created order and a participant within God's saving history."[8]

Many evangelicals in the States are taught in churches and parachurches that to accept the findings of critical scholarship is by default an act of rebellion and unbelief. Yet if the scriptures only contingently bear upon believers' relationships to God, there exists an appreciable

7. One mechanism that faith communities have used to reliably pass on the gospel story is a functional educational system. D. Carr observes that in ancient cultures "[o]ral and written modes are integrally intertwined in the process of transgenerational cultural reproduction." See Carr, *Writing*, 139.

8. Paddison, "Authority of Scripture," 448. In this chapter, I might be interpreted as compensating for what Paddison identifies as "one of the imbalances of blueprint theologies of Scripture, namely their inability to connect revelation *with the time of its reception* [my italics]" (460).

hermeneutical space between believers and scripture that believers are able to spiritually transcend. In some respects, then, the acceptance of critical scholarship can actually be a demonstration of faith, a genuine exercise of spiritual understanding. One way to illustrate what I mean is to reflect on how believers are already in the habit of making spiritual judgments *before* they ever reach for their Bibles. Jesus brings this to light, for example, in Mark 2:27, which might be anagogically paraphrased to the following effect: *scripture was made for humans and not humans for scripture.* Conservative evangelicals tend to regard Christ as one who taught and understood scripture in the same inerrantist manner that they do today. For example, to conservatives it seems only natural that one should collate a handful of inferences from scripture and insist that scripture clearly teaches the popular American inerrantist view. Furthermore, *because of this* inerrantists conclude that it behooves believers today to continue to uphold inerrancy. Yet conservatives seem all too unaware that whenever they do this they themselves illustrate how by virtue of their own intentionality and inter-subjectivity, believers are hermeneutically situated to transcend the biblical texts. They transcend the texts, for example, in their pre-interpretive act of collecting "inerrancy-friendly" texts to begin with, the texts they are wont to identify as relevant for supporting inerrancy in the first place.

In this context, D. Kelsey's observations come to mind:

> In the arguments we examined, Scripture was in fact almost always used as data, rarely as backing, and never as warrant. . . . The tendency to rely on Scripture only for data arises out of a concern simply to explicate God's Word and not to fall into a kind of churchy editorializing about the state of the world. But it causes theology to shirk its critical responsibilities and turn into a paraphrase of Scripture or an outline of the logical interconnections among concepts in Scripture.[9]

W. Webb goes further in his analysis of evangelical approaches to scripture. Although strict adherence to a "static hermeneutic" represents a good faith effort to draw pastoral conclusions based on "actual words on the page," "surface perceptions are not always an accurate reflection of reality."[10] Readers of the Bible *must* sit in judgment of it. In fact, doing so is an integral part of reading scripture—of reading any text for that mat-

9. See Kelsey, "Appeals," 17.
10. Webb, *Slaves*, 55.

ter. The evangelical hermeneut is *already* in the habit of transcending biblical texts in their every attempt to apprehend the purposes behind God's provision of scripture.

Returning to Jesus' Sabbath saying transmitted in Mark 2:27, E. Schweizer notes: "Jesus' attitude, however, is more radical: To him the law is a gift to man, not only in exceptional cases, but as a general principle." In other words, there are far greater implications for the saying than a less stringent understanding of the Sabbath. In Schweizer's view, Christians are precisely the ones spiritually situated to appreciate this given their chronological position in redemptive history. If they are not careful, however, faith communities can experience developments in ideology that actually cause scripture to become a cultural hindrance to the building up of God's kingdom. In other words, sociological and political factors can become insidiously operative to make scripture spiritually burdensome to believers—a burden, it goes without saying, God never intended it to be. In my view, the conservative evangelical construal of scripture enables just this kind of predicament to obtain via its strict doctrine of full inerrancy. When all is said and done, contemporary inerrantism is simply too prone to abandoning the redemptive intentions of scripture, intentions that evangelicals should take a more active interest in identifying and responsibly engaging.[11] Olson says as much in his own diplomatic way: "The fear that in much conservative theology a good systematic theology can replace the Bible is not entirely unrealistic."[12] It is not without reason that biblical scholars like K. Sparks have begun urging inerrantists to consider how it might not always be wrong for believers to "trump" scripture, that is, if they can find ways to do so in an authentically principled and scriptural manner.[13]

Some conservative evangelical students are independently coming to similar conclusions, not through the influence of unbelieving critics (as inerrantists like to allege) but as a natural result of their own cultural immersion in inerrantist communities, communities that espouse and promote "scripture-only" mindsets.[14] Conservative evangelicalism in the

11. Compare Webb's idea of adopting a "redemptive-movement hermeneutic."

12. Olson, *Reformed*, 154.

13. See Sparks, *God's Word*, 295. Olsen describes this in terms of preferring narrative to didactic statements. See Olsen, *Reformed*, 176.

14. Christian believers are thought to receive the gospel story from 1) scripture "alone," 2) tradition "alone," or 3) from a combination of scripture and tradition. By

States can be charitably interpreted as a full-throttled attempt to augment the material and scope of a scripture "alone" approach to Christianity to create a "biblical" tradition, putatively based wholly in scripture. What conservatives want to be able to say is that they have diligently gleaned a tradition that is truly "from the Bible" and which also can be identified both as their own and as that of historic Christianity.[15] In response to modern pressures, conservative Protestant traditions foster a scripture "alone" mindset that purports to sift scripture for express doctrinal statements and "necessarily" deduce "the whole counsel of God" from these clear propositions.[16] Variations of this strategy can serve the conservative impetus well. After all, conservative Protestants are after an account of scripture that is supple enough to have scripture surrogate as its own "tradition" without having to concede that scripture is somehow insufficient and without needing to explicitly invoke an actual church tradition—an actual, temporal and artifactual culture diachronically produced over the course of a community's history. Unexpectedly, however, the very process of constructing faith with a scripture "alone" mentality has forced some students to experience firsthand the delimiting frustrations inherent to a "scripture alone" procedure.

A growing number of "post-evangelicals" see themselves now as *post*-evangelical precisely because their spiritual journeys have gradually brought them to what appears to be the "end" of evangelicalism. One way to understand "end" in this context would be to take it to refer to a terminal boundary for evangelicalism, a place on the religious spectrum that indicates, at least on the face of it, that one has ventured "beyond" the cultural and theological confines of conservative evangelicalism, somehow managing to have culturally and theologically gone "outside" it. A second way to understand "end" is to take it to refer to the *telos* of evangelicalism, evangelicalism's *raison d'etre*. "Post-" in this sense suggests that a believer has come to gain a fresh understanding for what it really means *to be* evangelical, for what the underlying purpose

---

"tradition" I mean the total religious culture produced by the communities who incorporate the gospel story into their religious "grand narratives."

15. The extent to which evangelicals have failed to accomplish this was confirmed for me recently in a church membership class where the teacher unwittingly asked, "Where do you see the gospel in the Nicene Creed?" and not a few participants responded, "I don't."

16. Bovell, *By Good and Necessary.* For analogous developments in Roman Catholicism, see Powell, "Canonical Theism."

of evangelicalism *is*, or at the very least, *what it is supposed to be*.[17] Not without irony, a post-evangelical has come to spiritually appreciate that a scripture "alone" rubric ultimately entails a scripture-tradition hermeneutic, not unlike the ones already operative within scripture itself. In other words, an authentic way of "converting" to post-evangelicalism is to realize—after trying one's best to faithfully adopt a scripture "alone" mentality—that scripture itself is inherently "traditional," drawing believers into hermeneutical engagements that are *already* thoroughly embedded in communal and cultural understandings, understandings that cannot help but be intrinsically *extra*-biblical.[18]

To help see this, consider how evangelical scholarship tends to occupy itself with the recovery of scripture's "original" message. The assumption is that scripture can only be granted divine authority when believers are able to access those messages that scripture genuinely offers. In other words, evangelicals believe that there can come a point when reading scripture as a community where the "tradition" that is carried on by the community drowns out the voices that scripture is offering. When this happens, the communities have become too active, as it were, in their transmitting of the messages of scripture and have inadvertently "added" to these messages in such ways as to potentially obscure the messages or possibly even negate them. In an effort to guard against this, conservative evangelicals argue for the adoption of their scripture "alone" mentality, a mentality where scripture is to be given absolute priority, especially when ecclesial bodies come together to derive their statements of faith. Insofar as possible, as evangelicals communally read their scriptures and pass along the messages they believe the scriptures relate, priority must be given to scripture's own messages over against other considerations. As church history shows, this becomes ever more crucial when what scripture teaches and what a community's history, culture or tradition promulgates actually come into conflict. The evangelical mind, then, takes it for granted that a sustained and meticulous study of the scriptures is paramount for spiritual health, with every aspect of biblical study commanding the highest attention.

---

17. Whether this "new" evangelical perspective ultimately takes one "beyond" the pales of traditional American evangelicalism remains to be seen.

18. For more on the problems that "historical understandings" of faith pose for sola scriptura, see Williams, "Tradition," 362–64.

Evangelicals are faced, then, with having to decide which facets of scholarly inquiry are most suitable for the theological study of scripture. A controlling paradigm that directs evangelical investigations of scripture is this: "What, according to the Bible, is in fact going on when God speaks?"[19] T. Ward, to take a recent example, thinks the most promising way to broach this question is to consider first the relation between God's action and his words and then between God's words and human words. From there, one can ponder the relation between Christ's words, God's action and God's person and then reflect upon the relation between Christ's words and human words. Only after this preliminary theological groundwork is laid will one be in a position to properly consider the relation of God's word to the Bible. The upshot of all this, explains Ward, is that "[t]he supreme form in which God comes to encounter us in his covenant promise is through the words of the Bible as a whole. *Therefore to encounter the words of Scripture is to encounter God in action.*"[20] Yet an obvious and primary encounter of God in action is routinely overlooked by conservative evangelicals. According to the conservative's own position, there is an overwhelmingly obvious (at least it *should* be obvious) example of God acting in history lying at the heart of the evangelical project: that is, God's genetic action of giving his communities scriptures.

God's putative action of delivering scriptures to his people over the course of redemptive history should suggest itself to evangelicals as a primary locus of investigation if one is going to approach faith from a scripture "alone" perspective. In fact, the main way to properly understand scripture at all is precisely through an historic and cultural investigation of the scriptures themselves from their geneses through to their culmination as canons. When this is done, one begins to appreciate in what ways scripture is *not* in a position to constitute one's faith. More realistically, it should be culturally and sociologically incorporated into a broader spiritual dynamic that operates *historically* within broader religio-cultural matrices. For the scriptures both receive and direct communal developments. Scripture works together, through and with, religious culture. Its end is the building up and strengthening of believing communities' relationships with God and via the "ladder of abstraction" God's relationship to the world through them.

19. Ward, *Words of Life*, 20.
20. Ward, *Words of Life*, 48.

In a nutshell, the scriptures are God-breathed, a living and active component of God's revelatory economy. As such, they are always *useful* for the historical development of the various ways in which believing communities conceive and express faith. Scripture cannot but be *useful* for helping faith communities participate in God's redemptive program in culturally appropriate ways. Their usefulness, however, is of a peculiar sort: scripture uniquely strengthens believers in their kingdom-building capacities, holding both for a context of communities sharing belief in Jesus Christ and also the context of their wider participation in and contribution to artifactual world-culture (see 2 Tim 3:16–17).[21] All this is through the Spirit.[22] Furthermore, scripture is a primary means of providing historical and cultural direction to spiritual commitments already in place between faith communities and God and also amongst each other. The key is to understand that the hermeneutical process is always a work in progress. Therefore, understanding which aspects of biblical criticism are fruitful for the study of scripture at any particular juncture is an ongoing task of critical discernment. The point to stress is that this act of discerning is already underway even *while* constructing an evangelical bibliology (not merely *after* a bibliology has been set in place).[23] From one standpoint at least, then, "hermeneutics has less to do with biblical interpretation *than it does with biblical interpreters* [my italics]."[24]

Contrast this with how many conservative writers agree with a position like Ward's, insisting that learning about what happens when God "speaks" has to take priority over every other consideration, particularly "if what we eventually say about our understanding of the Bible

21. Compare Goodrick, "Let's Put," 486: "I would put 2 Tim 3:16–17 into English something like this: 'For Scripture, alive as it is with the vitality of God himself, is valuable for indoctrinating people, for rebuking people who should know better, for correcting people who do not, for guiding people, so that God's man can be completely equipped for every good work.'"

22. Compare Holmes' recent call for the reintegration of "the inner illumination of the Spirit, a regenerate heart and a commitment to prayer" with contemporary biblical hermeneutics. Even better is H. van den Belt's developing position: "If the *autopistia* of Scripture implies that the discovery of its authority depends upon the witness of the Spirit, it is preferable to see the doctrine of Scripture as an aspect of the doctrine of the Spirit." See Holmes, "Kings," 411; van den Belt, "Scripture," 446.

23. I try to dissolve the Old Princeton distinction between biblical "teachings" and "phenomena" in chapter six below.

24. Briggs, "What Does Hermeneutics," 69.

as the 'Word of God' is going to be true and coherent."[25] To achieve this, Ward, for example, immediately looks to the Old Testament and draws his readers' attention to biblical accounts of creation. Yet these pericopes have already been translated, already been interpreted and already been appropriated into English on believers' behalf before they can even begin to read them. I do not want to come across as pedantic or as wanting to restrict believers' access to scripture, but the point should be observed that what Ward is attempting to do as he "does" bibliology stands at the *back-end* of (or at least midway through) the hermeneutical process. This may be an indication that evangelicals are prone to engage in bibliological discussions without an adequate regard for the hermeneutical complexities that have already been set in motion. I should make clear that what I am after is merely a preliminary hermeneutical "depiction" of what inerrantists are already in the habit of doing when they read scripture, a phenomenological exploration of "hermeneutical ontology," as it were, *co*-doctrinally undertaken *within* evangelical bibliology itself and not *pre*-doctrinally stipulated as if probing for "the conditions of possibility" of reading scripture.[26] As F. Watson has rightly sought to clarify, "There is no question here of seeking a *foundation* [italics in original] for the doctrine of Scripture in general hermeneutical theory."[27]

That said, whatever else one believes regarding the Old Testament as scripture, it is manifestly a human, cultural and historical artifact, an artifact bearing remarkable semblances to other artifacts of its time. The OT itself is a heavily redacted compilation of ancient religious literature replete with culturally-laden notions, motifs, and images that have been transmitted to posterity in ancient and foreign languages, all involving long and complicated histories. As is well known, there are other cultural artifacts contemporary to various parts of the Old Testament, being both chronologically and geographically proximate to them and more or less close in literary "type." At this stage in evangelicalism's own historical development—after two hundred plus years of critical biblical scholarship—the very act of reading the Old Testament is known to call upon hermeneutical processes that have yet to be properly appreciated by inerrantists.[28] These hermeneutical processes cry out for pre-theological

---

25. Ward, *Words of Life*, 20.
26. Compare Webster, "Hermeneutics," 316.
27. Watson, "Hermeneutics," 142.
28. M. Pickup chides inerrantists for not being more sensitive to New Testament us-

discussion, as it were, *before* (or at least while) trying to map out all the options for what inerrancy might possibly mean—much less theologically entail—for us as believers in Christ in the twenty-first century. Yet these kinds of discussions, J. Webster points out, "can only be settled 'metaphysically,' that is, by working out what the text is, who we are as its interpreters, and what ends we are to pursue as we read it."[29]

Even as divinely inspired, the many writings comprising the Old Testament have been written, redacted, and compiled by numerous persons who lived in a variety of places and time periods. Let us presume that all persons primarily involved in these activities were "believers." By virtue of being hermeneutically active participants in the diachronic production of scripture, the biblical tradents were already ontologically committed to a faith relationship with God. At the same time, the biblical writers could not help but utilize contemporary cultural expressions as they sought to give voice to these relationships by fundamentally incorporating already existing traditional and communal deposits into the very production of scripture. Over time, some of the scriptures that were written became more permanent parts of an already vibrant cultural and historical matrix. These writings were dialectically absorbed into the complex of historical traditions that typifies community life. Traces of these developments are noticeable even in the earliest scriptures but tend to be more explicitly instantiated in later scriptures, particularly in their re-appropriation of earlier scriptures for subsequent cultural expression and trans-generational usage.[30] At every point, it is from within an historical, cultural-communal perspective that the conception and articulation of faith takes place.

What a Bible reader finds in the scriptures, then, never ceases to be fundamentally historical, cultural, and traditional, even when we acknowledge its status as "word of God." In retrospect, K. Koch came to recognize that "[t]he theology of the [nineteenth] century talked much about 'the Word,' but unpardonably neglected the importance of speech." Something similar might be said of conservative evangelical bibliology. For as Koch notes, speech requires more than philological and linguistic

---

age of the Old Testament according to midrashic hermeneutics. From this perspective, critical scholars have done a much better job of acknowledging these procedures for what they are. See Pickup, "New Testament."

29. Webster, "Resurrection," 138.

30. See, for example, Sanders, *Torah*; Fishbane, *Biblical Interpretation*.

investigation: "Linguistics still starts from the notion that the sentence is the unit of human speech, but speech is not in fact restricted to the utterance of sentences: it takes the form of the larger unit of the *literary type* [italics in original] of speech, which has a definite sociological function. This applies not only to the human word, but also to the Word of God as it is found in the Bible."[31]

What this means is that searching out the meaning of scripture, which conservative evangelicals identify as *the* task at hand, is a far more complicated affair than conservative evangelicals tend to assume in their articulations of inerrantism. A properly evangelical, scriptural hermeneutic should routinely involve the spiritual appreciation of what Fishbane describes as an "inner-biblical dynamic of *traditum-traditio* [that is] thus culturally constitutive and regenerative in the most profound sense."[32] A properly evangelical-hermeneutical appreciation of scripture will constantly be in flux, for researchers' own theoretical understandings of the cultural fabric of scripture are also hermeneutically formulated. As such, they too are—at their very core—open to perpetual change.[33] In other words, the goal for conservative evangelical theology—to faithfully promote a scripture "alone" perspective, a conception of scripture that is always under construction—should be to adopt a perspective on scripture that is itself radically "scriptural."

If conservative evangelicals are really interested in developing a sense for God acting in history—if they are serious about learning how God reveals himself to believing communities in history—they can do no worse than to turn a blind eye towards the theological significance of God's incarnational activity in the production of God-breathed scriptures within culture and history. If conservative evangelicals believe scripture to be God's word—that the best way to understand this is to concede divine action in God's scriptural "speech-acts"—they should be more willing to focus on the *way* God has acted historically in his diachronic giving of a written "word" to faith communities.[34] An important

---

31. Koch, *Growth*, xiii.

32. Fishbane, *Biblical Interpretation*, 18.

33. Ward is representative of conservative evangelicalism when he insinuates that Warfield's arguments effectively anticipate any new data that biblical studies may uncover. See Ward, *Words of Life*, 88–89. I engage the Hodges' and Warfield's views below in chapter six.

34. Compare Allert, *High View?*

way that evangelicals can take first steps toward doing something like this is by becoming more sensitive to the hermeneutical traditions of the biblical tradents themselves within *their* respective socio-cultural matrices. By doing so, inerrantists will be in a far better position to develop a nuanced view of the Bible's inspiration.[35]

For example, Ward helpfully suggests that "the 'fullness' of God, which God was pleased to have dwell in Christ, also included the *words* Christ spoke."[36] He, along with many other conservative writers, appeal to the dominical discourses found in the Gospel of John as illustrations. Yet this places students in an awkward position, particularly once they realize: "The bread of life discourse (as well as the other distinctive Johannine discourses) preserves not the words of the historical Jesus but words about Jesus that derive from prophetic articulations of his importance to the Johannine group . . . Social memory processes are evident in the way that the words of Jesus were preserved and transmitted by various early Jesus-group writers."[37] Of course, students do not need to draw this specific conclusion in order to appreciate the general point I seek to make here. D. Allison explains:

> [Some believers] may, for instance, fret upon learning that many modern scholars do not believe that Matthew wrote Matthew or that Jesus spoke the discourses of John. They may also, depending on their background, find themselves vexed upon becoming persuaded that the old props—miracles, eyewitness origins, the proof from prophecy—have seemingly fallen to the ground and are in need of being themselves propped up or maybe abandoned as everlasting ruins. Such individuals have awakened from their dogmatic slumbers and cannot go back to sleep.[38]

Consider another example. In *Words of Life*, Ward relates his understanding of "covenant" to the context of what God has done for Israel, a people "redeemed by this gracious and sovereign act of God in the exodus."[39] Yet a student inquiring into the nature and authority

---

35. Compare chapter six below where I insist that those who disagree with a full inerrancy position are not denying the Bible's "teaching" on inspiration but only trying to understand the nature and extent of its inspiration.

36. Ward, *Words of Life*, 38.

37. Williams, *Stewards*, 181–82.

38. Allison, *Historical Christ*, 4.

39. Ward, *Words of Life*, 28–29.

of scripture from an evangelical-hermeneutical standpoint might be advised to proceed more carefully, in a manner more consistent with critically-sensitive dispositions.[40] For even a conservative scholar like Sparks admits that "[the historical evidence] suggests that our biblical accounts of the exodus may have been shaped by literary embellishment and creative theological elaboration as much as by historical events."[41] To wit, the most informed summaries to date of the relevant archaeological evidence conclude that "the exodus story, one of the most prominent traditions in Israelite common memory, cannot be accepted as an historical event and must be defined as a national saga."[42]

Similarly on form-critical grounds, the conservative, "canonical" approach of B. Childs observes:

> the influence of the mythological language from the sea battle affected the transmission of the tradition of the Reed Sea. Particularly in the poetic passages the language of creation as a victory of the sea monster soon fused with the language of redemption at the sea. By the time of the Priestly writer the language of splitting the sea, of drying up the waters which were part of the myth, had become stereotyped vocabulary for describing the Reed Sea event.[43]

The point to take away is that there is a real cultural history to scriptural thought, a broader cultural fabric within which the scriptures fully participate and it is precisely within this cultural world that they

40. Thiselton has recently outlined a "dispositional" account of belief. See Thiselton, *Hermeneutics of Doctrine*, 35ff. One of the main motivations behind this account is to be able to emphasize how "belief becomes articulated precisely when someone denies it, distorts it, or attacks it in the hearing of Christian believers." In the present chapter, I am pondering how to articulate a doctrine of scripture precisely when the conservative evangelical position is critiqued *and the critique is found to have merit*. In my view, post-evangelical views will conceive of the formulation of doctrine as hermeneutical encounters with "questions that arise." By contrast, American inerrantist views of scripture shy away from hermeneutical polyphony and perpetuate biblical criticism as a "freestanding problem."

41. Sparks, *God's Word*, 100. Sparks concedes that "our theological judgment on these matters can be wrong just as easily as our historical judgment" (320–21).

42. Mazar, "Patriarchs," 60. Finkelstein in the same volume finds the stories about the patriarchs, about the exodus, and about the conquest all "wrapped in late-monarchic realities" (55).

43. Childs, *Book of Exodus*, 223. S. Richter, for example, misses a tremendous opportunity to guide lay persons through some of the critical issues that have definite implications for evangelical theologies of scripture. See Richter, *Epic of Eden*.

ideologically operate. In fact, it even appears to be the case that cultural considerations so inherently inform scripture's stories and teachings that such aspects can no longer be construed as merely "human" glosses over what God has inerrantly "spoken." Culture is a fundamental, hermeneutical dimension that evangelicals need to become more ready to acknowledge and engage as we revisit the question, what *are* the scriptures and in what ways are they revelatory? Every effort must be made to more adequately understand scriptural literary "types", preferably *before* asking these questions (or at the very least, *while* we are asking them).

Canonically speaking, the churches lay claim to a specific kind of "grand narrative," and communities throughout the world continue to celebrate them. The narratival framework they all adopt proclaims God's redemptive program as definitively advanced in the gospel of Jesus Christ, a gospel finding its basis in its story of death and resurrection. Most churches understand this framework to be revelatory, yet what some evangelical communities are realizing is that though the grand narrative is indeed revelatory, the means by which it has been revealed to churches involves a fundamentally cultural and historical economy.[44] The extent to which God has chosen to reveal himself and his redemptive program via particular historical and cultural matrices has only recently begun to inform evangelical bibliology. Inerrantist bibliology can only stand to benefit from more openly reckoning with the theological ramifications of God's deciding to reveal in this way.

To illustrate, consider Akenson's brilliant literary and cultural insight into the hermeneutical contingencies that have been intrinsically woven into the conceptual grammar of the New Testament:

> Therefore, when we see some of the more vibrant of the ideational components of late Second Temple Judahism [*sic*] being pulled together in a manner that is both religiously creative and pragmatically inventive, we must accept the possibility that this great work-in-progress might well have been achieved with another religious persona as its totem. All the major components are stock items, right off the shelf of Second Temple Judahism [*sic*], and they could have been made to fit a number of contemporary factional leaders. (Would a "New Testament" with John

---

44. The present claim is that revelation is always historical and cultural, not that culture is revelatory. Compare Olsen, *Reformed*, 196–97. We might not agree with Olsen, however, on whether scripture is "necessary" (although we may have a different sense of "necessary" in mind).

the Baptist as the central figure have been all that different?) The specific icon given centre stage was not so important as were the motifs and symbols that were assembled around the figure.[45]

Leaving for the moment Yeshua of Nazareth—"out of the picture entirely" as Akenson asks us to do—there is a very important observation to make. The early "Jesus communities" made full use of the conceptual tools available to them when they formulated their initial understandings of the Christian gospel. In other words, the biblical tradents themselves made ample recourse to pre-existing cultural traditions.[46] The phenomenon is not restricted to the New Testament; we have already mentioned how this happens frequently in the Old Testament, too.[47] The creative use of existing traditions in both the Old and New Testaments—to the extent of reworking preformed traditions under the names of well-known prophets or apostles for theo-political purposes—demonstrates not only how radically off the conservative evangelical understanding of biblical authorship is, but how radically an inerrantist understanding of what scripture is has to change.[48] Furthermore, Watson makes the historical theological observation that for contemporary Protestant doctrines of scripture "canonicity is the foundation."[49] Yet even here, tremendous advances in canon studies are prompting a fresh set of evaluations:

> To attribute so much significance to the canon in its final form, and to play down the means for discerning its history, is perhaps to put too much weight on a single segment of the tradition and one particular element of the believing community. Is it enough to acknowledge that canon resulted from a process, and that other factors besides theological ones played a part, but then deny the relevance of this for a theological explication of the canon?[50]

There is a danger, then, of "failing to reckon with the naturalness of the canonical texts" by "proposing an immediate relation between God and the texts." According to J. Webster, the understanding of scripture as "God-breathed" can thus wrongly be called upon to "short-circuit all

---

45. Akenson, *Surpassing Wonder*, 231.

46. See, for example, Flusser, *Sage*.

47. See Enns, *Inspiration*; Sparks, *God's Word*; and Harlow, "Creation."

48. See, for example, Ellis, *Making*; Neihuis, *Not by Paul*.

49. Watson, "Hermeneutics," 126.

50. Spina, "Canonical Criticism," 182.

historical processes" and to present the biblical texts as if they were not in fact "texts," that is, as if they were "ideal" and not as they are, "dirty."[51]

What inerrantism needs now more than anything else is for students to conscientiously take up this kind of work in their own researches to determine if and in what ways inerrancy might be rehabilitated. In virtually every quarter, for example, it has become commonplace for evangelicals to make less guarded hermeneutical concessions to sociology of knowledge. One tenet of interest—especially as it applies to biblical studies—is that "One cannot understand a text unless particular questions are asked of it, and these questions are prompted and informed by the preunderstanding of the world the interpreter carries with him as he initially approaches the text."[52] What is new and exciting, however, particularly in *evangelical* biblical studies, is the realization that the ways the biblical authors pre-understood *their* religio-cultural world was generically stipulated to them by a common social space populated by both the biblical tradents *and* their contemporaries (and not "primarily" by scripture, or at least by scripture unmediated). In R. Rohrbaugh's words: "the individual's universe of perception is both his own . . . and at the same time that of his society, [with the latter being] largely responsible for both giving and maintaining all structures of meaning."[53]

Unfortunately, American inerrantists seem inordinately reluctant to develop such ideas in bibliology. M. Pickup suggests that a strict adherence to grammatical-historical exegesis is partly to blame.[54] Yet a more fundamental reason may lie in the fact that inerrantist understandings of canonization seek to plausibly "[address] a variety of historical

---

51. Webster, "Dogmatic Location," 31. Webster also warns of the transformation that takes place from a dogmatic standpoint if the canon is subsumed by history of religions: "once [canon] comes to be viewed as part of the history of religions, the term 'holy' seems less and less appropriate" (17).

52. Rohrbaugh, *Biblical Interpreter*, 23.

53. Rohrbaugh, *Biblical Interpreter*, 22–23, which applies equally to the interpreter and the producer of the text.

54. See Pickup, "New Testament," 137: "[what we observe in the NT is] the tendency to read OT statements in something other than their grammatical-historical sense." This stands in considerable tension with both inerrantist exegesis and inerrantist doctrine of scripture. Compare Enns, *Inspiration*, along with Noll's comments: "What Enns seeks would require more critical self-consciousness than most scholars have been able to tolerate. . . . Christian exegetes need to be probingly self-critical about the religious and philosophical foundations of grammatical-historical interpretation." See Noll, *Jesus Christ*, 142.

periods in which scripture was reconceptualized" and "articulate the principles of transformation by which a canon is constructed," but they will never be able to make definitive "claims about the origin of canon."[55] This theoretical conundrum deeply troubles most conservatives in the States given their profound concerns with always upholding the *divine* origin of scripture.[56] However, this need not be as troubling as it may initially sound. Surely there is a way to articulate a post-evangelical (or even post-inerrantist) view of scripture that is still inerrantist enough "in spirit" to garner wider support. In the present climate, contemporary discussions regarding scripture are poised to develop in any number of interesting ways, but only time can tell which will prove the most bibliologically fruitful.[57]

55. Quotes adapted from Wyrick, *Ascension*, 384. Authorship and canon are not easily correlated. This raises uncomfortable questions for inerrantists. Add to this the observation that inerrantists tend to hold "historical" and "scientific" truths in parity with "theological" ones in their definitions of inerrancy. Therefore, if inerrantists prove unable to locate an "historical" origin for the canon of scripture, how much less will they be able to identify a theological one? Peckham admits this as an inherent weakness to "intrinsic canonicity" approaches to canon-determination yet he is not willing to accept it as a "defeater." Watson proposes that the pre-Reformation churches should be seen as wrestling with what books finally belong in the canon while the Reformation churches should be seen as investigating what *role* the canon plays for the churches.

56. This helps explain why inerrantists keep looking to prophecy as a model for scripture. See, for example, Beale, "Can the Bible?" Compare J. Barr: "Nothing is more important in fundamentalist tradition than the idea of the prophet, the man to whom it is given to speak the words given him by God. . . . The prophetic paradigm is central to the tradition of fundamentalist thought. . . . [F]rom the prophetic paradigm fundamentalism derives two essential positions. First, the prophetic paradigm extends not only over strictly prophetic parts of scripture, but over the entire body of scripture. . . . Secondly, the prophetic paradigm is used to convey implications of the *sort* of truth that must reside in scripture." See Barr, *Escaping*, 20. Compare the paradigmatic role given to the "prophet" for understanding inerrancy in Grudem, "Scripture's Self-Attestation."

57. Unfortunately, the culture of fear currently plaguing contemporary inerrantism has made the burden fall to students to not only create a social space within which they might critically explore the options but also to "prove" to everyone else that what they are doing will be fruitful in the long run. In other words, students are being deprived of developmental opportunities that come with making creative mistakes, which is where the real learning typically occurs. See, for example, Yarbrough's ill-advised passivity: "At the very least, groups that uphold inerrancy can afford to abide in their time-tested convictions for now while they serve Christ and wait and see. Will those presently opting to abandon inerrancy fare better than the Protestant mainline and others who have been conducting the experiment of decoupling a more sacrosanct God from a less sacrosanct Scripture for many generations, thus far with ominous results?" See Yarbrough, "Embattled Bible," 14. At this rate, inerrantists are virtually guaranteeing that there will

A. Torrance reminds us that God is not only "veiled by the human form of his revelation," he is also "revealed to humanity *because* of this veiling." Torrance looks to Barth's writings for theological inspiration, clarifying that *hermeneutically speaking*:

> There is the horizon of the people and culture of the biblical period; then there is our horizon in the twenty-first century. But there also has to be another human horizon, through which God is present by the Spirit and which facilitates the transformative integration of these two horizons—what we might call the "mind of Christ."[58]

What Torrance calls "another human horizon" I have described above as a "cultural," "historical," and "traditional" matrix of societal and communal depositories "through which God is present by the Spirit." The "transformative integration" which Torrance envisions is in the process of being uncovered by some evangelical bibliologists in the otherwise "natural" formation of scripture. From an inerrantist standpoint, then, these are the kinds of hermeneutical considerations that need to be theologically incorporated into contemporary evangelical bibliology.

What *is* scripture and how is it revelatory? These are questions that evangelical students need to begin asking afresh. Their answers will have important implications for their doctrines of inerrancy. The more in line a doctrine of inerrancy can be with what scripture is and how it is revelatory, the better it will serve upcoming generations of evangelical students. Admittedly, the broader evangelical world is not likely ready for a post-evangelical account of "inerrant" scriptures. Even so, important, preliminary steps must be taken in the meantime toward rehabilitating inerrancy. Perhaps along the way some other more credible bibliology might eventually even be constructed. If evangelicals really intend for some "high" view of scripture to remain relevant for the academic and spiritual formation of students—or if evangelicals hope to credibly use inerrancy at all—these are the types of questions that need to be addressed.

Some of the recent inerrantist literature I have come across features authors making provincial judgments to the effect that those critiquing inerrancy have simply not demonstrated enough familiarity with the

---

never be any breakthroughs, or that if there are, it will almost certainly not be an inerrantist who is responsible for it.

58. Torrance, "Can the Truth Be Learned?," 158.

doctrine to begin suggesting revisions. In my view, there is no need for students interested in criticizing inerrantism to be required to explicitly interact with the Chicago Statement of Biblical Inerrancy, for example.[59] The conservative inclination to artificially restrict students' dialogue partners to one "statement" or another is evidence that an impetuous traditionalism has set in over the course of decades of protecting against "liberalism." The prevalent inerrantist tendency of placing these kinds of ad hoc, bibliological burdens on students seems to me to border on emotional and spiritual manipulation. The evangelical students I am trying to reach will not be much helped by artificially turning their bibliological clocks back two or more generations.[60] The Chicago Statement, to continue with the current example, is programmatically incapable of fundamentally addressing today's students' concerns.

That said, in a gesture of good will and in an effort to keep the dialogue open to as many students as possible (including those raised on positions *like* the Chicago Statement) I will devote the next two chapters to trying to explain why the Chicago Statement is not a bibliological resource to which I can refer students in good conscience.

59. See, for example, Beale, *Erosion*; Churchouse, "Defining and Refining;" Yarbrough, "Embattled Bible;" and Sexton, "How Far Beyond?"

60. Compare Witherington, *Living Word*, xviii.

3

The Chicago Statement of Biblical Inerrancy and the Truth of Biblical Narratives

A FTER A BRIEF PREFACE, the Chicago Statement of Biblical Inerrancy provides a "summary statement." The first point reads: "God, who is Himself Truth and speaks truth only, has inspired Holy Scripture in order thereby to reveal Himself to lost mankind through Jesus Christ as Creator and Lord, Redeemer and Judge. Holy Scripture is God's witness to Himself." Although the impression given by the Chicago Statement is that its tenets are all supported by scripture, a number of philosophical assumptions are tacitly called upon by inerrantists to help them theoretically underwrite it. In this chapter, I briefly explore issues surrounding the belief that God should be a "God who is himself Truth and speaks truth only." Of particular interest is the importance of *function* for modeling truth, particularly scriptural truth, and for determining "truth-claims" made by biblical narratives. These issues I address in the next chapter. In this chapter, I question why inerrantists should expect biblical narratives to always participate in a specific kind of language game, one that has rules that allow for truth bearers *to be made true* by correspondence with states of affairs in reality.[1] My suggestion is that when evangelicals engage the issue of inerrancy they over-commit biblical narratives to being true by correspondence.

Truth is not a topic one broaches lightly. The literature on truth is immense and there is little I can say that will indicate ways out of the metaphysical thickets. On the one hand, contemporary metaphysics is not concerned with a God who is himself truth and who speaks only truth. On the other hand, inerrantist writers proceed as if a diversity of

---

1. Compare Longman, "Storytellers."

theories of truth were not extant. Most inerrantists appear content to say, "Truth is what is really the case," and leave it at that.[2] Nevertheless, work remains to be done regarding the metaphysical perplexities that come with truth-talk, especially truth-talk purporting to describe how God inspired biblical narratives to be "true." How biblical narratives are true has yet to be satisfactorily treated within evangelical bibliology.

The phrase, "God, who is himself Truth," I have not found in scripture. Nevertheless, evangelical believers have no qualms about affirming it. Nor should they, for "God who is himself Truth" has an estimable pedigree. For example, if one moves in Reformed circles, one can appeal to the Westminster Confession of Faith or to such theological luminaries as John Owen.[3] If one moves in non-denominational, evangelical circles, one can appeal to J. Feinberg's magisterial work on the doctrine of God.[4] Finding prominent evangelicals who declare something like "God who is himself truth" is not difficult, but to describe what one *means* by saying "God is Himself Truth and speaks truth only" is a different matter.

For example, the WCF does not elaborate on what is meant by the phrase "God (who is Truth itself)." In keeping with its language game of public confession, it defers to scriptural passages that describe God's role in prophetic utterances. John Owen (*Works*, 1.79), for his part, provides the following explanation:

> God himself is the first and only essential Truth in whose being and nature the springs of all truth do lie. Whatever is truth—so far as it is so, derives from him, is an emanation from that eternal fountain of it. Being, truth, and goodness, is the principal notion of God; and in him they are all the same.

Feinberg also offers an explanation: scripture claims repeatedly that only God is truly God. He goes on to say: "God is truth because he always tells the truth," which he understands to mean "whatever God says matches the way things are."[5]

---

2. Perhaps some readers are sympathetic to the extreme views expressed in Moreland, "Truth." I have tried to critique Moreland's views in Bovell, "Pragmatism."

3. WCF at 1.4 mentions "God (who is truth itself)," and John Owen writes, "God himself is the first and only essential Truth." See *Works of John Owen*, ed. W. Goold (Edinburgh: T & T Clark, 1882), 1.79.

4. Feinberg writes: "Our God is also a God of truth. He knows the truth and only speaks the truth." See Feinberg, *No One Like Him*, 370.

5. Feinberg, *No One Like Him*, 372. Feinberg goes further and asserts: "To say that God's

Altogether, there appear to be at least four points (one primary and three subsidiary) that evangelicals seek to make when they declare God to be Himself Truth who speaks truth only. The primary tenet is 1) God in his very Being is (among other things and in a way that preserves his simplicity) one of the transcendentals: Truth.[6] From this tenet stem three subsidiary claims: a) God is truly God; b) God is truth because he always tells the truth; and c) whatever God says matches the way things are.[7]

Now to say that God "is" in some way the transcendental Truth is not the same as saying that God is truly God, nor is it the same as saying that God is truth *because* he always tells the truth or that whatever God says matches the way things are. Each of these contentions may prove to be corollaries, but to say one of these things is not automatically to say the others, at least not without elaboration. When evangelicals affirm, "God is Truth," they often have in mind something like John Owen's phrase: "the springs of all truth do lie" in him. For better or worse, Owen describes what he means in terms of metaphysical "emanation." Conservatives who are bothered by the "un-biblical" language of "emanation" could say instead something like: "in his lordship attribute of authority, [God] is the very standard of truth for his creatures."[8] Either way, the basic aspect of truth evangelicals appear to be after is that whatever truth (lower-case 't') humans may encounter in the universe ultimately derives its truthfulness from God's transcendental Truth (capital 'T'). If this is the claim inerrantists are making in the Chicago summary, then some important questions to ask would include: "what is Truth"? "what is 'truth'?" and how important for either is the notion of "how things are"?[9] In this chapter, I will focus on the second question, referring to

-----

laws and statutes are true means that they correspond to the way things should be."

6. The transcendentals, by the time John Owens was writing, had become the main interest of metaphysics. According to Gracia, Duns Scotus was probably the first thinker to claim that metaphysics primarily occupies itself with "unity, truth, goodness, and whatever else is a transcendental attribute of being, as well as the relation of being to its transcendental attributes, and the relation of the transcendental attributes among themselves." See Gracia, "Suárez," 121.

7. Compare Berkhof, *Systematic Theology*, 69.

8. Frame, *Doctrine of God*, 477. Frame employs the language of "source and standard" when he discusses God's qualities in relation to those of creation (364, 366). Berkhof observes that considerations of the Absolute in philosophy do not always coincide with God in theology but concedes that there are times when this can happen.

9. Another critical question is *how* does truth "get" its truthfulness from Truth?

the first only insofar as inerrantists tend to do when they attempt to gain their bearings for addressing the second question.

Many conservative evangelicals see, "what is truth?" as a theological question and are quick to look to scripture for help in determining an answer.[10] R. Nicole has helpfully catalogued the different notions of truth that appear in the Bible, commenting on the various words in scripture that seem to him to describe the concept. Nicole observes that truth in the Bible principally denotes "faithfulness," "conformity to fact," and "completeness."[11] According to Nicole, when God is called "the God of truth," "the implication is that He is the only true God and that as God He sums up in Himself the fullness of faithfulness and truth."[12] Nicole further observes that what God says will always conform to fact. When Berkhof sums up the Reformed view, he makes the same basic points: to say that God is Truth is to say that God *fully answers to the idea of the Godhead, is perfectly reliable in His revelation, and sees things as they really are.*[13]

Interestingly enough, the description of the virtues of truth offered by B. Williams in his "State of Nature" fiction do not substantially differ from the biblical and theological descriptions just mentioned. (Williams' inquiry is explicitly naturalistic.) Williams observes that given any hypothetical community of human persons who are able to communicate, the basic communicative dispositions of "accuracy" and "sincerity" will always prove desirable.[14] Accuracy has to do with providing information that is reliable and correct. Sincerity has to do with providing information without lying or deceiving. Even from a naturalistic standpoint, anyone dependent upon a society's shared pool of information, on account of what Williams calls "an epistemic division of labor," will tend to hope

10. Geisler adamantly claims: "Every Christian should get his view of truth about the Bible from the Bible." Feinberg, for his part, repeatedly objects to looking to the meaning and use of biblical words to inquire into the meaning of biblical concepts. See Geisler, "Concept of Truth," 336; Feinberg, "Relationship of Theories," 16–19, and Feinberg, "Truth, Meaning and Inerrancy," 26–27.

11. Nicole, "Biblical Concept."

12. Nicole, "Biblical Concept," 289.

13. Berkhof, *Systematic Theology*, 69.

14. It is interesting to note that Williams' two naturalistic virtues of truth seem to be the same as those that Moreland and Craig identify as "[t]wo aspects of the biblical conception of truth," namely faithfulness and conformity to fact. See Moreland and Craig, *Philosophical Foundations*, 131.

that those who are in the business of contributing to this shared pool of information are both accurate and sincere every time they do so.[15] In bibliology, this is where the rubber hits the road for inerrantism.

Evangelicals find themselves methodologically committed to an exclusive corpus of religious writings for their religious beliefs and practices. In many ways, the compilation of sacred literature recognized as scripture by evangelical communities acts as their shared pool of religious information. In order for their spiritual understanding of Christianity to be conducive to eternal salvation, there is a profound hope that whoever historically contributed to this shared pool of religious information was both accurate and sincere when they did so.[16] One way to ensure that scripture, as a shared pool of religious information, exemplifies both virtues of truth is to insist that scripture has somehow been inspired by God. Irrespective of the precise manner by which God inspired the Bible, once God becomes one of the contributors to the shared pool of religious information, the information contained therein gains the potential for displaying the twin virtues of accuracy and sincerity to the utmost degree. And if God turns out to be the principal contributor to the shared pool of information or, better yet, the sole contributor to the pool, then there is a sort of guarantee that the information contained in scripture will, by its very nature, display the virtues of accuracy and sincerity to maximal degrees. As Feinberg notes, "Inerrancy becomes *necessary* because of the divine element."[17]

At least two issues arise. First, what *kind* of contribution did God make to the shared pool of information, with respect to the composition, redaction, and compilation of scripture? Second, what virtues of truth are exemplified by scripture (and in what ways are they exemplified)? Consideration of the first question I leave for another time.[18] A preliminary discussion of the second is what I present below.

---

15. See Williams, *Truth*.

16. Feinberg helpfully explains why accuracy is paramount from an inerrantist point of view: "[W]hy would one want to rest his eternal destiny on a book that is factually mistaken, even if those errors did not come as a result of willful deception?" See Feinberg, "Truth, Meaning and Inerrancy," 26.

17. Feinberg, "Meaning of Inerrancy," 282.

18. Thiselton glibly states how God-inspired scripture is God's business, not ours. See Thiselton, *Hermeneutics*, 350.

What virtues of truth are exemplified by scripture once it is accepted that God has inspired all parts of scripture equally? According to Feinberg:

> Inerrancy means that when all facts are known, the Scriptures in their original autographs and properly interpreted will be shown to be wholly true in everything that they affirm, whether that has to do with doctrine or morality or with the social, physical, or life sciences.[19]

To help his readers understand what he means by "true," Feinberg defers to Aristotle ("To say what is, is, and what is not, is not, is true") and also to Tarski ("Truth is defined in terms of language . . . in terms of sentences . . . and . . . in terms of *correspondence*").[20] However, theories of truth that emphasize correspondence with reality raise a number of controversial issues. For one thing, there remain open questions regarding what people have in mind when they talk about "reality," but before continuing further, I would like to make a few preliminary remarks.

I have always been skeptical of philosophers who doubt intuitive notions of reality, e.g., by challenging the existence of objective reality. But when I came across physicists R. Peierls and R. Omnès saying things like: "I don't know what reality is . . . Again, I object to your saying reality. I don't know what that is," and "I would say that I am certainly not a realist . . . because I cannot understand what it means," I began to reconsider.[21] If those who devote their professional lives to science have become this reluctant to talk about physical reality, whence the Chicago Statement's confidence in assuming correspondence to *metaphysical* reality as intrinsic to its understanding of scriptural truthfulness? Not only this, but I have come across analogous remarks in my readings in the philosophy of mathematics. Moore, for example, writes:

> For it is the same compelling urge to step back and reflect self-consciously on our own set-theoretical practice that makes us think both that there must be a definite grouping together of all that we are dealing with and, correlatively, that this grouping together might exclude what it could just as well have included . . .

---

19. Feinberg, "Meaning of Inerrancy," 294.

20. Feinberg, "Meaning of Inerrancy," 295.

21. See Davies and Brown, *Ghost in the Atom*, 74,75 and Omnès, *Converging Realities*, 245.

The thought persists that we have a limited point of view, though there is no satisfactory way of saying so.[22]

By parity of reasoning, I began to realize postmodern criticisms of metaphysics may actually have something positive to contribute to inerrantism, with one important aspect having to do with how inerrantists construe biblical narratives as being "true."[23]

W. Welsch, for example, agrees with the parameters that were set for truth above: "truth is a characteristic of sentences" and "sentences belong to vocabularies or language games." He goes on to explain, however, that after subjecting Rorty's anti-representational argument to rigorous analysis he finds it "sound in every respect." According to Welsch, "Rorty has, at least according to all standards known today, achieved a valid refutation of the representational model." Rorty is not popular among evangelicals but it appears he has affected progress in metaphysics. If so, evangelicals should not hesitate to welcome it. Welsch traces some of the fallout in metaphysics from Rorty's philosophical work: "The idea of a reality-in-itself, an alpha-reality, is in *stricto sensu* impossible, because it can only occur within a language game . . . Our talk of reality is always the talk of a 'reality-under-a-certain-description.'"[24] It seems to me that if Welsch is right, there are ramifications for inerrantism, specifically pertaining to its insistence upon biblical narratives being true by correspondence.

22. Throughout, Moore is drawing attention to an acute sense of self-awareness now present in mathematics. He suggests humans, being finite, will often find themselves at pains to express what they cannot express. For example, when contemplating the implications of the Löwenheim-Skolem theorem he concludes: "Our best advice is surely that offered by Wittgenstein: to pass over in silence what we cannot talk about." See Moore, *Infinite*, 170, 171. Bronowski claims—though it has come as somewhat of a surprise—that scientists are more or less in the same boat. He describes the situation as a "crisis in mechanism": human attempts to speak about what it is that they do seem to inevitably unleash self-referential paradoxes. In his view, *science* can still continue as a discipline, but *scientists* are left shrugging their shoulders, admitting: "This is simply how we do things; so far it has worked for us." Compare Sternberg's remark about how those involved in hermeneutics must come to accept "that branch of acrobatics known as lifting oneself by one's bootstraps," either that or resign themselves to the fact that nothing can be accomplished in interpretation. See Bronowski, *Origins of Knowledge*, 85; and Sternberg, *Poetics*, 16–17.

23. Evangelical reflections on truth that incorporate postmodernist insights include: Williams, "Scripture"; Franke, *Manifold Witness*; Knight, *Future for Truth*; and Hicks, *Evangelicals and Truth*.

24. Welsch, "Richard Rorty," 170–71, 173–74.

If talk of reality is always conducted under certain descriptions, that will have implications for truth relations by which sentential descriptions are thought to correspond to reality. Thiselton observes, for example: "The biblical writings are clearly not committed to a formal 'correspondence theory' of truth as a *general* theory, but biblical writers regularly use 'truth' in the non-technical sense of *what corresponds with the facts of the case*." "Truth . . . remains a *polymorphous* [italics in original] concept, often context-dependent for its meaning."[25] The Chicago Statement, by contrast, pre-commits the Bible to truth by correspondence, setting out a bibliology that even defines God in terms of it.

To their credit, inerrantist writers emphasize two important strengths of correspondence theories: 1) Correspondence seems to describe our intuitive understanding of truth; and 2) Correspondence seems to be presupposed by its rivals.[26] I do not dispute these strengths.[27] Yet I do think inerrantists have not gone far enough to incorporate critical postmodern insights into their understanding of how biblical narratives relate to reality or how these narratives might be wholly true.[28]

Consider E. Wright's musings, for example. According to Wright, in order to communicate at all, humans must proceed *as if* the Real objectively conforms to our various projections. However, that the Real should conform *in toto* to human projections is not guaranteed. Not only this, but a metaphysical paradox persists such that our very interactions with reality indicate that conformity to reality should be questioned. Wright

25. Thiselton, "Does Lexicographical?," 284–85.

26. See, for example, Moreland and Craig's phenomenological and dialectical arguments in *Philosophical Foundations*, 139–41. Compare Geisler, "Concept of Truth," 335–36, and Larkin, *Culture*, 231–37.

27. That said, the evangelical arguments for how every other conception of truth presupposes truth as correspondence appear to me metaphysically myopic. As Schindler notes, truth can appear to come last or it can appear to come first. This will depend on where we decide to place our emphasis—the showing (beauty), the giving (goodness) or the expressing (truth): "The order [of the transcendentals: truth, beauty, goodness] is not static but circumcessive, and we would upset the circumcession if we allowed them to move, as it were, only in one direction." See Schindler, *Balthasar*, 370. As far as I can tell, many of the inerrantist arguments upset the circumcession of transcendentals in order to drive home a specific aspect of expression by making their understanding of truth metaphysically primary.

28. Geisler cautions inerrantists not to get sidetracked from focusing on what counts as error by trying to provide a theory of truth. But as Slob notes: "Perhaps, accounting for mistakes is really what theories of truth are about." See Slob, *Dialogical Rhetoric*, 11.

finds the intersubjective dynamic so striking he observes that those who defend realism are "exhorting us not to question the trust that binds us together."[29] They make a salutary *ethical* gesture by bringing to light their commitment to human communication. In Wright's view, however, they do not help philosophy along with its work in metaphysics.

In the tradition of philosophical hermeneutics, several writers acknowledge that in order to converse, conversation partners must trust they belong to the same "subject matter." There is an implicit expectation that a common subject matter provides an intersubjective meeting place where conversationalists can successfully engage each other. This acts as a universal constant, without which human intersubjectivity would not be possible. Conversing subjects exhibit a fundamental trust for the duration of conversations. That is the condition for intersubjective interactions.[30] Generally speaking, then, experiences of the Real are mediated through intentionality, an intentionality that is linguistic at its most elementary level.[31] This is a point on which the continental, analytic, and pragmatic traditions all seem to agree.[32] As Welsch explains, expressions like "real" and "reality" "already contain . . . a particular exposition of the X to which they refer, moreover an exposition that is anything but self-evident."[33]

In Wright's view, pre-theoretic affirmations of the Real as a singular and external reality serve as a methodological fiction for the sake of intersubjectivity.[34] Humans *must* take reality for granted as a precondition of intersubjectivity. Nevertheless, suspending judgment on reality as a singular, external Real is not the same as asserting that the Real is not real. Phillips brings this out in several of his essays. To say that contemporary metaphysics has gotten things wrong in its conception of human contact with reality is not the same as saying that humans are not in contact with reality.[35] As Moore has recognized, any argument that comes across as a defense of antirealism must be understood as "a *realist*

---

29. Wright, *Narrative*, 124.

30. See Bubner, "Ground of Understanding," 72–73.

31. Gill explains that as fundamental as language is to intentionality, it should not be thought to exhaust intentionality. See Gill, *Mediated Transcendence*, 116.

32. Compare Wheeler, *Deconstruction*.

33. Welsch, "Richard Rorty," 172.

34. Wright, *Narrative*, 107.

35. Phillips, *Religion*, 40.

attempt to justify anti-realist circumspection."[36] And this is as it should be: *some* kind of reality always remains in sight.

Wright is intrigued by the way the Real corrects intentional subjects' projections; he happily affirms the Real. Lynch, too, understanding truth as pluralistic, has an interest in validating reality. Informed by a relativistic Kantianism, Lynch argues:

> Truth concerns the way the world is.
> Pluralism holds that the way the world is, is relative to a scheme.
> So pluralism must hold that truth is relative to a scheme.[37]

Lynch commits to a pluralistic understanding of truth without denying realism. He adopts a minimal realism, to be sure, but it is realism nonetheless.[38]

The concern I have about the Chicago Statement's emphasis on "God, who is Himself Truth and speaks truth only" has to do with the way it emboldens students to uncritically presuppose a simplified, unified "how things are" mentality while reading biblical narratives, dialectically reinforcing a metaphysical expectation for a "how things are" correspondence. The correspondences inerrantists discern between truth-bearers (whether sentences or propositions) and truth-makers (facts or states of affairs in reality) are notoriously mysterious. This helps obscure from students some of the more serious difficulties.[39] The main problem involves the way correspondence theories cannot say much about facts or states of affairs. Williams explains: "There is no account of facts that at once is general enough for the purpose and does more than trivially reiterate the content of the sentences for which it is supposed to be illuminating the truth-conditions."[40]

36. Moore is referring to "the case for antirealism." See Moore, *Points of View*, 244.

37. Lynch, *Truth in Context*, 137. Lynch defends himself from two of the most common objections to pluralism by explaining that although every truth might be relative to a scheme, our concept of truth is not and that although pluralism might be true relative to every scheme, that is not the same as saying that pluralism is true not relative to any scheme.

38. Compare Engel who remarks that minimal realism is "more real than it is minimal." See Engel, *Truth*, 122.

39. Proponents of correspondence do not consider mysteriousness a problem, but Slob presses correspondence theorists: "The only reason, thus, why we would prefer the correspondence theory to a deflationary theory is exactly a *substantial* [italics in original] clarification of what it is to correspond." See Slob, *Dialogical Rhetoric*, 15–16.

40. Williams, *Truth and Truthfulness*, 64–65, summarizing Davidson's well-known

Inerrantists like Feinberg tend to object that critiques such as these confuse talking about what truth is with talking about how to decide whether a given sentence is true.[41] After all, there are those who are interested in truth precisely for what significance it holds for epistemology. For example, Ducasse writes: "It seems to me evident that the only sort of way of defining truth and falsity capable of being useful for the purposes of a theory of *knowledge* [italics in original] is in terms of the activities and experiences by which truth or falsity get known, as these activities are observable in the cases where truth or falsity admittedly do get known."[42] The Chicago Statement, for its part, is interested in establishing an inerrantist bibliology, but it gives students the false impression that the pertinent questions have already been satisfactorily answered. The Chicago Statement prematurely forecloses inquiry precisely where the problems are the most pressing: what should believers understand when they affirm biblical narratives are wholly true? *Are* there ways of asking for clarification on correspondence without having to ask how one can *know* a sentence is true? *Are* there ways to ask for clarification regarding how to decide if a sentence is true without having to be in a position to actually decide whether a sentence is true? The jury is still out on such questions.[43]

Consider Article IX of the Chicago Statement, which reads: "We affirm that inspiration, though not conferring omniscience, guaranteed true and trustworthy utterance on all matters to which the Biblical authors were moved to speak and write." Feinberg interprets this as saying that whatever the biblical writers affirm in any matter they write about will be wholly true. Evangelicals are interested in providing a rationale for believing that the Bible is true in theology, particularly with respect to an evangelical understanding of personal salvation. To help accomplish this, inerrantists believe something *like* the Chicago Statement is

---

objection. Williams notes that there is also the more general problem of individuating facts for any purpose. Correspondence theorists propose ways around this critique. See, for example, Vision, *Veritas*.

41. Feinberg, "Relationship of Theories," 4–5.

42. See Ducasse, "Facts," 326–27.

43. Compare Kunne, *Conceptions of Truth*, 24: "How can we understand sentences that allegedly express truths beyond justifiability?" Or from the other direction, Engel, *Truth*, 118: "But a conception of truth *conditions* can hardly be alien to a conception of *truth*, for how could one fail to have a conception of these conditions, without having a conception of *what* they are the conditions *of* [italics in original]?"

required.[44] This is where truth as correspondence reinforces for evangelicals a rigid pattern of thinking regarding what biblical truth entails: in every way available biblical narratives should be understood as corresponding to reality, and this correspondence is made good by actual states of affairs. In other words, the states of affairs that correspond to what biblical narratives affirm are what make the scriptures true. In their effort to emphasize scriptural truth, inerrantists place an emphasis in biblical narratives' correspondence to reality.

G. Osborne's discussion on truth in Scripture's historical narratives illustrates the inerrantist thought process in action. According to Osborne, when dealing with scriptures that narrate history, one should search for scripture's truth in two ways: 1) via a correspondence between an event or speech reported in the narrative and what actually happened in history; 2) a correspondence will also obtain between the *theology* affirmed by the narrative and the theological message of the rest of scripture.[45] Osborne explains that readers of the Bible must grow in their appreciation of how its historical accounts and theological teachings are integrally related. Thus believers should expect scripture to be wholly true on levels deemed appropriate to history and theology respectively. Both the historical and theological dimensions of truth are involved in every historical narrative of the Bible and both facets of truth are to be understood in terms of truth as correspondence. The inerrantist expectation, then, is that in whatever ways correspondence is achieved for the biblical genre in question, the Bible never fails to correspond to a state of affairs. This is the only way biblical narratives can count as true.[46]

Kevin Vanhoozer offers similar advice to inerrantists.[47] He explains that when it comes to scripture, "[t]ruth is the fit between text

44. The Chicago Statement's "summary statement" insists: "The authority of Scripture is inescapably impaired if this total divine inerrancy is in any way limited or disregarded, or made relative to a view of truth contrary to the Bible's own; and such lapses bring serious loss to both the individual and the church."

45. See Osborne, "Historical Narrative." Stated in this way, one wonders whether Osborne remains captive to "Hume's metatheological dilemma" (that there are two types of truth: truths between ideas and truths among facts). See MacDonald, *Karl Barth*, 4–5.

46. Some articulate the matter as follows: "If those parts of the Bible that can in principle be checked by empirical investigation are shown to contain error, on what basis does one maintain that the doctrinal, nonempirical matters are infallible?" See Erickson, "Biblical Inerrancy," 390.

47. To clarify, it is Osborne who is following Vanhoozer, "Semantics."

and reality, between what is written and what is written about." Yet, in Vanhoozer's view, it is important to remember that "there is more than one kind of fit." Each of the different types of biblical literature corresponds in different ways "to this or that aspect of what is really the case."[48] He claims the biblical literature always speaks about something in a specific way.[49] Appropriating speech-act theory, he terms the act of speaking, *locution*, and what one accomplishes by speaking, *illocution*. According to Vanhoozer, biblical truth is to be found in illocutions. On this account, a biblical author employing phenomenological descriptions is not necessarily affirming the phenomena. How to distinguish what is being *affirmed* from what is being *said* depends on the literary genre involved.[50] Yet inerrancy is always the result: "When properly interpreted, the Scriptures are utterly reliable because they are infallible—not liable to fail—no matter what God is doing with them."[51] Although Vanhoozer uses the term "correspondence" to describe biblical truth, he extends its normal connotation to include pragmatic aspects of truth (faithfulness, etc.). Still, at the core of Vanhoozer's construal is a correspondence account of truth: "the truth of Scripture is that quality of the biblical text that, as God's communicative act, ensures that what is said corresponds to the way things are when interpreted rightly and read in faith."[52]

What are the truth-conditions of scriptural narrative that allow us to say it is true?[53] What are the truth makers for biblical narratives if they are construed as God's speech-acts? Once again, the question arises as to whether inquiring into the truth-conditions of scripture is tantamount to checking to see if scripture is true.[54] For example, Stiver observes: "It

48. Vanhoozer, "Lost in Translation?," 103, 104.

49. A popular definition of discourse: "Discourse (spoken or written) occurs when someone says something about something to someone." See Westphal, *Whose Community?*, 79.

50. Or as Thiselton puts it, the language game employed dictates what can "count as" true.

51. Vanhoozer, "Lost in Translation?," 113.

52. Vanhoozer, "Triune Discourse (Part 2)," 72.

53. Greidanus explains that it is not required that a reader demand absolute historical accuracy from the narratives but there must be some "historical core" without which the theological message evaporates. Oswalt understands scripture to be claiming: "you should believe what we say because what we say grows out of things that actually happened." See Greidanus, *Preaching*, 31–32, and Oswalt, *Bible among Myths*, 155.

54. A distinction is made by Kirkham between the "metaphysical project" and the "epistemological project." See Kirkham, *Theories of Truth*, 23–28.

is one thing to determine what historical conditions are necessary. It is another to assess their truth."[55] At this stage of the game, inquiring into the truth-conditions of scripture is not the same as doubting its truth.[56] And inquiring into the truth-conditions of scripture—in ways that cause students to doubt the truth of scripture *as correspondence*—is not tantamount to proposing unbelief. Furthermore, even when doubts arise as a result of a genuine "faith seeking understanding" approach to bibliology, the types of doubts that arise tend to *illuminate* the faith in ways that would probably not have been possible had the doubts never been allowed to occur.

One question to ask is: what truth-conditions would make a "narrative speech act to succeed"? Similar to Osborne, Stiver suggests there are two kinds of truth-conditions that can make a narrative speech act succeed: "affective" and "representative."[57] Affective conditions for truth are the criteria by which narrative speech acts can be said to have accomplished their goals. Representative conditions for truth are the states of affairs in reality that have to obtain for the narrative speech acts to succeed. Stiver stipulates that biblical narratives are true in at least these two ways. In my view, it is wiser to mandate that only one of the truth-conditions be met for the narrative to count as true.

Even so, sometimes it will not be clear what the goal of a narrative speech act might be or what states of affairs are being indicated. M. Hesse

55. Stiver, "Ricoeur," 65–66.

56. Unfortunately, Bullock teaches that inquiring into the historicity of biblical narratives is a task properly done in apologetics but not in theology. In my view, Bullock's position not only encourages inerrantist students to take over-defensive postures toward critical examinations of the historicity of biblical narratives, it also erects an artificial wall between these kinds of historical critical questions and doing evangelical theology. When theology is done independently, as it were, then it will only be natural for practitioners to slide into apologetic mode whenever issues of historicity come up: their entire theological construct is at stake! Furthermore, students immersed for several years in evangelical philosophical and theological studies will emerge from their studies genuinely surprised that a given biblical narrative's historicity is extremely doubtful. "This can't be! Why didn't anyone tell me?" they might respond and gradually become spiritually disaffected. Otherwise, they will simply disallow its very possibility on philosophical and theological grounds. Compare how many evangelical Christians who had heard Davis Young lecture on geology were expecting his research to "marvelously confirm" the Bible (as they understood it). They could hardly contain their anger after hearing what he had to say. See Bullock, "History and Theology"; Davis, *Biblical Flood*, ix.

57. Stiver has the Gospels in mind. See Stiver, "Ricoeur," 64–65.

draws attention, for example, to "speech acts that have the *form* of prop-ositions, in that they must surely be understood to have some relation to *truth*, but which are couched in metaphoric or other tropic language for which criteria of truth are not clear cut."[58] Another consideration comes from rhetorical criticism where "a [biblical] text's predominant genre does not necessarily reflect the author's purpose."[59] Yet another consideration involves prophetic texts where the meanings of words are often not as they appear. The same goes for narratives that incorporate accounts of prophets (and their prophecies) into their storylines.[60] My contention is that the reading of biblical narratives is plagued by so many hermeneutical complexities that when "biblical truth" is construed as correspondence with reality, it does not adequately capture the nature of that truth. Even worse is that it can culturally prove a hermeneutical distraction. For starters, a preoccupation can develop with "establish-ing Scripture as a bullet-proof shield against modern historical-critical challenges."[61] It would be helpful if students could be given a chance to explore other options in metaphysics, but since the Chicago Statement for all intents and purposes forecloses critical discussion regarding how most fruitfully to understand how the Bible is "true," it should not be recommended to students as a helpful guide for constructing their ideal of scriptural authority, particularly as it touches upon scripture's "truthfulness." In a contemporary philosophical textbook, for example, A. Burgess and J. Burgess teach students that "[a]ll theories of truth, deflationist or inflationist are controversial."[62] The Chicago Statement, by contrast, gives students no indication whatever that philosophy (as usual) still has plenty to sort out.

If students presuppose that God is a God who speaks truth only and God is believed to "speak" through scripture, then they will be predis-posed to uncritically assign genres to biblical literature that seem most easily understandable as God speaking truth to them. In our modern (or hyper-/post-modern) culture, this means reading biblical narratives

58. Hesse, "How to Be," 93.

59. Möller, "Words," 377.

60. See Sandy's paper given at the ETS annual meeting in San Antonio, "Inerrancy of the Illocution." Online: <http://wordoftheday.reclaimingthemind.org/papers/ets/2004/Sandy2004/Sandy2004.pdf>. Accessed: 19 November 2009.

61. Stiver, "Theological Method," 172.

62. Burgess and Burgess, *Truth*, 132

as biblical "history" since history is easily conceived as corresponding to facts. If these facts are not stipulated as actual states of affairs, which is what makes correspondence metaphysically possible, then the prospect of a scriptural narrative being true is already precluded by virtue of definition. For this reason, students will resist construing narratives as "stories" since stories qua stories defy their pre-theoretical inclination toward construing (and establishing) truth by correspondence. Suggesting that biblical narratives are stories, therefore, has the same practical effect upon inerrantist students as not only suggesting that the God they believe in is untruthful *but that the redemption they are hoping for is an illusion.*

Even when students are taught to acknowledge the literary dimensions of biblical narratives, they will instinctively follow Osborne and Stiver and demand that scripture "doubly" correspond to reality with one strand of biblical truth corresponding to history (understood as "what actually happened") and another strand of truth corresponding to theology (understood as what the Bible theologically communicates through its literary activity). Whatever genre sensitivity students acquire in their classes is reflexively and emotionally overridden by an underlying existential concern over whether inerrancy can be upheld for every truth the Bible claims.

In an article criticizing McGowan's recent effort to rehabilitate inerrancy (by calling it infallibility), P. Helm takes McGowan to task for the charge he inveighs against inerrantists, namely that "inerrantists reduce the Bible 'to a set of propositions.'" To help illustrate McGowan's alleged "misunderstanding," Helm "adds the usual prefix" to three biblical sentences he claims to take almost "at random" (Mark 8:8, 27, and 33):

7. (It is true that) they took up the broken pieces left over, seven baskets full.
8. (It is true that) (Jesus asked) "Who do people say that I am?"
9. (It is true that) (Jesus said) "Get behind me, Satan!"[63]

Helm then proceeds to point out that (7) is the only one of these statements that can be true since it is the only one that is a proposition. This is a curious thing for Helm to say but at the same it highlights some of

---

63. Helm, "B. B. Warfield," 30, discussing McGowan, *Divine Authenticity.*

the complexities that inerrantists commonly overlook. One question to ask, for example, is what is the "biblical sentence" in (8)? Is it, "Who do people say that I am?" or is it, "*Jesus asked*, "Who do people say that I am?"[64] Another question arises as to whether we are in a position as readers to immediately subject biblical sentences to this type of analysis, particularly "at random." In other words, is it appropriate to restrict our investigations to the properties of "biblical sentences" as we try to understand how the Bible is true? Might there be larger units of discourse that need to be identified first *before* these types of analyses even take place? When Helm supplies his parenthetical phrase "Jesus asked," is he not implying as much?

Helm specifically states that the error he has uncovered in McGowan's views "rests upon a simple misunderstanding." In my view, Helm could hardly be more wrong; there is nothing simple about the claim he appears to be dismissing. Helm clarifies: "Questions and commands are not 'propositional statements.' Nevertheless, questions, commands, exclamations, aspirations, vows, and so forth, as well as statements, are all included in the inerrantist's basket." Very well. But is "*Jesus asked*, 'Who do people say that I am?'" a statement or a question? There are two levels of discourse here that need to be distinguished. The biblical narrator is stating what the character Jesus asked in his story. So although Helm is right to identify Jesus' question as a question, he seemingly ignores everything that has to do with the *story* the evangelist is telling.[65] The evangelist appears to be making a statement: "Jesus asked, 'Who do people say that I am?'" The statement involves the *narratival* claim that Jesus asked a question. The question itself, however, has no bearing at all on whether the narrator's statement is a statement. In other words, we should not be so quick here to "flatten" biblical narratives to a sequence of "first-order biblical sentences." This seems to me to raise at least the following two questions: 1) Is the narrator's claim qua statement-made-within-the-telling-of-a-narrative a propositional *truth*-claim? 2) What are the truth-conditions that would make such a proposition true?

Unfortunately, Helm's analysis with its stress on propositions shows little to no interest in deciding such matters. He explains: "For questions,

---

64. Mark 8:27: "Jesus went forth, and his disciples, into the villages of Caesarea Philippi: and on the way he asked his disciples, saying unto them, Who do men say that I am?"

65. He does the same thing for (9).

commands, and the like can each be inspired, delivered unerringly by their speakers and/or unerringly recorded. They are facts recorded by Scripture." The question to pose, which Helm regrettably overlooks, is whether the statement "Jesus asked, Who do people say that I am?" is a fact recorded by Scripture. Is Jesus' question a question he unerringly delivered as its speaker? Is the fact that Jesus delivered a question being unerringly recorded by the evangelist? While the latter two questions might be helpful for inerrantists like Helm to consider, they seem to pre-judge the matter, silently passing over some of the more pertinent issues. According to Helm, adding "it is true that" as a harmless prefix is "simply a linguistic device" that helps readers "assert" biblical sentences as facts. But why all the hurry to assert biblical sentences—sentences appearing in *narratives*—as facts?

Above I related Helm's examples 7–9, let us now turn to examine his first three examples:

1. (It is true that) Miss Muffet sat on a tuffet.
2. (It is true that) Miss Muffet ate curds and whey.
3. (It is true that) a Big Spider frightened Miss Muffet away.

Helm supposes for the sake of discussion that these are true and claims that the propositions (1) *Miss Muffet sat on a tuffet*, (2) *Miss Muffet ate curds and whey*, and (3) *Miss Muffet was frightened by a spider* are "nothing other than expressions used to record or report bodily states (like sitting) or actions (like eating) or reactions (like being frightened)."[66] In my view, Helm may reveal here his own over-willingness to propositionalize, for the complication at issue lies not in how propositions (1), (2) and (3) seek to express the "content" of the original sentences (1–3) but with the supposition that the sentences are "reporting" anything at all. He remarks:

> Of course the report of someone being frightened is not itself a case of being frightened, and it may not have a frightening effect on those who hear the report. A report of someone being frightened using language that rhymes is different from a report without a rhyme. But then a recipe for haggis is not itself haggis, nor a photograph of Edinburgh Castle itself Edinburgh Castle.

66. Helm, "B. B. Warfield," 28.

Helm then moves on from here to further develop his critique of McGowan's book, but this is precisely where more needs to be said.

What is the relation of the recipe to the thing that it is a recipe for? What is the relation of the photograph to the thing it is a photograph of? If biblical narratives are automatically conceived as "historical reports," it is no wonder inerrantists are so concerned about ultimately finding correspondences since inerrantists would be expecting them to be reports *of* something. But even Helm has recognized "a considerable hermeneutical burden on any would-be interpreter of special revelation. For he has to determine the exact limits of each kind of revelation, otherwise it may happen that the mistaken beliefs of men would be equated with the special revelation of God." According to Helm, there is a kind of special revelation that "reports" or "records" and another kind that "endorses" or "discloses." Both kinds of special revelation are to be found in scripture, but according to Helm, it is up to hermeneutics to help distinguish between them.[67]

And so we see how important philosophy has come to be for the Chicago Statement of Inerrancy. Inerrancy requires of students that they take unwavering stances on a number of complex philosophical issues that, in the broader philosophical literature, remain as open problems. These include truth, hermeneutics, and philosophy of literature, to name a few. Regarding the last, I briefly note that according to Larmarque and Olsen, "The constitutive conventions of literary practice are those that make a work of literature what it is: i.e., a work with aesthetic value. Roughly speaking this value is assumed to reside in two principal dimensions of the literary work: the imaginative and the mimetic."[68] I suggest one of the reasons the Chicago Statement proves so unhelpful is that it omits the pre-bibliological discussion of what the Bible is, of what the Bible might turn out to be, of how *imaginative* it is. It jumps the gun by trying to state upfront: " '[I]nerrant' signifies the quality of being free from all falsehood or mistake and so safeguards the truth that Holy Scripture is entirely true and trustworthy in all its assertions." Only after this does the Chicago Statement mention anything about history being treated as history, poetry as poetry, and so on. But inerrantists have already stacked the deck. For what type of literature *is* the Bible? Or more to the point, *what kind of literature is biblical narrative?*

---

67. See Helm, *Divine Revelation*, 90.

68. Lamarque and Olsen, *Truth*, 261.

Lamarque and Olsen helpfully remind us that although "a literary work can give form to a subject or a story which need not be invented by the author," "many literary works do, wholly or to some extent, consist of descriptions and stories which are made up or constructed."[69] And this brings us to the inerrantists' sticking point: Can scriptural narratives be "poesis," that is, "invention rather than report, story rather than history?"[70] Inerrantists tend to say, "No," because, as I have suggested, according to them the only way for biblical stories to be "true" is if they correspond to reality. A God who "speaks truth only" can only inspire stories that correspond to reality.[71]

Yet even Helm has to distinguish between reporting and disclosure, recording and endorsement, when writing about scripture as special revelation. He cautions that readers of scripture bear a hermeneutical burden of figuring out which is in view in specific passages. Thus I find his critique of McGowan all-the-more perplexing. In 1976, however, the devisers of the Chicago Statement officially convened to decide upon how to present inerrantism as a viable cultural option for the late 20th century. With so much at stake, they appear to have taken a gamble, finding it politically expedient to overconfidently expose the entire tradition to the imminent prospect of methodological deconstruction:

> We are conscious too that great and grave confusion results from ceasing to maintain the total truth of the Bible whose authority one professes to acknowledge. The result of taking this step is that the Bible that God gave loses its authority, and what has authority instead is a Bible reduced in content according to the demands of one's critical reasoning and in principle reducible still further once one has started.

The Chicago Statement is an apologetic effort to provide evangelicalism with a way to ensure that its theology corresponds to reality. The Bible's authority is respected only insofar as its correspondences can success-

---

69. Lamarque and Olsen, *Truth*, 262. Fishbane considers poesis to be an important part of "the practical imagination of Jewish exegesis."

70. Lamarque and Olsen, *Truth*, 262.

71. Inerrantists give lip service to being able to entertain other possibilities by pointing to Jesus' parables. By acknowledging there are parables in the Bible, inerrancy supposedly allows for "stories" in the Bible, but this maneuver is similar to Helm's focusing on the question Jesus is said to have asked rather than tending to the various levels of narratival discourse.

fully resist "the demands of one's critical reasoning."[72] For those who subscribe to the Chicago Statement, the way in which the Bible's narratives correspond to reality must be sufficient for its "account of the outline of doctrine from which our Summary Statement and Articles are drawn" to also be true. This list includes: the fall of Adam, the election of Abraham, the time of the exodus, the receiving of the Law by Moses at Sinai, and the life, death and resurrection of Jesus.

For better or worse, all these doctrines were constructed on the basis of the churches' decision to read biblical narratives as reports. And since Christians also believe that God "speaks truth only," when "historical" readings of the biblical narratives lose credibility *as* reports, a natural response is to try to cut bibliological losses by tying (in whatever way possible) the churches' decision to read biblical narratives as reports to cardinal beliefs regarding God's own truthfulness.[73] This way, suspicions applied to the churches' decision to read scripture historically can be recast (via inerrantist philosophy) as being tantamount to "apostasy," for only an unbelieving spirit could provoke someone to doubt God's veracity.[74] But as T. Pavel observes: "it is not always easy to discern regularities that belong to the literary genre from those engendered by the representation of social conventions established outside the literary exchange."[75]

Every religious community possessing a set of scriptures will have to find creative ways to "reactualize the ancient word of God for the present hour."[76] It is an arduous and continuous process. By paying special attention to the way inerrantists have already done this for them, students can learn a great deal about the cultural dynamics at work within contemporary American inerrantism. The cultural interplay between inerrantists and the wider non-inerrantist Christian world has been

---

72. Compare J. Barton Payne's surmise that traditional hermeneutical practices "have shifted in function from that of an X-ray for exposing meaning of Scripture to that of a cloak for avoiding it," and that this is even the case in "conservatively-oriented publications." See Payne, "Hermeneutics," 94.

73. Beale, for example, enlists the book of Revelation in his inerrantist attempt to force this very conclusion. See Beale, "Can the Bible?"

74. Thus inerrantists' frequent appeal to Gen 3:1. J. Morrison, for example, adopts this motif throughout his monograph: *Has God Said?*.

75. Pavel, *Fictional Worlds*, 127.

76. The phrase is taken from Fishbane, *Garments*, 38.

one of repeatedly drawing lines of hyperbolic, "here I stand" sorts.[77] The culture of fear that persists within inerrantism is a consequence of the way inerrantists have decided to expose the entire tradition to critical investigation and then call upon inerrancy to be its ad hoc Protector. J. Orr observed this over a century ago:

> This view still finds an echo in the note sometimes heard—"If the inspiration of the Bible (commonly some theory of inspiration) be given up, what have we left to hold by?" It is urged, e.g., that unless we can demonstrate what is called the "inerrancy" of the Biblical record, down even to its minutest details, the whole edifice of belief in revealed religion falls to the ground. This, on the face of it, is a most suicidal position for any defender of revelation to take up.[78]

Instead of belaboring just how much the inerrantist position sounds like bibliolatry, let us focus instead on exploring alternate ways for engaging some of these issues. To paint a better picture of what rehabilitating inerrancy might entail in the present culture, let us further explore the idea that scriptural narratives, whether true or not, are, well, *narratives*.

---

77. For the latest pertaining to the historicity of Gen 1–3, see the recent editorial in *Christianity Today*, "No Adam, No Eve, No Gospel." Online: <http://www.christianity-today.com/ct/2011/june/noadamevenogospel.html>.

78. See Orr, *Revelation*, 197–98.

4

Inerrantist Appeals to Speech Act Theory and the Truth of Biblical Narratives

THERE IS A SCENE in 1 Sam 5 where the Israelites bring the Ark of the Covenant out to the place of battle. As the Philistines recognize that the ark is a supernatural source of strength for the Israelites on the battlefield, they fearfully cry, "God has come into the camp!" But to everyone's surprise, the Philistines manage to capture the ark, which symbolizes not only the toppling over of the Israelites' army but also the toppling over of the Israelites' god. Yet when the Philistines take the ark away to the temple of *their* god and place it next to an idol there, the idol is later found toppled over on the ground beside where the ark is. The Philistines then replace the idol with another one and return the next morning. This time they find the idol not only toppled over, but also its head and hands are cut off and its torso alone is intact.

Before long, the Philistines grow very sorry they ever decided to bring the ark into their land. As the narrative unfolds, they move the ark from place to place in successive attempts to escape the hemorrhoids the ark repeatedly inflicts upon whoever is in possession of it. After seven months, the ark is finally set free, but since nobody wants to contract hemorrhoids by getting too close to it, the Philistines enlist the help of two unattended cows to take the ark from their land. The cows are left alone to travel in whatever direction they wish as they moo along their merry way. Nevertheless, the Philistines remain anxious over what will become of the ark lest, after all this, it should end up in their land again. So they secretly follow the ark, making sure it cannot see them. (They are afraid that if it sees them it will turn and give them more hemorrhoids). The cows eventually travel to Beth-Shemmesh. From there, the ark safely finds its way back to the land of the Israelites. The story elicits a good chuckle, if not outright laughter, from hearers/readers.

Taking up issues raised in the last chapter, how would someone who affirms the Chicago Statement read this story, knowing (in advance) that what it affirms has to be wholly true? If truth is understood primarily in terms of correspondence and if God is viewed as speaking truth only, inerrantists may feel obliged to say 1) the narrative is true in the history it recounts and 2) the narrative is true in whatever theology it affirms. I suggest this double tiered approach to biblical truth will not sustain students for long, particularly as they progress in their studies and allow their studies also to inform their faith.

That the 1 Sam narrative has the initial effect of making readers laugh should be brought to bear upon what range of dispositions readers might appropriately display towards it. Although the narrative might naively read as a report of "history," that the series of events recounted prompts laughter as a genuine response may indicate that the narrative is following rules belonging to language games other than reporting history. The prompting of laughter in this case may be an opportunity for the reader to train herself to read the pericope more competently. During subsequent readings of biblical narratives readers develop sensitivities they would not have been able to utilize on a first reading. As readers become more attuned to the literary practices in which a particular narrator is participating, they become better prepared to further explore what they are reading.

Evangelical interest in speech acts began with the realization that locutions are not the whole story, illocutions play an important role, too. Here I suggest that *per*locutions also pertain to the truth of narrative speech acts, even if they are not always recognized as being central to communicative acts. Nevertheless, their relevance to evangelical bibliology is beginning to receive some attention. For example, Vanhoozer in recent research explains: "Perhaps the most radical part of my thesis is its implicit claim (now explicit!) that any future evangelical doctrine of Scripture ought to include an account of the reader's interpretive agency and action."[1] In the last chapter, we saw that Vanhoozer finds biblical

---

1. See Vanhoozer, "Triune Discourse (Part 2)," 78. Once perlocutions gain the attention they deserve, I would not be surprised if it marks the end of evangelical interest in scripture as "God's speech act." On the unwieldiness of perlocutions for speech act theory, see Marcu, "Perlocutions."

truth in illocutions. To him, the question, what does it mean to say that the 1 Samuel narrative is wholly true? would be the same as asking, what illocution is involved in the narratival speech act?

We have already seen that *sentences* are what philosophers emphasize as being true or false.[2] The illocution, however—what an author is *doing* via the locution—does not appear amenable to the assigning of such truth values.[3] One question that comes to mind is, how can the illocutionary force of a story be regarded as true or false when the locution is the proper locus of truth value? The most straightforward way to respond, it seems to me, is to understand the illocutions as being intrinsically committed to the truth of their associated sentences, that is, the truth claims ostensibly being made by the locutions. One inerrantist strategy, then, might be to insist on a locutionary reduction by which the collapse of the illocution into the locution not only preserves the truth function of locutions but also purports to express the "truth" of the illocution by means of the "truth" of the locution since they are made out to be the same. If this can be programmatically done, then as far as truth is concerned, illocutions are nothing more than the affirmation of locutions, or at least nothing in and of themselves *without* the affirmation of locutions.[4]

Unfortunately, this kind of locutionary reduction is not always easy to accomplish, nor is it desirable. Oftentimes, Bible readers have the preliminary hermeneutical work of positing what language games the biblical tradents are engaged in. Then as they work their way through

---

2. Many philosophers do not want to bother with the ontological baggage that comes with talking about *propositions*. On the division of labor in philosophy of language between sentences and propositions, Searle explains: "The fundamental *use* of the word 'true' in assessing speech acts is to appraise members of the assertive class of speech acts. But the fundamental *concept* of truth is defined not in terms of statements but in terms of propositions." See Searle, "Illocutionary Acts," 40.

3. A related point is made over and again by D. Z. Phillips: practices and conventions cannot be true or false.

4. Another strategy is to deny that illocutions are the proper locus of biblical truth. Compare Geisler: "[W]hy something is said does not determine the meaning of what is said. The meaning of many passages of Scripture is understood apart from knowing why they were uttered in the first place. . . It is not the purposes of the biblical authors that are inspired; the propositions of Scripture are inspired." Contrast Vanhoozer: "Inspiration means not only that the words (locutions) are God's but that the word-acts (illocutions) are ultimately God's." See Geisler and Nix, *General Introduction*, 61, and Vanhoozer, *Drama*, 67.

discrete pericopes, they are better positioned to attempt to discern biblical truth-claims. Language games span the gamut of human communicative action. These include: describing an appearance, reporting an event, giving a measurement, and so on. Inerrantists seem to agree that biblical narratives, especially those in the "historical" books, are playing the language game of "reporting events." Accordingly, they expect that narratives will always correspond with states of affairs.[5] I suggest this kind of approach evinces a misguided zealotry for the Bible's truthfulness, construed in overly narrow terms of correspondence to facts.[6]

Could it be that the operative language game for our 1 Sam pericope, for example, is "making up a story and telling it"?[7] Furthermore, illocutions are not always singular because narratives tend to accomplish several things simultaneously.[8] I suggest it is the *spiritual-theological* illocution evangelicals are ultimately after. Nevertheless, inerrantists insist that one of the truth-makers for biblical narrative must be the state of affairs that comply with the rules of the language game, "reporting an historical event." Why? As far as I can see, the reason has to do with how inerrantists have decided in advance on what the truth-maker for narrative truth-bearers has to be.[9] During the process of determining the truth-maker, evangelicals try to steer clear of tensions that persist between evangelical intuitions regarding truth (involving accuracy and sincerity) and the prospect of there being illocutions for narrative

---

5. This approach to biblical narrative is arguably one of the defining features of the evangelical heritage. Compare MacDonald: "The tradition of Reformation exegesis construed all such genres as history in the ordinary sense of the term." See MacDonald, *Karl Barth*, 93.

6. Geisler argues that a correspondence view of truth can include non-correspondence theories, but the reverse cannot be made to happen. He explains: "Furthermore the passages where truth is used propositionally cannot *all* [my italics] be explained as truth in a strictly intentional and personal sense, that is, a sense that is not necessarily factually correct." The dispute is not about "all" passages but rather "some" or perhaps "many." David provides an interesting discussion on "bridge principles" between truth-making and truth-as-correspondence. For my part, I agree with Thiselton: "What truth *is* or *consists in* [italics in original] varies from language-game to language-game." See Geisler, "Concept of Truth," 333; David, "Truth-making"; and Thiselton, "Faith," 189.

7. See Wittgenstein, *Philosophical Investigations*, 12e.

8. Wolterstorff, for example, encourages Bible readers to conceive of scripture as "double-agency discourse." For a summary, see Wolterstorff, "Promise of Speech Act."

9. The language is borrowed from Sundholm, "Existence," 20.

speech acts that have little to do with truth so understood, at least within a framework of having narratives correspond to facts.

Inerrantists find questions like, "Is the 1 Sam narrative accurate?" and "Is the storyteller being sincere?" relevant questions to ask from the perspective of their doctrine of scripture. For them, asking these questions is tantamount to asking, "Is the Bible true?" But by asking these questions, inerrantists are appealing to something like Grice's conversational maxim of quality: All conversationalists are expected to "[t]ry to make a true and sincere contribution" to conversations. According to Vanderveken, the maxim of quality makes sense for "assertive utterances made in a special kind of discourse," but when the maxim gets generalized into broader illocutionary logic, it translates into a non-specific rule with the force: "Let your illocutionary act be successful."[10] In other words, to be accurate and sincere are sensible goals for *descriptive* illocutionary acts, but for other acts like deliberative, declarative and expressive ones, accuracy and sincerity simply do not translate well.[11] If inerrantists are claiming that the only way biblical narratives can follow the rule, "Let your illocutionary act be successful," is by their reporting actual historical events, then that seems to say more about *inerrantist readers' expectations* than it does about the Bible as an inerrant text.

In a summative article on the Philistines, C. S. Ehrlich writes: "Although [the 1 Sam pericope related above] may be based on an actual capture of the ark by the Philistines, in its current context it serves a symbolic function to underline the power of God and his ark."[12] Note how Ehrlich mentions that the story may loosely correspond to a state of affairs. *However, the reader's interest should clearly be on the function the story serves.* Inerrantist writers, however, are not generally satisfied with focusing on function, especially to the relative neglect of locutionary referents (whose truth, it is supposed, will be made good by actual states of affairs). They would be happier to establish some historical reference as a baseline truth condition for as many of scripture's narrative speech acts as they can. I lay the blame for this on two unwarranted bibliological assumptions: 1) If God inspired scripture, it must be *accurate* at all appropriate levels of discourse (including history, science, etc.) in order for it to be true, and 2) If the tradents of the biblical literature were *sincere* in

10. See Vanderveken and Kubo, "Introduction," 14–15.

11. Vanderveken and Kubo, "Introduction," 19.

12. Ehrlich, "Philistines," 784.

their contributions to the biblical texts, then the language game operative in and among the various parts of scripture will be plain to believing hearers/readers.[13] This second assumption—that the language game in which biblical writers are participating will be plain to the hearer/reader—impinges conceptually on the first.[14] It influences the first by predisposing inerrantists to understand it in a particular way.

To see this, consider what would happen if a fellow believer were to suggest to an inerrantist: Initially, several biblical narratives appeared *as if* they were historical narratives; however, many of them—after subsequently engaging them in more careful (re-)readings—seem more fruitfully understood as sagas and legends rather than recounting actual history (at least as we understand history today). The inerrantist would likely respond that to suggest the narratives are legends is to call the sincerity of the biblical writers into question.[15] This is not something an inerrantist would ever want to do because in their view these kinds of suggestions effectively render the entire Bible untrue since they practically imbue scripture with indeterminate amounts of what V. Poythress calls "muck."[16] Generally speaking, inerrantists are fearful of a slippery slope: if scripture is not held to be true and sincere in everything it affirms, there is the possibility (the likelihood?) that scripture will not be true and sincere in anything it affirms.[17] To help guard against this, a distinction is maintained between history and fiction, and the idea that fiction should be literarily embedded in scripture's historical narratives is culturally construed as being tantamount to blasphemy.

13. Compare this second assumption with Martin's remarks in "Special Revelation," 70–71.

14. This second assumption is different from supposing scripture's meaning will always be evident. It also differs from the practice among evangelicals of encouraging Bible readers to use clearer passages for the elucidation of obscure ones. The assumption supposes that if the book of Judges, for example, seems to us to be "history" then it must be historically true. In other words, to suggest that Judges is not history is to impugn the sincerity of the biblical writers themselves (to say nothing of their accuracy).

15. R. Gundry once suggested that portions of the Gospel of Matthew were written as midrash. The inerrantist response was unkind to say the least.

16. See Poythress, "Problems." Poythress is concerned that if the "clear" passages are not accurately and sincerely conveyed, what can we say about the less clear passages in scripture?

17. Bart Ehrman has been adduced as a possible example of this. See Bovell, *By Good and Necessary.*

For example, Bergen is not even willing to concede that a biblical character's utterance in a given narrative is the creative literary invention of the biblical author. He explains:

> Biblical analysts outside of the conservative evangelical tradition would suggest that the producers of canonical texts formulated comments that they then placed within the mouths of their characters. Conservative evangelical commentators deny that this inventive kind of authorial activity occurred within biblical narrative, but are willing to concede that activities such as editing, summation, and encapsulation of characters' comments did take place.[18]

Bergen insists that even the speeches recorded in biblical narratives must correspond to reality. In the case of characters' speeches, the narrator's characters (referring here to the actual people the characters are thought to represent) must have actually spoken words close enough to those reported in scripture in order for a correspondence to still hold. In short, historical narratives in scripture must always participate in the language game of giving a report.

The same concern lies behind S. Davis' position on the historicity of the Gospels in contradistinction to N. Wolterstorff's application of speech act theory to scripture. Davis disclaims that he is not an inerrantist, yet the tenor of his objection to Wolterstorff's approach is similar to one that an inerrantist might make. Davis writes:

> I said that adopting Wolterstorff's proposal would present the Christian church with a big problem. This is because his proposal would require a hermeneutic for distinguishing between those Gospel texts that are meant as actualities and those that are meant only as plausibilities. . . . How will we refute [those who say that the resurrection of Jesus was not meant to be an actuality]? I suppose by showing them that the chapters at the end of the Gospels simply do not read that way: that is, the evangelists thought of themselves as reporting sober fact. But surely that is true of just about everything we find in the Gospels (again, with the possible exception of Mark's chronology, Luke's grouping together of episodes with similar themes, and so forth).[19]

18. See Bergen, "Authorial Intent," 363, n. 5.

19. Davis, "What Do We Mean?," 96.

What Davis is fearful of is similar to what troubles Bergen above. In order for the Christian faith to be true, it is necessary to maintain some baseline correspondence to historical reality throughout the Bible's historical narratives, whether they are in the OT, the Gospels, or anywhere else in the Bible. Establishing a baseline for truth via historical correspondence to states of affairs may be of paramount concern to modern inerrantist believers, but these were not the primary concerns of the ancient biblical tradents, those involved in preparing the biblical documents for posterity. Wolterstorff is right to emphasize this—and I do not think this can be emphasized enough—"But there are other purposes that these portraits of Jesus serve, and other purposes—so I suggest—that they were meant to serve, than the purposes of the modern historian of the traditional sort."[20]

The Chicago Statement's declaration about God being Himself Truth and speaking truth only unhappily predisposes inerrantists to expect biblical narratives to participate in descriptive illocutionary acts by affirming the accuracy and sincerity of what is being described in the narrative. This shortchanges biblical truth. Wolterstorff is to be commended for his efforts to get believers talking about an "illocutionary stance of biblical narrative," for it does not seem appropriate to assume that the maxim of quality *must* be everywhere in effect in order for scripture to be true. That biblical narratives may temporarily suspend the maxim of quality does not necessitate that scripture cannot achieve "truth" by way of its broader illocutionary logic.[21] Generally speaking, biblical narratives are not being read competently when they are read strictly in terms of accuracy and sincerity, particularly when the language game in play does not have the maxim of quality among its rules of performance.

Above, I mentioned two assumptions: 1) the truthfulness of scripture demands accuracy in terms of correspondence, and 2) the truthfulness of scripture demands sincerity in terms of its participation in obvious language games. Taken together, the two assumptions work to obscure a major bibliological problem still requiring explicit treatment from inerrantists: *It is not always easy to tell the difference between his-*

---

20. Wolterstorff, *Divine Discourse*, 259.

21. Compare Martinich and Stroll, *Much Ado*, 70: "Suspending [the Maxim of Quality], even for large parts of discourse, does not change the fact that the maxim is not suspended for the whole."

tory and fiction in narrative hermeneutics. As Walhout remarks: "If we had only the narrative events, we would have a hard time telling whether the narratives in novels like Stephen Crane's *The Red Badge of Courage* and John Steinbeck's *The Grapes of Wrath* were intended as accounts of what actually took place or as fiction."[22] The inability to decide whether a work is history or fiction, based on narrative events alone, is not a hermeneutical problem unique to modern fictive literature. If anything, the problem is compounded in the case of biblical narratives on account of the considerable historical and cultural gap separating modern readers from the ancient world that produced them. Extra-textual factors must play a crucial role for figuring out what language games are in play. Even when a form of ancient historiography is involved, "[k]nowing *that* historical realities underlie the work does not immediately help us, in the absence of additional resources, to know *which* part originated where."[23]

Some inerrantists try to theologize the hermeneutical predicament by (mis)identifying the situation as an instance where rebellious sinners are seeking to mitigate or even undercut scripture's divine authority. Unfortunately, this description entirely misconstrues the important hermeneutical role humans play in their active contributions to the divine communicative act. Not only that, but it seems spiritually naïve, on a practical level at least, to limit the authority of biblical narratives to what inerrantists arbitrarily think *should* lie "behind" the text. The active role of the reader does not abolish scripture's authority, it merely complicates it by giving it human form.[24] Try as they may to keep hermeneutical complications from muddying their bibliological waters, inerrantists can no longer afford to ignore how "the reader is led, or perhaps more strongly, even *compelled* [italics in original] by the great author, to think and reason, in the gaps and afterlife, about the moral and philosophical hypotheses expressed in the fictional work of art."[25] This is not to suggest that the Bible is best regarded as an entirely fictional work or even as literature, but to insist: "There has to be a genuine tension, a real pos-

---

22. Walhout, "Narrative," 101.

23. Compare Sternberg, *Poetics*, 23–30. See also Sparks, *God's Word*, 212–27. Quote is from Mason, "Encountering the Past," 107.

24. To paraphrase Westphal, *Whose Community?*, 65. For a discussion of the "three-dimensional integrity of biblical authority," see Thiselton, "Can 'Authority?'"

25. Kivy, *Performance*, 113.

sibility of treating the scriptures as 'mere literature' until the 'signs' are interpreted aright."[26] To help illustrate the point, let us consider a second pericope, this one from 2 Sam 12.

There is a scene in 2 Sam 12 where the prophet Nathan enters David's presence at the Lord's behest and delivers an urgent message.[27] Nathan tells David that an incident has occurred involving two men, one rich and one poor. The rich man did not want to use one of the many sheep from his own flocks to feed a guest who was visiting. So he took the poor man's only lamb and prepared it for the guest instead. When King David hears this from Nathan, he assumes that everything Nathan says is true. Nathan, after all, is the selfsame prophet who communicated to David the Lord's promise for an everlasting dynasty. What Nathan said on that occasion was accurate and sincere, surely the same holds for what he says here as well. One might even speculate further that David always worked under that assumption: everything Nathan says in his prophetic capacity has to be accurate and sincere. That this man of God could give a false report in his capacity as prophet is not something David likely entertained. Either way, the story relates that David unreservedly commits himself to the truth of Nathan's story. Thiselton notes: "David construes [the fictional 'world'] as factual and . . . fully enters it."[28] David takes the accuracy and sincerity of Nathan's report for granted even though (unbeknownst to him) there is no state of affairs to which the report corresponds.

By the time it occurs to David that Nathan's report does not correspond to a state of affairs, it is too late. It no longer matters whether the report is accurate, for, in an important way, David is already committed to the truthfulness of the report. What I mean by this is that David has already existentially committed himself to the truthfulness of what Nathan is *doing* via his report. Thiselton concurs: "David has *lived through* [italics in original] the experience of the fictional world . . . He cannot now change his stance without loss of face and transparent hypocrisy."[29] One

---

26. Young, *Virtuoso Theology*, 178.

27. Whether Nathan is relaying this report after God had shared it with him during an earlier prophetic state or he is speaking "live" while in a prophetic state is unclear. The narrator indicates, though, that the Lord had sent Nathan to David, but the prophetic formula: "Thus says the Lord" does not appear until midway through the account.

28. Thiselton, "Communicative Action," 164.

29. Thiselton, "Communicative Action," 164.

might say, then, that the truth of this particular report does not lie in the accuracy or sincerity of the locution or even in terms of correspondence. The truth is rather more complicatedly located in the illocutionary and perlocutionary aspects of the total communicative act. This is not to say one could not find other sentences (or propositions) purporting to assert the truthfulness of Nathan's report. The point is rather that *the sentences that comprise Nathan's report* do not themselves qualify as truth-bearers, at least not directly, and certainly not in ways that inerrantists otherwise expect given a correspondence theory which treats locutions only.

At the Lord's direction, the prophet Nathan makes up a story and tells it to David, the focus clearly being on what he will accomplish by the telling of the story. The language game of making up a story and telling it serves here as the communicative mechanism by which David could be made to recognize his unconscionable sin and own up existentially to its severity. Again, any number of sentences (or propositions) might be called upon to describe what Nathan is doing. Any number of sentences (or propositions) might be called upon in an effort to "get at" what Nathan (and ultimately, God) is "saying" to David. *Yet none of this can be allowed to obscure how Nathan was participating in a language game that David did not immediately recognize.* One might even say that it was precisely David's failure to recognize what Nathan was doing that contributed to the speech act's resounding success. That David did not recognize Nathan's language game does not abrogate Nathan's sincerity. That Nathan's "report" did not corresponded to a state of affairs does not mean his prophetic rebuke was not true on account of inaccuracies. It rather suggests that what the virtues of accuracy and sincerity entail for a given communicative act can shift (and indeed have shifted) in accordance with the language game in operation. Nathan's telling of a story seems to work by virtue of analogy, a complication introduced to the communicative act by acknowledging the importance of illocutions and perlocutions. After all, "telling stories really is a separate language game . . . not on all fours with illocutionary language games, but is parasitic on them."[30]

Inerrantists have generally been reluctant to consider truth in biblical narratives in terms of other language games besides "giving a report." Instead, they move to corner the truth-market with a litany of slippery slope arguments. I have also come across arguments from guilt: if "giv-

30. See Searle, *Expression*, 67.

ing a report" is not the default language game in play then that would leave us lording our autonomous, "critical" methods over scripture as opposed to submissively receiving scripture as God's word. Some buttress the strategy by insisting God would not make up and tell stories, not when they appear to sincere Bible readers *as if* they had actual, historical referents (when in reality they do not).[31]

One problem with this line of thinking involves an inappropriate application of truth as correspondence to all biblical narratives.[32] The locus of truth becomes confused. Wolterstorff describes the predicament well: "The doctrine of biblical inerrancy amounts to claiming that everything said by any biblical author was said by God."[33] This version of the inerrantist formula is inherently problematic.[34] What scripture "says" is not always "really" what scripture is saying to its hearers/readers. There is no guarantee that the biblical narratives' language games will be clear to most readers. Perhaps the language games can only become clear after a lifetime of hermeneutical training. In fact, there is nothing keeping the church from taking centuries or even millennia to learn how to read biblical narratives "well."[35]

Inerrantists themselves are making similar points. J. Walton, for example, explains:

---

31. Ward concedes: "Inerrancy does not set down any principle that requires certain sections of Scripture to be treated as intended to be largely historical or largely metaphorical." See Ward, *Words of Life*, 194.

32. Interestingly enough, Richard Rorty judged fiction to be an excellent vehicle for illustrating the weaknesses inherent to all correspondence theories of truth: "The importance for philosophy of truth about fictions lies in the role which solutions to this problem play in deciding what to say about truth in general." See Rorty, *Consequences*, 110.

33. See Wolterstorff, "Importance," 45.

34. Compare Geisler's "sound argument" for inerrancy:
    1. The Bible is the utterance of God.
    2. God cannot utter falsehood or error.
    3. Therefore, the Bible is without error.
See Geisler, "Inerrancy," 2.

35. J. Kugel chastises all biblical scholars, particularly narrative critics: "Now . . . to hear the Bible with, as it were, biblical ears is not necessarily the sole form of critical enquiry; but it sometimes seems that even when we assign ourselves the task of listening 'with biblical ears' we fall woefully short. Our own 'literary competence' continuously imposes itself on the texts we read." See Kugel, "Bible and Literary Criticism," 229. What I have in mind does not require a generic aptitude of literary competence but rather an ever-increasing sense of hermeneutical awareness.

The worldview of antiquity was lost to us as thinking changed over thousands of years, and the language and literature of the ancient world was buried in the sands of the Middle East. It was only with the decipherment of the ancient languages and the recovery of their texts that windows were again opened to an understanding of an ancient worldview that was the backdrop of the biblical world. This literature and the resulting knowledge has made it possible to recover ways of thinking that were prominent in the ancient world and has given us new insight into some difficult biblical texts.[36]

Given the increased hermeneutical capacity that comes with advances in scholarship, churches can constantly improve upon, even correct, preliminary readings of scriptural narratives. In this respect, Sanders is absolutely right in insisting that "Enlightenment study of the Bible can be viewed as a gift of God in due season."[37] One of the most prominent of recent examples is expressed well by J. R. Porter's concessive remarks: "In fact, it is only the comparative method, and even the comparative method 'on a grand scale,' which enables us in many cases to identify the presence of folklore elements and folklore motifs at all in the life or literature of any given group, to answer the question 'how do we know whether a particular piece of evidence is an example of folklore or not?'"[38] As Harlow observes, since "ancient narratives do not typically announce their genre or pronounce on their own historicity . . . the best we can do is pay close attention to clues within the text about how it should be taken, with a sidelong glance at similar texts that are roughly contemporaneous with it."[39]

I suggest that the truths of illocutionary narrative speech acts become easier to appreciate when the apologetic distraction of defending locutionary correspondences is deliberately set aside. The problem might be stated another way: "The pre-critical mode of interpretation

---

36. See Walton, *Lost World*, 171.

37. Sanders, "Challenge," 15.

38. Porter, "Folklore," 5. Compare Enns, *Exodus*, 58–61.

39. Harlow, "After Adam," 181. Commenting on Gen 1–11, for example, he explains further: "Having done this for many years now, I have come to share the view that the narratives in Genesis 1-11 were probably written and read as both paradigmatic and protohistorical—*imaginative portrayals of an actual epoch in a never-to-be-repeated past that also bears archetypal significance for the ongoing human situation* [italics in original]."

distorts the use to which the meaning of the final form is put."[40] When applying scriptural inerrancy to biblical narratives, instead of asking, "Does the narrative correspond to reality?" evangelicals might consider asking, *"To what use does the canonical text put the biblical narratives?"*[41] For example, one biblical language game found in scripture involves the "scripturalizing" of extant stories.[42] Here biblical tradents engage in a literary practice where they read sacred stories "in conjunction with one another," and end up interpreting them in tandem. J. Maxwell Miller offers the following example:

> Among the component parts, the regnal period reckonings recorded for the rulers of the Divided Kingdoms probably have the strongest claim to authenticity. We suggested earlier that these reckonings, along with the synchronisms, may have been calculated originally on the basis of data which was derived ultimately from official court records. But as they stand now these regnal period reckonings appear to be excessively long. One possible explanation is that they were adjusted intentionally in order to accord with the framework as a whole. That is, the post-Exilic chronologers may have found it necessary to expand some of the regnal periods in order to achieve the 480-year era which they believed to have extended from Solomon's founding of the temple to the end of the exile.[43]

Another biblical language game that might help students reconceptualize the truth of historical biblical narratives is the common ancient usage of what Steinmetz calls "second narratives."[44] Davies' work may prove relevant here. In his view, biblical tradents engaged in various literary practices where layers of history and fiction come together in the Hebrew Bible for the collective expression and transmission of Israel's cultural memory.[45] Yet another biblical language game involves describing present circumstances in light of "the prophetic past."[46] Inerrancy cannot exempt scriptural narratives from participating in such language

40. MacDonald, *Karl Barth*, 139.

41. Compare Sandy, "Inerrancy of the Illocution."

42. See Smith, *Priestly Vision*, 159.

43. Miller, *Old Testament*, 77.

44. See Steinmetz, "Uncovering."

45. See Davies, *Memories*. Compare Lindars, "Elijah."

46. Sanders, "Hermeneutics," 8.

games simply because these complicate the inerrantist construal of biblical truth as correspondence.

The operative rules in scripture's various language games methodically grant the biblical tradents "greater license in the reconstruction of events [than a correspondence model allows for], including dramatizations of events and speeches of which there could be no factual record."[47] Inerrantists may insist they seek to engage scripture "plainly" and in good hermeneutical faith, but that does nothing to prevent believing communities from discerning a plurality of language games, each with a different set of rules appropriate for its performance. After all, "it is one thing to believe the Bible to be true; it is another to understand what it says."[48] In fact, Long insists: "one's discernment of the particular truth claims of the Bible requires that more specific genre decisions be made."[49] More to the point is not so much what the Bible might *say* in this or that pericope, but what it could possibly *mean* for us today. And as L. Alexander reminds us, when exegetes in the ancient world looked to make these kinds of hermeneutical decisions, they deliberately did so in ways that could imaginatively "unfreeze the revelatory text."[50]

J. Sanders' vision for a "canonical criticism" was suggested to him by this very observation: Judaism and Christianity prized their respective authoritative traditions precisely because of their cultural and ideological *adaptability*. He explains: "As soon as need be, [Judaism and Christianity] broke into the frozen text and made it relevant to the next problem faced, and for the most part they fragmented the texts in order to do so—no matter how much we moderns may regret it."[51] Reflecting on similar phenomena, J. Kugel observes that in antiquity changes affecting genre identification, the revising of traditional interpretations, and even emendations to the biblical texts themselves "may [at first] have been accompanied by a little wink, but soon the winks disappeared."[52] B. Lindars perceives related strategies throughout his examination of the NT authors' "apologetic" interests:

47. Organ, *Is the Bible?*, 8.

48. Long, *Art of Biblical History*, 300.

49. Long, *Art of Biblical History*, 301.

50. Alexander, "This Is That," 202.

51. Sanders, "Biblical Criticism," 163.

52. Kugel, *How to Read*, 518.

Generally quotations in the New Testament have not been selected with complete regard of the original context. Their meaning has been already fixed by the process of working over whole passages which seem most relevant to the Church's fundamental doctrines. The analogy of the Habakkuk Commentary has suggested a definite rule of interpretation in this process: the events of redemption are the regulative factor, and provide the key to the meaning of scripture. Moreover, we observed in the same source a distinctive method of exegesis, whereby this interpretation is clarified by means of subtle modifications of the texts which are used . . .[53]

All this to say that the same scripture can function as God's word in different ways to different communities in different times and locations; or as J. Dunn puts it, a dialectic will always persist—it even underwrites much of the NT itself—between the historical relativity of the scripture reader on the one hand and the historical relativity of the scriptural text on the other.[54]

It is interesting to note, however, that Long, an inerrantist biblical scholar interested in the historicity of biblical narratives, is eager to "make the point that questions of truth value and truth claim are essentially distinct," while T. Ward, an inerrantist theologian interested in bibliology, discourages inerrantists from "[making] a distinction between Scripture's overall purpose and its individual statements that Scripture itself never makes."[55] More confusing still is that, in another place, Ward affirms "both that Scripture is God's speech act and God speaks polyphonically." There is a diversity of positions regarding what readers should expect from the Bible's inerrant narratives. That said, J. Webster once lambasted postliberal theology for what he perceived as an over-emphasis on local stability. Perhaps his warning applies all the more to conservative evangelical bibliologists: Take care not to rob bibliology of "its exploratory character," that in the process of trying to establish their local inerrantist identity conservative churches not lose "a lively self-critical awareness of its own limits and what lies outside them."[56]

53. Lindars, *New Testament Apologetic*, 17.

54. Dunn, *Living Word* (2e), 106.

55. Long, *Art of Biblical History*, 301; Ward, *Word and Supplement*, 304; Ward, *Words of Life*, 138.

56. Webster, "Locality," 5.

At times, inerrantist biblical scholars appear but all too ready to halt the exploratory character of evangelical bibliology. Long, for example, raises a series of questions that only inerrantists writing in an apologetic mode would pause to ask: "Is the fact that trees do not talk sufficient reason to label Jotham's speech a fable?" "[The story of Balaam] too has its 'fabulous elements,' but do these elements alone make it a fable?"[57] What Long is afraid of disrupting is a sense of theological stability that inerrantist bibliology seems to theoretically afford him. It comes as no surprise that Long enlists divine inspiration to "more than adequately guarantee [the biblical narrators'] access to their subject" and to further guarantee that "the authority of the Bible's pictures of the past (whatever may be the differences between them, and however incorrectly we may at times view them) is as secure as the authority as the One who inspired them."[58] For Long, all indications of fable must be treated the same in order to safeguard the resurrection, with the practical effect that "unless one is willing to argue that the book of Numbers as a whole must be characterized as fable, there appears to be no valid literary reason to label the Balaam stories as such."[59] This is a perfect example of inerrantists pitching their bibliological starting points so high that the only alternatives left for students to consider are somewhere unacceptably "down" the slippery slope.[60]

If inerrantists refuse to permit narrative function to inform their hermeneutics of biblical language games, inerrantists will consign themselves to the unfruitful game of always finding ways to make it possible for there to be correspondences between biblical narratives and states of affairs in reality, misunderstanding this to be the only way biblical narratives can be true.[61] It is precisely such an insensitivity to language games that prompts potential allies of evangelicalism to conclude: "Evangelicals

---

57. Long, *Art of Biblical History*, 315.

58. Long, *Art of Biblical History*, 329, 330.

59. Long, *Art of Biblical History*, 313.

60. Dunn, *Living Word* (2e), 100.

61. Long (*Art of Biblical History*) gives lip service to attending to these kinds of issues but prejudges the matter and prematurely flattens the entire hermeneutical playing field. He invokes a principle proposed by R. Bergen to the effect that larger units of discourse should generally be allowed to dictate what language game is in play in the lower levels of discourse. Readers may recall our brief interaction with R. Bergen above and his insistence that the speeches reported in biblical narratives had to correspond to speeches made in reality, whether by summation or encapsulation.

entered a dead end when they committed themselves to that doctrine [inerrancy]."[62] If inerrantists continue to impose the rule of correlating narrative locutions to states of affairs in reality, the possibility that biblical narratives can be wholly true by virtue of being "trustworthy as a communication of that which God wanted us to know through the story" is categorically precluded.[63] Should not inerrancy at its very best work to keep this from happening?

62. Wolterstorff, "Importance of Hermeneutics," 45.

63. Barr, *Escaping*, 86.

5

Anti-Apologetic Philosophy:
On Giving Students Room Enough to Breathe

W HAT I AM SUGGESTING is that if inerrantists could somehow condition themselves to lower their guard and become comfortable
with a more generic idea of Christian disclosure[1]—as opposed to an
ultra-"high" paradigm for an inerrant set of scriptures—the hermeneutical enterprise may suggest surprising ways to foster spiritual growth.[2]
Yet to approach scripture with expectations of any kind would require
students to already have a theology-in-motion, even before approaching
scripture. However, many segments within conservative institutional
Protestantism—segments largely responsible for the religio-cultural
outlook of inerrantist students under their care—still operate as if the
intent of scripture can be found simply by opening up the Bible and
reading it.[3]

Furthermore, students tend to approach the Bible confident they
already possess a more or less accurate idea of what the overall intent of
scripture is. Indeed, if they did not already possess a basic understanding of its significance, they would not trouble themselves with reading
it and studying it as much as they do, much less with paying tens of

1. One way to accomplish this is to be mindful that God inspired the canonical biblical narratives for a very specific purpose, perhaps "to reveal Himself to lost mankind
through Jesus Christ as Creator and Lord, Redeemer and Judge," but even this may be
too specific. See Barr, *Escaping*, 86.

2. Compare the benefits brought by the advent of narrative criticism. See Powell,
What is Narrative?, 85–91.

3. This is not a caricature. Hermeneutical naivety is very much a part of both popular and institutional evangelical culture. A fundamental impetus for pursuing scriptural
studies in the first place is the assumption that a biblicist foundationalism is both possible and desirable. See Bovell, *By Good and Necessary*; and Bovell, "Two Examples."

thousands of dollars on specialized training with hopes of learning how to properly interpret it. In short, the Bible occupies a central position for their faith, believed to be the actual word of God. Imagine their sense of betrayal, then, as students begin to encounter what I call the "academic-apologetic dilemma." Over the course of years of schooling, students are gradually presented with contemporary findings in a wide array of research programs, each containing an entire field's worth of theory and data. As these new domains of knowledge are explored both in and outside the classroom, whether these will ultimately prove compatible with inerrancy is not typically given immediate consideration—and this is how it should be. However, as students mature in their knowledge of the disciplines a form of cognitive dissonance can develop.

The academic-apologetic dilemma, as I call it, is arguably encountered in its most acute form by students of biblical criticism. J. Kugel describes the tension in contemporary biblical studies:

> Apologetics are a sign of an underlying anxiety. The anxiety in this case derives from the inescapable fact that, in light of all that modern scholarship has discovered, the Bible necessarily looks very different from the way it looked only a century or so ago. Yet these commentators still want it to be the Bible in the old sense— divinely inspired (at least in some attenuated way), a guide to proper conduct and proper beliefs, a book of truth and not falsehood, as free of error and internal contradiction as possible, in short, despite everything they know, a book still worthy of being called the Word of God.[4]

My target audience for this book (post-inerrantist students) will likely agree that Kugel has identified a real problem, perhaps *the* problem, or at least one that evangelicals have not taken enough care in addressing. How can students maintain a high view of scripture "despite everything they know"? If one were to interpret the recent spate of books on inerrancy as a theological sign of the times, they might deduce that God is calling the present generation of bibliologists to work together to find a plausible, salient way of culturally dismantling inerrancy's academic-apologetic dilemma. The first step, I submit, is to encourage students to come to terms with Kugel's main contention. In almost every imaginable way, the Bible we know today is simply not the Bible of the early or medieval, or even Reformation, churches: ours is vastly different from

---

4. Kugel, "Appendix," 12.

the one churches utilized when originally constructing our theological inheritance.[5] It should come as no surprise, then, that those Protestant traditions that place disproportionate emphases on the authority of scripture will be precisely the ones positioned to experience the most profound changes.

Intuitions to this effect may be what are prompting inerrantist leaders—systematicians primarily and historical theologians, too—to publicly voice the fears of their representative traditions. After all, few people like being told to change their ways. But when it comes to inerrancy, the run-of-the-mill, human resistance to change seems to morph into something like an eschatological intransigence. The main concern appears to be that any change in bibliological outlook (particularly like ones considered in earlier chapters) quickly lead to heterodoxy. In fact, depending on the cultural mood of the churches-at-large constructive re-conceptualizations of inerrancy can be made to appear so radically different from what was previously accepted as the norm that for all intents and purposes the proposals might as well be deemed apostate.[6]

Whenever inerrantist institutions try publically to respond to such concerns, they inadvertently precipitate (and sometimes even foster) a culture of fear. The cultural climate they affect stymies imagination and forestalls much needed conceptual developments in bibliology. Thus the onus is awkwardly placed on *students* to persevere on their own in spite of enormous pressure to conform to inerrancy's inherent conservatism. Yet in order to be effective, students require just the opposite: they require *freedom* to carry out their work. What students decide to do with inerrancy now is bound to influence inerrantism's future as a viable cultural force. And what inerrantism needs more than anything else is help conceptually transitioning from outdated bibliological assumptions that were born in a seventeenth century culture to ones fully conversant with what people are thinking today. I propose one fruitful approach is to encourage students early in their studies to face Kugel's challenge head on. They might begin by asking, what is it about inerrantism that causes evangelicalism's brightest students to become so influenced in their

5. For example, see any number of articles by R. Rohrbaugh. For instance, the collection in Rohrbaugh, *New Testament*.

6. In his classic, *Christianity and Liberalism*, Machen took up this strategy to great effect.

scholarship by inerrantist apologetics that someone like Kugel should refer to these and other researches as "biblical criticism lite"?

It will do no good for students to dispute this or that critical finding and then methodically ground an entire bibliology on the precarious successes of this or that disputation. A more promising way, I suggest, might be to question Kugel's overall understanding of theological method. For Kugel makes it sound as if students must stop reading scripture devotionally until they can give a satisfactory account for why believers should read scripture at all. But perhaps this way of putting things is problematic. Perhaps the fact that Kugel should find himself in a position where he *can* pose this kind of dilemma is itself an indication that the operative model of scripture is faulty.[7] For example, if I were really pressed to provide a rationale for why I read scripture devotionally, I would honestly find myself at an initial loss for words. I know that I should continue reading scripture; of this I have no doubt. It is just that I am simply unable to say as much as I would like with respect to *why*. The answer I keep coming back to is that I recognize on some tacit level my devotional reading of scripture is meeting something like a primal, spiritual need. According to D. Bloesch, "The Bible might be likened to a drinking fountain whose water is drawn from an underground spring. The water of life is hidden, and we therefore have access to it only by means of this fountain. Unless we go to the fountain and drink from it, our spiritual thirst will not be satisfied."[8] So long as that remains to be the case personally, I will continue to contemplatively read scripture and listen to scripture being read.

A second thought is this: what if what Bloesch had to say about scripture is about all that *can* be said about scripture? "Scripture is authoritative because it is penetrated and filled with the Holy Spirit. . . . The notional or conceptual meaning of Scripture is available to natural reason but not its revelational or existential meaning."[9] What if this is as far

---

7. Compare Springsted, "Theology."

8. Bloesch, "Sword," 16.

9. See Bloesch, *Holy Scripture*, 129–30. Vanhoozer, for one, takes issue with this, insisting: "what the Spirit does *through* the text is not unrelated to what the authors, human and divine, have said." See Vanhoozer, "Very Idea," 171. It would have been better had Vanhoozer written: "*All things being equal* or *many times* what the Spirit does *through* the text is not unrelated." In my view, not only does the human author not always say what the divine author says and the divine author not always say what the human author says, but the Spirit can and sometimes (often?) *does* through the

as an evangelical bibliology can sensibly hope to venture?[10] Interestingly enough, coupling the experience I have when reading scripture with my belief that the Holy Spirit is somehow active during my reading (perhaps as Bloesch says, "penetrating" and "filling" scripture) I arrive at A. Plantinga's consideration pertaining to the Holy Spirit at work "in my heart": "[U]pon having the experience in question, I acquire the belief directly, without the benefit of argument." There is simply no argument to form on the basis of "the experience or phenomenology accompanying the working of the Holy Spirit." Much rather, "I form the belief immediately upon having the experience in question."[11] This is not to say that evangelical students should not *try* to probe more deeply into bibliology, but that whatever approach they ultimately take should be conceived as an attempt to gain a clearer sense *of what students are already in the habit of doing*, with hopes of gradually increasing in what might be called "wisdom."[12] It is in this spirit that R. Briggs advises believers that "the implied reader of Scripture will have to be someone who is patient, a long-term reader of considerable perseverance, and strikingly tolerant of quite extraordinary diversity in almost every way relevant to the reading of the whole canon."[13]

Most evangelical students are familiar with the idea of "biblical" wisdom. They may even call to mind its culmination in the Apostle Paul's assertion that Christ is the wisdom of God. What I have in mind by wisdom, however, has more often been associated with philosophy than theology and is described well by J. Gill: "the acquisition of Wisdom through sincere and reflective involvement with the enduring

---

text what neither author happens to be "saying." Just think of how many times the Spirit works through the text in spite of how terribly off our interpretations tend to be. Compare Harris, "Scripture."

10. Compare Daley's comment regarding the Trinity: "[T]rinitarian language always resists further explanation; it simply confesses, proclaims." See Daley, "Foreword," x.

11. See Plantinga, "Comment," 129-30.

12. In chapter two above, I made mention of how fruitful it may become for inerrantists to look to scripture's own bibliological "habits" for further bibliological insight since, as F. Watson observes, a "'scriptural doctrine of scripture' is not forthcoming." See Watson, "Hermeneutics," 125. In this chapter I am suggesting that by following the churches' spiritual instinct to believe that there will always be more to learn from a divinely inspired scripture, inerrantists should be encouraged to hermeneutically pursue more aspects of *our own experience* of scripture reading, particularly as a cultural and historical part of God's redemptive economy.

13. Briggs, "Bible before Us," 22.

and axial questions of life." Gill counsels that "life, like philosophical activity, is a process in which one can only begin where he or she is and through which we can only proceed one step at a time."[14] Students should approach bibliology in the same way, right where he or she is and by proceeding one step at a time with whatever questions they have.

A turn to philosophy seems only natural at this point.[15] K. Harries points out, for example, that historically speaking philosophy always gains in importance whenever long-held traditions are culturally upset.[16] This is why the medieval Boethius, for instance, when wrongfully imprisoned decided to write a "Consolation of *Philosophy*" and not a "Consolation of *Theology*," a gesture the Church of his time was unready to comprehend. Reflecting on the nature of philosophy, Harries writes: "Philosophy, as I understand it, has its origin in a sense of homelessness that is intimately linked to the demand for authenticity."[17] I submit that this is precisely where more evangelical students are finding themselves, particularly with respect to their views on scripture, asking for example: how can I authentically conceive of what God has wrought through what turns out to be an "accidental" book *that I already know as scripture*?[18]

Like many who attend conservative schools, I initially felt absolutely sure that whatever else the Bible turned out to be, it had to be inerrant, and this expectation was something I assumed before I began to read scripture seriously. But as I was brought to think more critically about what it was I actually expected the Bible to be (first in a sort of armchair kind of way, then with the help of some training in philosophy and biblical studies), I found myself bemused. On the one hand, I knew the Bible had a reception history such that it always held a unique place in the spiritual life of the churches. On the other, since I had not come to know what made the Bible "unique" from reading the Bible firsthand, how is it that I should claim to know ahead of time what the Bible should

---

14. Gill, *Metaphilosophy*, 2, 3.

15. In their discussion of "wisdom," Shults and Sandage acknowledge that "[t]he human spirit longs to understand its relation to the sacred, to interpret the ultimate meaning of its identity in relation to that which is beyond its comprehension." Even here, philosophy plays a crucial role. See Shults and Sandage, *Transforming*, 67. On the importance of philosophy, compare Shults, *Christology*.

16. Harries, "Philosophy," 61.

17. Harries, "Philosophy," 61.

18. See Beal, *Rise*. Figuring out where to put what when also fits in to the "biblical" picture of wisdom (e.g., Isa 28:23–29).

turn out to be? What began to strike me as far-fetched was not that there were more or less well established ways for American evangelicals to read their Bibles,[19] but that the Bible always had to say the same thing to everyone who has ever read it. Somehow I had come to believe that what dispensational inerrantists believe today is approximately the same thing churches worldwide have believed, and that this has more or less been the case since the beginning.[20] I had to modify this position, however, as I began to read writings from the early church. The understanding in my faith community was that the early church had quickly fallen away from scriptural teachings. As unbelievable as this may sound, such a conclusion was easily drawn from cursory readings of the Apostle's Creed, for example. The Apostle's Creed makes no mention at all of justification by faith, substitutionary atonement, or the inerrancy of the Bible. How could it possibly be "biblical"?[21] At the same time, my faith community understood that what the Bible teaches is supposed to be absolutely "clear." Everyone accepted it as an obvious fact of redemptive history that God would have made provision for all churches throughout history to have direct access to his eternal truth through the Bible.[22] A very important component of that truth was said to be the fundamentalist construal of inerrancy.[23] Over time, this became harder for me to maintain.

19. Reception theory holds that "[w]e learn who we are as a result of our tradition and our position in it. But in order to learn how we belong to a tradition, we must first learn how to listen to it." See Parris, *Reception*, 301.

20. A common evangelical belief that Smith explodes. See Smith, *Bible Made Impossible*.

21. R. Briggs also raises issues with this fundamentalist "leap of understanding," at least with respect to justification by faith: "if Luther (inadvertently) created Protestantism out of reacting against Catholicism, then Paul, fourteen centuries earlier, must have been basically arguing about what Luther was arguing about, and therefore early Christianity was essentially reacting against a form of Jewish works-righteousness . . . On this view, Christianity offers freedom from a Jewish legalism which today's reader assumes was a lot like medieval Catholicism. This is a powerful and widely held theological reading. It is almost certainly mistaken . . ." See Briggs, *Reading*, 57–58.

22. Abraham is exactly right when he decries that inerrantists have made salvation "hinge on a very particular range of epistemic doctrines." See Abraham, "Foreword," xi.

23. Consider, for example, Woodbridge, *Biblical Authority,* particularly the overwhelming praise it has received from within inerrantism. Yet as Bloesch observed: "[Woodbridge] accuses Rogers and McKim of being overly selective in their quotations in order to advance their case. While this charge has some merit, one can show that Woodbridge too is selective." See Bloesch, *Holy Scripture*, 137.

While taking math classes at a secular college, it began to occur to me that 1) all Western thinkers writing before the modern period (including Christian theologians) were operating with a fundamentally different understanding of physical reality than the one we possess today; and 2) when the biblical tradents were active producing scripture the views current in the Near East were arguably even more different from those dominant in the premodern West than ours are from the premodern West.[24] I came to see that an immense historical "chasm" separates present day inerrantists not only from understanding our own inerrantist traditions but especially from appreciating how the biblical tradents likely conceived of their "scriptures." Even so, it was not until I enrolled as a biblical studies major that I could really appreciate the depth of the problem. The theological giants responsible for constructing our church traditions were largely active before we came to know about other ancient Near Eastern literatures, for example. Couple this with the fact that our traditions were already fully formed by the time any of the finds at Qumran were made public. What these and other discoveries have shown is that the ideational contexts for properly understanding what the biblical writers were likely trying to say and do through what they wrote were all but unknown for most of Christian history!

One last phase of my scholarly development bears mentioning. While studying the history of philosophy I began to realize, as M. Holmes points out in an article on Origen, that "prior to Luther nearly everyone of any significance employed the concept of 'multiple sense' of Scripture, and the interaction of this idea with their doctrine of inerrancy must be examined."[25] This means that even if a theological luminary sounds to us like he is talking about "inerrancy" he likely meant something quite different from what inerrantists today understand by the term, which raises an important question: How can inerrantists claim they understand not only *that* but *in what specific ways* the Bible is "inspired" even before coming to the Bible to see what qualities it actually possesses? If inerrantists claim to accept only what the Bible teaches (implying the reason they know what special qualities scripture possesses is because they have read it and understand its teachings), how have they managed to recognize what constitutes a biblical "teaching" *without already having an expectation for what a biblical teaching should look like*?

24. See, for example, Young, "Mathematical Approach"; and Bailey, "Biblical Math."
25. Holmes, "Origen," 231.

It is not uncommon for philosophy to stumble upon these kinds of "performative" conundrums.[26] According to S. Cavell, conceptual puzzles comprise an inescapable part of doing philosophy; they inevitably arise, he explains, during the course of getting a better handle on what we are already in the habit of doing: "This is the sort of thing that happens with astonishing frequency in philosophy. We impose a demand for absoluteness (typically of some simple physical kind) upon a concept, and then, finding that our ordinary use of this concept does not meet our demand, we accommodate this discrepancy as nearly as possible."[27] A similar tendency in philosophy is mentioned by H. Wang: "More precise artificial concepts are introduced to substitute for vaguer intuitive concepts so that before long one forgets what started the whole thing off."[28] I submit that this happens in inerrantism whenever bibliologists try to spell out with more precision than appropriate the nature of scripture's authority. It leads us into false-dichotomous approaches like "To which do we give priority, theology or biblical studies?" One problem is that it encourages believers to expect to arrive at definitive answers to their questions. A further concern is that it incites believers to enlist what would otherwise be tentative proposals into the service of more aggressively styled apologetic defenses of the faith.[29]

From one vantage point at least, I would say that an unfortunate characteristic of evangelical inerrantism is an undue emphasis on maintaining an overly vigilant, "apologetic" spirit. This cannot help but contrive something of an artificial environment for doing evangelical bibliology. In terms of the philosophic distinction between dialogue and dialectic, apologetics persistently coaxes students into less imaginative modes of thinking, holding their spiritual instincts captive to restricted sets of social practices, which as a consequence become putatively gov-

---

26. Meno's paradox (from Plato's *Meno*) besets contemporary discussions in evangelical bibliology. Compare the exchange between Waltke and Enns in *WTJ*. A similar problem also attends the classical discussions of Old Princeton surrounding biblical "teachings" and biblical "phenomena." See chapter six below.

27. Cavell, *Must We Mean?*, 77.

28. Wang, *Beyond Analytic*, 207.

29. Despite its apparent irreverence, compare the nugget of truth contained in Johnston's glib remark: "there is something to the view that what is called orthodoxy is just a motley bunch of heterodoxies that have caught on." See Johnston, *Surviving Death*, 105.

erned by the dictates of logic and dialectic precisely at the wrong phase of theological construction. D. Nikulun describes dialectic as follows:

> Any disagreement must ultimately be resolved and brought to a standstill in a well-established conclusion. This conclusion can occur either through the sublation of contradictory opposites (which, although they struggle against each other, are nevertheless united and reconciled within a closed and finalized system) in speculative, systematic dialectic, or through a productive disagreement of non-understanding that is suspended by understanding in the interpretive hermeneutical dialectic. Or disagreement may be overcome in logical, formal dialectic by means of an argument that is meant to be universal and binding, such that everybody (every "rational being") must agree with and accept the force of the deduction obtained.[30]

The third scenario Nikulun mentions is a situation some inerrantist apologists unwittingly present to students as a primary feature of evangelical bibliological discourse. However, in order to help re-establish a sense of emotional and spiritual stability there will be those who need to seriously question, or even doubt or abandon, inerrancy. As a result, such students may begin to interpret their genuine questioning and doubting in a negative light, as if in and of itself, such doubt and questioning is indicative of some negative spiritual development, which only gets compounded when other unwanted, *apologetic* implications are pointed out. Students may begin to think, for example, that they are being "irrational" or that they are stubbornly refusing to consider pertinent evidence. These preliminary concerns can quickly snowball into a deep-seated worry that their very relationship with God is being called into question in the most fundamental way possible for students who are inerrantists. Such students can become paralyzed by the hyperbolic rhetoric of some inerrantist apologists, who ironically intend to *uplift* students' faith.

In my view, a complete rethinking (if not reworking) of inerrantist philosophical culture can help predispose students to take more theoretical initiative.[31] What I am after is a more welcoming ideological space where students can easily create existential-bibliological niches, as

---

30. Nikulun, *Dialectic*, 88–89.

31. I am reminded of J. Smith's remarks regarding knee-jerk reactions he engendered from inerrantist students in the audience at a conference he had recently spoken at. See Smith, "Response," 226, n. 1 and n. 2.

it were, wherein to do their research, places where they can freely engage in inerrancy's constructive critique and rehabilitation, acknowledging full well that this might even lead to its eventual deconstruction and abandonment. A risky proposition, I know, but the key is that students must be *free* to do their work: they must be free primarily to *make mistakes*. It is only by making genuine mistakes that students will actually learn anything of value. And the cultural climate could not be better for making pedagogical adjustments in bibliology. For even in contemporary analytic-philosophy-at-large, there is nobody "telling us what can and cannot be said": "There's nobody doing any serious policing nowadays in analytic philosophy."[32]

This is certainly good news for those inerrantist students who are desperately looking for ways to get their apologist friends and acquaintances off their backs so that they can go about their academic work without being made to feel guilty. Although some may interpret this as a willful escape from reason, there are times when students will need to be given room to emotionally regroup and ideologically refresh their minds.[33] There is nothing unreasonable about honestly re-assessing the contemporary bibliological landscape in order to better appreciate what other traditions (and other religions) have accomplished, whether on inspiration, the authority of scripture or any number of related topics. Philosopher R. Rhees once candidly wrote: "I admit that there are difficulties about the questions of what we learn from the history of philosophy; and these are connected with the point that in philosophy every generation has to start from scratch."[34] If evangelical students, marking

---

32. So Wolterstorff, "Postscript," 2.418, 419. Admitting it has its drawbacks, Wolterstorff explores how this is largely a positive development.

33. By the same token, I do not want students to become "enemies" of reason either, becoming "confirmed in their disposition not even to consider rational argument: as soon as they see it coming up, they can set it aside without bothering to read it, saying to themselves, 'Oh, yet more "If . . . then . . . if . . . then."'" See Dummett, "Theology," 238. Much rather, my point is quite similar to Wolterstorff's: "the absence of *any* big program has made it easier for the historians among us to get into the mentality of historical figures rather that squeezing them into our mentality," which gains us incredible perspective on the "social and cultural anxiet[ies]" involved. See Wolterstorff, "Postscript," 419.

34. Rhees acknowledges difficulties in describing what service philosophy (qua philosophy) provides to human thought: "I cannot sort this out clearly. I feel that I ought to be able to see how it goes, for it cannot be so very hard; but I never manage to." See Rhees, "Fundamental," 576. Wolterstorff points to how much more "rich, fascinating, illuminating, and provocative" history of philosophy has become compared to the time

a new generation, feel the need to "start from scratch," there should be allowances within inerrantist philosophy and culture for them to stave off apologetics long enough to try their hand at some bibliological prolegomena. Again, if there were ever a time in recent evangelical history where students might have a chance to make some genuine bibliological headway—a time where they might positively and actually contribute to evangelical theological re-construction—the present time seems to be as good as any.

Yarbrough recently remarked (to his consternation) that the work of P. Enns and K. Sparks will likely serve as "a rallying point for students and others."[35] Whether this turns out to be the case or not, Enns, Sparks, C. Smith and others are broadcasting what inerrantists have needed to hear for years. Unfortunately, having done their best to secure faith from heterodoxy, agnosticism and unbelief, some apologetic types are moving to convince students (and whoever else will listen) that there is really no room for anyone to think about changing their minds when it comes to inerrancy. Some apologists have sought to overcome the impression of theological diversity among evangelicals by "reducing apologetics to a single more crucial issue." As a result, "a question about these formulations is at once a challenge to the social contract at the heart of the evangelical identity."[36] Aggressively, they move to impress younger believers with rhetoric reminiscent of what M. Murray has called "sledgehammer apologetics."[37] "If you change your mind on such-and-such position," they say, "you will play right into the hands of (insert out-group)." At this point, inerrantist apologetic culture—or at least the way some evangelical leaders transmit the arguments of inerrantist apologists to students—can wind up presenting unnecessary "emotional hurdles" for students that will only have to be overcome in later years.[38]

---

when he was a graduate student at Harvard.

35. Yarbrough, "Embattled," 20.

36. Sheppard, "Biblical Hermeneutics," 84.

37. See Murray, "Reason," 11.

38. "Emotional hurdle" is a phrase W. L. Craig uses in his review of Murray's *Reason for the Hope Within* to describe something he himself had to overcome upon reading Murray's characterization of evangelical apologetics as "sledgehammer apologetics." Craig responds that no respectable apologist will fit this mold. Perhaps. But anyone who has attended a debate between a young earth creationist and, say, a professor of anthropology from a secular university will understand what Murray is getting at. See Craig, "Review," 130.

Apologists are obviously to be commended for doing all that they do in order to preclude harmful changes in those doctrinal areas that seem vital for faith. Dangers arise, however, whenever the forestalling of doctrinal development is accomplished by completely passing over how Christian traditions *must* change in order to survive. In their efforts to defend evangelical doctrine, it is not uncommon for apologists to use rhetorical strategies that deliberately link potentially peripheral tenets of faith to others that are more central. By explicitly associating less important doctrines with those that are more cardinal, it is hoped that while the lesser doctrines stand to gain in their contemporary significance, the whole will also be strengthened and thereby remain intact. Take, for example, apologist G. Habermas' proposal in the following argument in defense of inspiration:

> Although the doctrine of the inspiration of Scripture is usually rejected by critical theologians in spite of Jesus' view, we now have some solid grounds on which to reassert it. Using both traditional and critical paths to determine that Jesus firmly taught inspiration, we may reassert our earlier assumption that if God raised Jesus from the dead, then the most likely reason was to confirm the truthfulness of Jesus' teachings. If we are correct in this, then the inspiration of Scripture follows as a verified doctrine, affirmed by God Himself when He raised Jesus from the dead.[39]

An inerrantist can appropriate this defense-by-association strategy in support of whatever teaching she may be inclined to ascribe to Jesus. For the purposes of our discussion, what Jesus "taught" would be inerrancy. Now consider what options such an apologist leaves for students who are busy studying biblical studies (or researching in another field) and who while doing so come to believe they have landed upon independent reasons for doubting scripture's inerrancy. For example, if inerrancy is intrinsically linked by apologists to not only the teaching of Jesus but to his resurrection also, students will have to—in addition to finding the courage to go back to the bibliological drawing board—confute the apologetics tying inerrancy to more central doctrines.[40] This can prove exhausting. For since inerrantists have reduced apologetics

39. Habermas, "Jesus."

40. Habermas concludes: "In short, the doctrine of the inspiration of Scripture is anchored to the teaching of Jesus Christ, and grounded in His resurrection."

to one central doctrine, debating bibliology with them is commonly misinterpreted as inveighing against all apologetics generally. To take one instance, K. Sparks has been criticized for *arguing against* apologists whenever they defend the doctrine of inerrancy while *deferring* to their arguments while they defend the faith. But practically speaking, what else is he supposed to do?

In our adaptation of Habermas' argument, the options left for students to explore include: 1) downplay inerrancy as Jesus' view of scripture; 2) suggest that Jesus' view of scripture should not count as one of his "teachings"; 3) deny that inerrancy is one of the tenets God sought to verify by Jesus' resurrection; 4) challenge the understanding that Jesus' resurrection was a blanket vindication of all his "teachings," etc. For some students, in the midst of trying to decide which option seems most promising, a sense of emotional withdrawal can set in, an existential side effect, as it were, of relinquishing the certainty of social belonging that comes with affirming inerrancy. To make matters worse, there is something about inerrantist apologetic culture that gives the unmistakable impression there are quintessential, evangelical milestones that all believing students should be striving to achieve. First and foremost among them is the acquisition and maintenance of a maximizal degree of epistemological certainty. It is no small matter of convenience that the certainty sought is precisely the kind inerrancy brings to faith. Why, depending on the subculture, there may even exist the further expectation that the level of certainty brought about by inerrancy should hold not only for inerrancy qua doctrine but also for the reasoning process used to derive it, which involves, as it happens, accepting rather generous helpings of inerrantist philosophy. In secular philosophy, analogous cultural developments came to be seen as a quirk of modern Western intellectual history but among inerrantists it came rather to be identified as a centrality of faith.[41]

According to Cavell, over the course of its recent history philosophers have constantly sought assurances that the activity they professionally engage in is substantially more like logic than psychology, where

> "logic" is a matter of arriving at conviction in such a way that anyone who can follow the argument must, unless he finds something definitely wrong with it, accept the conclusion, agree with

41. For a preliminary account of this development, see Bovell, *By Good and Necessary*. See also Schreiner, *Are You Alone?*

> it. . .that constant pattern of support or justification whose pecu-
> liarity is that it leads those competent at it to this kind of agree-
> ment . . . *pattern* and *agreement* [italics in original] are distinct
> features of the notion of logic.[42]

There are historical reasons for this, but even more interesting are the
social motivations for emphasizing certain facets of philosophy over
against others, particularly its logical and linguistic aspects.[43]

In a fascinating account of the founding of the American
Psychological and American Philosophical Associations, J. Campbell
recounts how at the turn of the twentieth century philosophers felt a
good deal of pressure to address "the great disparity between the respect
and hope that they had for their discipline and the lack of any compa-
rable status in the eyes of so many others, both inside and outside of
academia."[44] That some traditions in philosophy conceive their discipline
as being more like logic than psychology does nothing to negate the observation that philosophy, as everything else we do, constitutes a human
practice. Along these lines, Cavell observes: "It is not necessary that we
should recognize anything as 'logical inference;' but if we do, there are
only certain procedures that will count as drawing such inferences."[45]
Logic, like painting, Cavell suggests, is a human convention and "only
someone outside such an enterprise could think of it as a manipulation
or exploration of mere conventions."[46] Cavell's point proves doubly important to us for outside the enterprise is precisely where many biblical
studies students live. In fact, according to D. Kinnaman in the face of
"compelling logical argument," the overall tendency is for "young people
[to] nod, smile, and ignore you."[47] This is likely because, in their minds
at least, clarity, rigor and consistency can no longer effectively disguise
how even the most tightly wound arguments are also being devised for

---

42. Cavell, *Must We Mean?*, 94.

43. Compare Wolterstorff's observation that one of the main reasons philosophers
can talk about this today (whereas they could not, say, thirty or forty years ago) is precisely because we live in a time of the demise of both positivism and ordinary language
philosophy.

44. Campbell, *Thoughtful Profession*, 74–75.

45. Cavell, *Claim of Reason*, 118.

46. Cavell, *Claim of Reason*, 119, summing up his observation that we will accept
something as painting but nothing a priori can tell us what that will be.

47. Kinnaman, *Unchristian*, 72.

socio-political ends as well, such as to justify a community's sense of identity or to legitimate the existence of a profession or institution.[48]

A first phase of inquiry, then, is to try to contextualize for bibliology what might "count as" a divinely inspired Bible for us as believers (i.e., insiders) in the twenty-first century. In what ways should philosophy (or theology) be allowed to dictate in advance what the Bible can possibly turn out to be? How can biblical studies and its variegated findings theoretically inform our exegeses by setting some preliminary boundaries of its own for the range of bibliological possibilities? And should we venture answers to these questions before approaching scripture or only after interacting with it at some length? Consider D. A. Carson's framing of the question from the standpoint of an inerrantist biblical scholar: "when various exegeses ('readings') of Scripture are proposed, the most probing question, then, is always this: What authority status does the Scripture have for the exegete concerned?" He reasons:

> if we are attempting a theoretical construction of the relation between biblical exegesis and systematic theology, the status of Scripture must be central to the debate. To word the problem more generically, no systematician has the luxury to avoid identifying what elements may and what elements may not be admitted into one's dogmatics and specifying the ground for these choices.[49]

Similarly, G. Osborne claims that one's view of scripture is pivotal for the direction one's exegesis will ultimately take. He observes that the hermeneutical possibilities open to exegetes are largely dependent upon their prior understanding of scripture's authority. Still, he is concerned to nuance this by approaching exegesis holistically while still deliberately keeping scripture at the forefront:

48. I will never forget a time when I was conversing with a student of postmodern philosophy. I found it curious that he should have such an absolutely negative opinion about Descartes while admitting he had not yet gotten around to reading him. So I asked him what he thought of Descartes' substance dualism and how if something like his position is not accepted then the matter of establishing identity over time, particularly before and after the resurrection, becomes problematic. How else would we be able to claim that the person resurrected is the same person both before and after the resurrection? He admitted that he did not know. He simply offered that he was more ready to concede that there is no resurrection than be "forced" to say that there is something good to be found in Descartes' philosophy. For an exploration of how humans might be "resurrected" without resorting to dualism, see Johnston, *Surviving Death*.

49. Carson, "Role of Exegesis," 54.

The biblical material becomes the inductive basis for theological formulation; the data itself in the end provides the basis from which dogma is "adduced." Yet [theological] formulation itself also proceeds from the deductive interpretation and collation of those texts as well as from the application of issues derived from the history of tradition.[50]

To his credit, Osborne presents a more robust description of the evangelical hermeneutical predicament: "for in every decision I am not only interpreting Scripture but am both reaffirming and interacting with a tradition."[51] One might note, however, that his hermeneutical inquiry is wholly committed to *affirming* a tradition that has already judged "revelation to inhere in scripture" and that has found "a consistent atmosphere of divine inspiration" there.[52] For both Carson and Osborne, the expectation that scripture must be inerrant seems to occupy a procedural role analogous to the one played by "reason" in certain traditions of philosophy, which is, according to Cavell, to "minimize distress" over social and historical arbitrariness by making it appear as if everything has an answer, suggesting to minds who are troubled with inquiring, that "no one has [the answer] if I have not [the answer]."[53]

Notwithstanding Osborne's plea for more tentative (and polyvalent) theological and hermeneutical "attitudes," one dogmatic statement he refuses to approach with suspicion is tacitly expressed in two parts: 1) the more a creedal affirmation "coheres" with the Bible the greater its authority and 2) "coheres with the Bible" should be strictly understood as finding support in the collation of "all the scriptural statements that address the issue."[54] Well enough. But now a *meta*-bibliological problem arises: the evangelical cultural dynamics that are already in play categorically preempt the possibility of real criticism. For inerrancy is both presupposed for doing biblical studies today, *and must have always come first*

50. Osborne, *Hermeneutical Spiral*, 385.

51. Osborne, *Hermeneutical Spiral*, 394.

52. Osborne, *Hermeneutical Spiral*, 387.

53. I find it interesting that inerrantist philosophy students seem attracted, by and large, to the more aggressive *ethos* of analytic philosophy. Cavell once spoke of a "worry" he had that "method dictates content; that for example an intellectual commitment to analytical philosophy trains concern away from the wider, traditional problems of human culture which may have brought one to philosophy in the first place." See Cavell, *Must We Mean?*, 346–47. Compare Wang, *Beyond Analytic*, 207–8.

54. Osborne, *Hermeneutical Spiral*, 396.

for biblical scholars throughout history in one way or another.[55] If this is not held to be the case then (inerrantist) Christianity will have no choice but to relinquish its psychological and apologetic superstructure.

Carson describes the putative thought pattern innocently enough: "historical theology may contribute to (though not utterly determine) the *boundaries* [italics in original] of systematic theology, which in turn, as we have seen, contribute to one's exegesis."[56] But V. Poythress's approach seems more transparent:

> One must get one's framework of assumptions—one's presuppositions—from somewhere. If one does not get them from healthy, biblically grounded systematic theology, one will most likely get them from the spirit of the age, whether that be Enlightenment rationalism or postmodern relativism or historicism. The idea of systematic theology influencing biblical studies begins then to look much more attractive; in fact, it is the only sane approach that takes with seriousness the corrupting influence of hermeneutical assumptions rooted in human rebellion against God and desire for human autonomy.[57]

A rhetorical trap has methodologically been set: any student who thinks twice about how inerrantists "biblically ground" systematic theology or who critically examines the *ethos* and *telos* of inerrantist bibliology is, *just by virtue of their doing so*, dismissed on account of "the corrupting influence of hermeneutical assumptions rooted in human rebellion against God."

This is an all too convenient development, especially considering that inerrantists themselves claim that what the Bible "says" always trumps in theology; however, inerrancy remains a *theological* construct. How is it, then, according to Carson and Osborne, that inerrancy should become the most fundamental consideration for doing exegesis? On all sides, the suggestion being made is that theology is primary to scripture, meaning the theological issues have to be sorted out *beforehand*, that is,

---

55. For an example of how this approach looks in practice, see Edgar and Oliphint, *Christian Apologetics*, where the authors repeatedly size up historic Christian thinkers with respect to how well they approached scripture and theology in biblicist, authoritarian ways, that is, according to the methodology proposed by C. van Til. I cannot think of a more ahistoric way to do philosophy, theology or biblical studies. See Lewis, *Testing*, 147–48; and Bovell, "Integrating History."

56. Carson, "Role of Exegesis," 57.

57. Poythress, "Kinds," 134.

before approaching scripture. So it would seem that inerrantists have a practical answer, at least, for the question: "Which is more fundamental to Bible reading, theology or biblical studies?" On the one hand, they claim scripture to be ultimate (at least it is supposed to be in theory). On the other, they insist that inerrancy must always inform, if not govern, one's exegesis.

Be that as it may, what I am suggesting is that the question itself is unhelpful. The Bible should never be viewed as "more fundamental" than anything else: inerrantists already expect scripture to be inerrant even before they read it.[58] As a consequence, whenever inerrantists turn to scripture, they will not entertain any other exegeses than those which appear to support inerrancy, going so far as to discount, or at least considerably downplay, observations that cause trouble for the doctrine. This has far-reaching, practical ramifications for students. When doing extensive research they will not always be in a position to magisterially control all the data they encounter (there is just too much of it![59]) to ensure ahead of time that inerrancy will survive.[60] What's more, they will be moving further and further away from the requisite *emotional* disposition for entertaining rehabilitation at all. The very impetus that normally compels researchers to improve upon their theories is theologically vilified from the onset as an exercise in human "autonomy," symptomatic of unbelieving "corruption" and deep-rooted, spiritual "rebellion."

Contrast this perception with Harries' explanation that a correlate of philosophy's "demand for authenticity" is precisely its "demand for autonomy." Given the context, it behooves me to clarify that the part of "autonomy" I am encouraging students to take up is that which will enable them as students-turned-philosophers to look at their bibliology *self-critically*, asking, "Is there a better way to construe inerrancy than the ones outlined thus far by inerrantists?" The idea is to pursue what

58. Compare Bovell, *Inerrancy*, 142: "the Bible has always operated (and continues to operate) as part of such a powerful cultural dialectic that it is not helpful to speak of it as an ultimate authority, especially in terms of practicalities."

59. The most recent assembling of scriptural problems inerrantists have yet to satisfactorily deal with is Stark, *Human Faces*.

60. Unless, as Sparks observes (*God's Word in Human Words*, 145–46, 168), they deliberately contrive a "safe-for-inerrancy" research environment for themselves, which is why so many evangelical colleges and seminaries think it important to advertise themselves as inerrantist by affirming inerrancy at the top of their statements of faith.

Harries calls "the philosopher's dream," by which he means doing critical philosophy, but with hopes of finally arriving at the "end" of philosophy.[61] This may be the only sensible way for students to proceed, particularly if they find themselves in a sub-culture where the fact that there are plenty of important thinkers outside evangelicalism who do not find apologists' arguments for inerrancy convincing is always explained away by appeals to their "unbelieving" worldviews.[62]

As we saw in chapter one above, inherent to the inerrantist view of bibliological disagreement is a soteriological framework that inculcates students to believe outsiders are not expected to see what insiders can see. Indeed, even my earlier appeal to Bloesch assumes something along these lines. Notwithstanding, when approaching the matter *as insiders*, it can become difficult for students to conceive of a bibliological "way out"—whether in order to become better students or perhaps more mature believers—without feeling they are reducing the faith to absurdity. By appreciating just how much room there is in philosophy for exploration—for *mistakes* to be made and for students to be allowed to *start over again*—they can continue with more confidence in their individual and collective efforts to regroup and reflect upon what options are still open to them.

For their part, Carson and Osborne are not fazed by the circularity of coming to scripture with inerrancy already in hand while at the same time saying they can read inerrancy "out of" scripture. In fact, they claim to escape circularity by appealing to a hermeneutical "spiral." It is not a circle to do as they do, they say, but rather a spiral. The image of a spiral has the advantage of suggesting a semblance of gradual hermeneutical progress, even allowing for the possibility (the inevitability?) of incrementally ascertaining what the Bible actually teaches.[63] A curious feature of this methodology, however, is its insistence upon inerrancy as an indispensable part of being able to successfully navigate the spiral in the first place. Notice how quickly the inerrantist's "hermeneutical spiral" leads right into another, this time "meta-", circle.

61. Harries, "Philosophy in Search of Itself," 61, 62.

62. For an example of this type of approach, see Edgar and Oliphint, *Apologetics*. For my part, I attempt a critique of worldview philosophy in Bovell, *Inerrancy*, 15–28.

63. Thus in *Scripture and Truth*, for example, Carson has the lead essay (by W. Grudem) trying to show that scripture teaches its own inerrancy. The effort is intended to confirm the inerrantist expectation that scripture *should* be inerrant. See Grudem, "Scripture's Self-Attestation."

Interestingly enough, when realists argue against antirealism they tend to rely upon three main types of arguments: default arguments, indispensability arguments and miracle arguments.[64] The first type assumes the reasonableness of realism and focuses on playing up the weaknesses of rival theories such as an inability to demarcate. This argumentative strategy resembles how inerrantists are wont to complain that there are no non-arbitrary ways to distinguish history from fiction once fiction is introduced to the historiographical parts of scripture. Another comparison can be drawn between this strategy and the inerrantist objection that there are no non-arbitrary ways to distinguish "faith and morals" from other biblical teachings.

The second type of argument, indispensability, asserts that the undertaking in question cannot be carried out without a prior methodological commitment to realism. This compares with the Chicago Statement's Article 19 which reads: "We deny that such confession is necessary for salvation. However, we further deny that inerrancy can be rejected without grave consequences both to the individual and to the Church." B. B. Warfield, who is discussed in the next chapter, takes this one step further and ties the fate of Christianity to that of inerrancy.

The third type of argument realists employ against antirealism suggests that the main reason human beings are successful in what they do is that by virtue of some "miracle," what humans seek to approximately describe and interact with is actually and truly there. Most students reading this book have come to a place where something like a miracle argument on behalf of the doctrine of inerrancy should have suggested itself by now, but because it has *not*, there are a growing number of reasons to suspect that the initial presumption of inerrancy is not as useful as it at first appeared, much less indispensable.

In fact, to some inerrancy seems to be in desperate need of rehabilitation, if not superseded by another, more promising bibliological theory. Instead of approaching scripture, then, with the expectation that scripture is already inerrant, such students become more and more inclined to turn a critical eye toward inherited exegeses and apologetic argumentation they had relied upon previously to "confirm" inerrancy. And since inerrantists themselves admit that they are coming to the Bible with inerrancy already in hand, the only way to properly scrutinize exegeses used in support of the doctrine is to suspend judgment

64. See Wylie, "Arguments," 287–88.

altogether. The hope is that students can be given some room to breathe, to more judiciously consider and compare various models and theories for scripture's inspiration. Of course, inerrancy's rehabilitation is what would initially be in view, but there remains the real possibility that inerrantist doctrine will be abandoned.

This is a risk students must be encouraged to take. Inerrantist philosophy and theology are inherently constructed to legitimate the cultural conservatism students are experiencing in evangelical churches. In these circles, philosophy and theology become more important for understanding scripture than studying scripture "on its own terms," that is, as a political, sociological and religio-cultural product of faith communities who operated in actual space-time history. The philosophy practiced within evangelicalism is often apologetically motivated, programmatically interested in supporting and defending inerrantist views of scripture. This leaves little cultural room for students to honestly appraise the doctrine where appropriate. However, judging by recent inerrantist responses to the work of post-inerrantist scholars, inerrantists are simply not willing to budge in their positions until *someone else* proposes an acceptable alternative to them. That means if post-inerrantists *are* interested in rehabilitating the doctrine or in exploring something else that promises to work better, then they are on their own. Either way, in all likelihood that "someone else" who is going to providentially accomplish this is a student somewhere today, but she will not be able to do anything without us giving her the room she needs to adequately weigh all her bibliological options.

6

Biblical Teachings, Biblical Phenomena, and Inerrancy at Old Princeton

IN HIS "SURVIVOR'S GUIDE" to evangelical theology, M. J. Sawyer makes mention of what he sees as an evangelical, bibliological consensus: "It is generally recognized within evangelicalism that if one begins with the teaching passages of Scripture and, having established the teaching, moves to the phenomena of Scripture, he or she will ultimately emerge with a doctrine of Scripture that embraces inerrancy. Whereas, if a person begins with the phenomena of Scripture and from the phenomena proceeds to the explicit teaching passages, that person will not embrace inerrancy."[1] P. Helm observes a similar pattern in Warfield in the course of arguing against A. McGowan's treatment of the same:

> At this juncture, the logical order of the procedure, the character of the path, is vital to Warfield's case. If, proceeding inductively, we were to begin with the phenomena of Scripture and the state-ments about inspiration together, giving to each of these data equal weight, we would be unable to challenge the phenomena by the statements. So the "real problem" of inspiration, as Warfield understood it, is "whether we can still trust the Bible as a guide to doctrine, as a teacher of truth."[2]

If Sawyer and Helm are suggesting there is a hard-and-fast rule between starting with teaching passages and arriving at inerrancy or beginning with phenomena and *not* arriving at inerrancy, surely they overstate the case.

I have objected elsewhere that the deductive arguments inerran-tists tend to devise, whether based on "biblical teachings" or theological

---

1. Sawyer, *Survivor's Guide*, 151.
2. Helm, "Warfield's Path," 40.

platitudes, do not *necessarily* imply their conclusions.[3] This observation alone is enough to lead students to consider whether biblical phenomena might help decide the question.[4] There is nothing preventing students, however, from concluding not only that the Bible's "teachings" do not lead to inerrancy by way of deduction or even induction but that there is a more fundamental misperception regarding "biblical teachings" in the first place. Even ceding that the Bible "teaches" its own inspiration (or granting further, its own "inerrancy") will not get inerrantists as far as they seem to think. E. Harrison explains this well: "One must grant that the Bible itself, in advancing its own claim of inspiration, says nothing precise about its inerrancy. . . . *The problem is to define the nature of that inspiration in the light of the phenomena contained therein* [my italics]."[5]

The present chapter seeks to apply some of the observations made in chapter five above to the inspiration and inerrancy of scripture: scripture's teaching passages *already* qualify in and of themselves as phenomena of scripture before they can be identified as "teaching" passages at all. To help illuminate this, hermeneutically speaking, with the idea that a preunderstanding of what and how the Bible "teaches" is always already in motion when doing bibliology, I will briefly consider what two inerrantist writers in the Old Princeton tradition have had to say on this topic.

Charles Hodge (1797–1878), the Old Princeton systematician par excellence, makes the following statement in (*ST*, 1.153): "The nature of inspiration is to be learnt from the Scriptures; from their didactic statements, and from their phenomena." And again (*ST*, 1.169), "Our views of inspiration must be determined by the phenomena of the Bible as well as from its didactic statements." In response to online conversation, Helm proffers that for Hodge there are basically two types of phenomena: "The first refers to apparent features of Scripture arising from internal consistency and the relationship between its teaching and established facts from elsewhere, which, if they are true, are relevant to

---

3. See Bovell, *Inerrancy*, 64–66.

4. In the article mentioned above, Helm tries to get around this by quoting Warfield and interpreting him to the effect that the approach taken involves *probability* with the probability being so high in this case that it might as well have the force of demonstration. Contra Helm, Trembath points out that since his "exegesis is completely dominated by systematic considerations," "Warfield's deductivism was even more pronounced than that of his mentor." This chapter suggests there is much truth to this. See Trembath, *Evangelical Theories*, 26.

5. See Harrison, "Phenomena," 259.

the denying of inspiration and especially of infallibility. . . . The second of the phenomena, the individual style of each biblical writer, is simply a datum for a developed view of inspiration, and so is relevant to our overall view of inspiration."[6] According to Helm, "there's an important difference in method between saying 'the phenomena must be taken into account' and 'the phenomena must be taken into account in a way that gives them parity with the teaching of Scripture respecting its own inspiration, or priority over that teaching.'" In other words, scripture affords theologians with explicit, didactic statements and these should act as control beliefs for the interpretation of phenomena as well as for the eventual articulation of a doctrine of inspiration.

I have argued against this general approach to theology elsewhere.[7] Yet even on its own terms, as more data becomes available, the phenomena in question may prove far more relevant than Hodge could ever have anticipated. For one thing—at least on the face of it—Hodge is writing *as if* one can approach the Bible "for the first time," as it were, with an eye toward constructing from scratch a conception of biblical inspiration. He advises that due consideration be given to both the "teachings" of scripture and the scriptural data. One question to pose to those who interpret Hodge the way Helm does is, how can phenomena *not* be "given parity" with the teaching of scripture if scripture's teaching is precisely what readers are in the process of establishing? How can a teaching that has not yet been distilled from scripture be given priority in its own construction? This suggests, as I claimed in the last chapter, that inerrantists are really not starting with scripture, but rather beginning with a church doctrine and moving ad hoc to confirm it. This they attempt to do through exegesis, which is conveniently equated with scriptural "teaching."

It seems to me that a major concern for Hodge was the unwanted prospect of theologians relying too heavily on passing fads in philosophy, particularly during the course of theological construction. Perhaps developments in biblical studies were not specifically on his radar.[8] Either

6. These two sentences have been inverted for readability. See Helm, "'Phenomena.'"

7. Bovell, "Two Examples."

8. It was Warfield who was writing in an evangelical and Reformed context where conservatives were being forced by developments in Europe as well as in the States to outline a *specific* position in response to growing threats posed by German higher criticism, which incidentally was about to find a "culminating expression to the documentary approach," both in Wellhausen's source-critical articles of 1876–1877 and his history of Israel published in 1878 and again in 1883. See Arnold, "Pentateuchal Criticism," 625–26. Prior to this, attacks on inspiration were largely philosophical and mainly

way, what Hodge could never have imagined is just how much scripture's cultural milieu would be further elucidated by future archaeological discovery. Even so, how could Hodge have practically advised that phenomena are only ancillary to the construction of a doctrine of inspiration? Is it not by means of phenomena that exegetes try to understand what scripture seems to be saying in the first place? Surely, Hodge would have agreed with S. McKenzie's basic hermeneutical dictum: "Each reader of a given text makes an assumption about the genre of that text. *The reader then adjusts that assumption in the course of reading according to the signals in the text and the reader's familiarity with literary and cultural conventions* [my italics]."[9] Indeed Hodge seems to admit as much himself, at least in his own way. For when it comes to formulating our understanding of "inspiration," Hodge requires that Bible readers make recourse to "the usage of antiquity, sacred and profane." Thus the idea of phenomena, as construed by Helm's interpretation of Hodge, should be allowed to broaden as our understanding of the usages of antiquity, both sacred and profane, become more expansive.

For his part, Charles Hodge seems to have in mind a meta-bibliological procedure that most scholars teaching at Princeton Seminary agreed to follow at the time—presumably the one spelt out by Hodge's son, A. A. Hodge (1823–1886), in *Outlines of Theology* (1860). It is interesting to note that A. A. Hodge clearly begins his discussion of inspiration with his received understanding of the churches' doctrine of inspiration already in hand. He then goes on to explain that this doctrine of inspiration has been and can be gleaned from 1) the statements of scripture and 2) the phenomena of scripture. What he says, however, is important to observe: the statements and phenomena both give "evidence as to the nature and extent of inspiration." So there is a generic idea of biblical inspiration that one should already possess as one approaches scripture

targeted mechanical theories of dictation. Old Princeton mobilized to put forward a philosophy (with the contemporary philosophical climate unmistakably in mind) that would make inspiration plausible again and to conceive, articulate and defend a theory of inspiration that did not involve dictation. Thus Scottish Common Sense Realism was integrated with Calvinistic anthropology and soteriology and older Lutheran ideas involving "concursus" were promoted as the real Church doctrine (over against dictation). As far as I can tell, it was the Graf-Wellhausen documentary hypothesis along with burgeoning evolutionary approaches to scripture and Christianity that helped Old Princeton define their own cultural-theological-ideological identity over against what quickly became "modern" or "liberal" thinking. See, for example, Woodbridge and Balmer, "Princetonians"; Harris, *Fundamentalism and Evangelicals*.

9. McKenzie, *How to Read*, 19.

and the nature and extent of this inspiration is indicated by a thorough examination of the statements and phenomena of scripture. I think this picture is somewhat different from the one Helm seems to paint above.

For A. A. Hodge goes further and states at once that "[w]e come to this question [of the truth of the inspiration of the scripture] already believing in their credibility as histories, and in that of their writers as witnesses of facts, and in the truth of Christianity and in the divinity of Christ." But to what extent does the truth of Christianity practically depend on the truth of the inspiration of scripture for its validity if one comes to the scriptural teachings and phenomena with it already in mind? And how are we to understand the biblical tradents' "credibility" as historiographers, for example, without knowing something about whether they intended to do historiography at all or what ancient historiography might typically have looked like in comparison to what historiography looks like today? What does "making up a story and telling it" (see chapter 4) look like according to ancient usage, sacred and profane, and what place would such language games have had in ancient historiography? Should ancient historiography really count as "giving a report" (see chapter 4) or as being a wholly reliable witness to "facts"? And if not, what is one to make of any apparent claims to the contrary within the texts themselves? What does the "truth" (see chapter 3) of the inspiration of scriptures have to do with the "truth" of scripture, or even the truth of Christianity and the divinity of Christ? At one point, A. A. Hodge makes a rather sweeping claim: "It is evident that if [the biblical writers'] claims to inspiration and to the infallibility and authority of their writings are denied, they are consequently charged with fanatical presumption and gross misrepresentation, and the validity of their testimony on all points is denied. When plenary inspiration is denied all Christian faith is undermined." Yet the entire discussion is clearly taking place on a "pre-"bibliological level, as it were; these issues come up before believers can even broach considerations of what inerrancy, for instance, might mean.

I submit that it is simply not a matter of setting statements against phenomena or phenomena against statements as Sawyer and Helm appear to suggest. It is more a matter of trying to better understand the "nature and extent" of the inspiration of scripture for our twenty-first century context. After all, inerrantists and post-inerrantists alike affirm the inspiration of scripture. What is at stake is rather the nature and extent of its inspiration; that is what is being contested. What can count as a biblical "teaching" given the types of biblical phenomena scripture exemplifies? According to A. A. Hodge, the phenomena of scripture, taken together, can help us establish at least the following bibliological characteristics:

> Every part of Scripture alike bears evidence of a human origin. The writers of all the books were men, and the process of composition through which they originated was characteristically human. The personal characteristics of thought and feeling of these writers have acted spontaneously in their literary activity, and have given character to their writings in a manner precisely similar to the effect of character upon writing in the case of other men. They wrote from human impulses, on special occasions, with definite design. Each views his subject from an individual standpoint. They gather their material from all sources—personal experience and observation, ancient documents, and contemporary testimony. They arrange their material with reference to their special purpose, and draw inferences from principles and facts according to the more or less logical habits of their own minds. Their emotions and imaginations are spontaneously exercised, and follow as co-factors with their reasoning into their compositions. The limitations of their personal knowledge and general mental condition, and the defects of their habits of thought and style, are as obvious in their writings as any other personal characteristics. They use the language and idiom proper to their nation and class. They adopt the *usus loquendi* of terms current among their people, without committing themselves to the philosophical ideas in which the usage originated. Their mental habits and methods were those of their nation and generation. They were for the most part Orientals, and hence their writings abound with metaphor and symbol; and although always reliable in statement as far as required for their purpose they never aimed at the definiteness of enumeration, or chronological or circumstantial narration, which characterizes the statistics of modern western nations. Like all purely literary men of every age, they describe the order and the facts of nature according to their appearances, and not as related to their abstract law or cause.

These are among the aspects according to A. A. Hodge (and, presumably, according to the elder Hodge and the other Princetonians as well) that can be learned from scriptural phenomena. Crying out for comment, however, is the preunderstanding that it would not be bibliologically fitting for the biblical writers to "[commit] themselves to the philosophical ideas in which the usage originated." Old Princeton is placing arbitrary limits on the extent of the biblical writers' participation in contemporary culture. "They use the language and idiom proper to their nation and class," they assert, "They adopt the *usus loquendi* of terms current among their people . . ." But why should the biblical writers, for example, evince an understanding of inspiration as per the *usus loquendi*—as per the thought patterns current in Second Temple Judaism—while not committing themselves to the philosophical ideas that would have suggested the usus loquendi as culturally functional in the first place? With the publication of the Dead Sea Scrolls, for instance, traditional answers to these kinds of questions are in dire need of a thoroughly critical re-evaluation.[10] To name just one topic, the DSS can help contemporary readers comprehend more precisely just how the biblical writers "arrange their material with reference to their special purpose, and draw inferences from principles and facts according to the more or less logical habits of their own minds." Although the modern mind might proceed by drawing inferences from principles and facts, the biblical tradents appear not to have operated so much on "more or less logical habits" but on prevalent hermeneutical practices that were thoroughly Jewish in nature, which were significantly different from ours. *The more familiar one becomes with the kinds of issues involved, the more obviously such factors begin to impinge on the nature and extent of inspiration.*[11] P. D. Alexander succinctly highlights the significance of contemporary developments. With the finding of the DSS and a codex containing the Palestinian Targum in its entirety:

---

10. Warfield (*Works*, 1.120) cites one R. Rothe approvingly for accurately clarifying that the NT authors have "the same theoretical view of the Old Testament and the same practice as to its use as among the Jews of the time." Biblical scholars are in a better position now to assess this claim than either Rothe or Warfield could ever have been. R. Bauckham writes: "The thoroughly Jewish character of the NT literature has been constantly demonstrated by the intensive study of this literature in relation to relevant Jewish literature," with the DSS being the most important of recent discoveries. Similarly, C. D. Elledge: "The scrolls have provided a priceless 'insider' perspective into the issues and conflicts that generated new religious and political parties in Second Temple Judaism . . . and have also contributed primary literary sources for the study of Jewish literature and theology in the period." To give an idea of just how illuminating scholars have found the non-canonical literature to be for understanding scripture, G. Oegema ponders, interestingly enough, whether the notion of "revelation" might profitably be extended to include some of the non-canonical material. See Bauckham, "Relevance," 91; Elledge, *Bible*, 97; and Oegema, *Early Judaism*, 22–37.

11. See, for example, Henze, *Companion*.

What became crystal clear from the study of Midrash was that the early Christians were reading the Old Testament in a manner typical of their time, and in doing so were often taking for granted post-biblical tradition. They were not responding to the Old Testament in an unmediated way, "face to face." Rather they were viewing it through the veil of contemporary Jewish exegesis.[12]

Another point calling out for discussion is Old Princeton's gratuitous supposition that the biblical authors would have always had in the back of their minds that whatever they wrote "spontaneously in their literary activity" should be "reliable in statement," and in all relevant cases faithfully "[describing] the order and facts of nature."[13] The extent to which Old Princeton was influenced by Scottish Common Sense Realism has been disputed by inerrantists.[14] Without entering this debate here, one might innocuously observe that Old Princeton seems to have presumed that it is part of human nature to have direct access to objective reality.[15] One inference that is being made is that the ancient authors responsible for the composition of holy scripture also enjoyed the same untrammeled, objective access to reality and, as such, would have naturally freely exercised such capacities whenever engaging "spontaneously in their literary activity." In other words, it would not have occurred to Old Princeton that the biblical tradents, as providentially selected human beings acting according to their true nature, could have done anything other than genuinely "describe facts."

If this is even partly right, the influence of Thomas Reid's and James Beattie's common sense philosophy can be detected in at least two ways. First, Old Princeton is championing a sort of scientific "encyclopaedism" where "the pursuit of scientific truth in accordance with the encyclopaedist conception is simply an expression of human nature." Second, the accumulation of scientific knowledge is taken for granted as being a gradual, almost linear, development marked by nearly continuous

12. Alexander, "Bible in Qumran," 35–6.

13. The question of reporting by way of appearances need not detain us here. See my remarks below and also in chapter four above.

14. See, for example, McConnel, "Old Princeton"; Helseth, "Warfield's Apologetical Appeal"; and idem., "'Re-Imagining' the Princeton Mind." Harris concedes that "[r]ecent claims about [the] effects [of Common Sense Realism] have been excessive." See Harris, *Fundamentalism and Evangelicals*, 95.

15. I leave aside the question of whether Hodge (and Old Princeton) thought that human nature had to be "redeemed" before this could obtain since either way both he and the biblical authors would have been thought to qualify.

progress.[16] Thus, it would be only natural for Old Princeton to insist, for example, that biblical writers wrote "in the language of common life." This contention in itself is not new. John Calvin, for example, taught that Moses (taken by him to be the author of Genesis) could only make mention of those parts of God's works that "meet our eye." This is the only way, Calvin explained, Moses could proceed in accommodation to human ignorance.[17]

At Old Princeton, however, there is an additional consideration: that the "language of common life" is based on "apparent and not upon scientific truth," indicating that the level of accuracy evident in the scriptures should only be commensurate to the level of science achieved by the ancients and the purpose of the writer in question. This way when it comes to any reference of "fact," the Bible can still be deemed accurate, particularly in the face of all extenuating scientific discovery. After all, as C. Hodge explains (*ST*, 1.171): "Theories are of men. Facts are of God. The Bible often contradicts the former, never the latter. . . . The Bible has stood, and still stands in the presence of the whole scientific world with its claims unshaken." By virtue of their very nature as providentially selected human authors, the biblical writers would have only done what is natural for any human being to do according to their nature as human and that is: describe facts.[18] Hence A. Kuyper's reluctant criticism of C. Hodge to the effect that he had "succumbed to the temptation of placing Theology formally in a line with the other sciences . . . [with] Theology, in like manner, [having] the data of this supernatural history."[19]

Furthermore, in his effort to guard against the influences of the philosophies prevalent in his own day, C. Hodge insists that inspiration should be conceived as a monolithic, even static, theological notion (*ST*, 1.158): "The idea of inspiration is therefore fixed. It is not to be arbitrarily determined. We must not interpret the word or the fact, according to our

16. Pakaluk, "Defense." 570, 567. For more on Scottish Common Sense Realism at Old Princeton, see Bow, "Samuel Stanhope Smith."

17. For a history of accommodation-talk and its application to scripture, see Benin, *Footprints*.

18. I have already suggested an alternate language game above in chapter four.

19. See Kuyper, *Sacred Theology*, 130. Helm, for his part, in his critique of Vanhoozer, insists that most critics of C. Hodge misrepresent him. He holds Bavinck and Kuyper responsible for initiating widespread misunderstandings: "Bavinck and Kuyper set the ball rolling, and it still rolls." See Helm, "Charles Hodge." Perhaps what I am suggesting here differs from what Vanhoozer and others have observed.

theories of the relation of God to the world, but according to the usage of antiquity, sacred and profane, and according to the doctrine which the sacred writers and the men of their generation are known to have entertained on the subject." I will leave it to others to discuss how to most helpfully conceive God's relation to the world.[20] At present, the point to take away is this: biblical "phenomena" are already being extended by Hodge to encompass whatever usages were prevalent in antiquity. What Hodge is ultimately after is a *modern* doctrine (singular) of inspiration that is informed by ancient usage (again presumed to be singular) and is consistent with the churches' understanding of it (singular) so that he may successfully ward off contemporary anti-religious ideologies (plural). In so doing, he conveniently allows for students of the Bible to ask a rather restricted set of questions wherever difficulties are encountered.

As one might expect, the questions he permits are in conformity with the parameters he already has in mind for scripture (*ST*, 1.169): "Do the sacred writers contradict each other? Do the Scriptures teach what from any source can be proved not to be true? The question is not whether the views of the sacred writers were incorrect, but whether they taught error? For example, it is not the question Whether they thought that the earth is the centre of our system? But, Did they teach that it is?" Such carefully selected questions stand side by side with summative statements such as the following: "It is enough to impress any mind with awe, when it contemplates the Sacred Scriptures filled with the highest truths, speaking with authority in the name of God, and so miraculously free from the soiling touch of human fingers."

This is because Charles Hodge proceeds from considerations of phenomena as they bear on what A. A. Hodge calls the extent and nature of inspiration to the ramifications of these same considerations on what Old Princeton refers to as "discrepancies." For some students today, however, the progression will seem awkward, if not artificial. Recent developments in biblical studies, for example, have caused the scriptural "discrepancies" encountered by students today to become fundamentally related to phenomena qua phenomena. This causes a glitch in Old Princeton's bibliological procedure since the phenomena were initially called upon to help the inerrantist tradition decide upon the nature and extent of biblical inspiration in the first place. As a consequence, students today are instantly positioned to *transcend* Hodge's recommended

20. For a recent proposal, see Wright, *Providence*.

approach. For by virtue of their historical location within the inerrantist tradition itself, they are socio-culturally poised to ask: were the questions that Charles Hodge thought to pose, considering their contrived and methdologically restrictive nature, suggested to him by the didactic statements in scripture or by the phenomena—*or was it perhaps by the lights of Hodge's own historico-cultural milieu that his questions seemed to him as the only ones permissible for readers of scripture to profitably ask?*[21]

As a doctrine undergoing (re-)construction, inspiration is currently open to the "believing," retrospective scrutiny of inquiring, inerrantist students. Of course, students may not always find it *existentially timely* to engage in bibliological criticism of this kind, but there are points during the course of academic study where *it may not be possible* to do otherwise. There may even be times when it makes perfect existential sense to de-constructively critique evangelicalism's inerrantist preunderstanding of scripture. Whether conversant with Hodge or not, the questioning might as well proceed along the following Hodgean lines (paraphrasing Hodge here): "The question is not whether the view of *inspiration* the sacred writer possessed is correct or incorrect but whether he is teaching error." Or again, "It is not the question, *whether they thought the Bible is inspired*? But, did they teach that it is?" Irrespective of what precise answers these and other questions may elicit, other more pressing concerns now arise regarding *our own* expectations for what "inspiration" is (should be?) in the first place.

Although by today's lights this is the most pressing issue, Old Princeton vigorously condemned its constructive consideration, much less entertained its positive development. Warfield (*Works*, 1.150) chides contemporary scholars: "Shall we then take refuge in the idea of *accommodation* [italics in original], and explain that, in so speaking of the Scriptures, Christ and his apostles did not intend to teach the doctrine of inspiration implicated, but merely adopted, as a matter of convenience, the current language, as to Scripture, of the time?" But what *do* we count as "incorrect" or what *should* count as "being taught" by the biblical writers and why? "Just because apostles believed something does not

---

21. See Seely, "Subordination." Compare Enns on Hodge's contemporary at Old Princeton, W. H. Green, Professor of Oriental and Old Testament Literature: "Throughout Green's writings we see assumptions he made that are more in keeping with the tenor of his times than with the character of Scripture." See Enns, "William Henry Green," 403.

mean they are actually teaching it" is the Old Princeton maneuver *for dealing with discrepancies*. (Is this not why the very distinction of believing and teaching was called upon in the first place? But this presupposes a theory of inspiration! How does making a distinction between what biblical authors *believed* and what they actually *taught* practically differ from saying there are incidental errors to be found here and there throughout scripture? Warfield walks a fine line indeed!) Old Princeton, then, follows the same procedure that they consistently deny their opponents *so long as it suits their sense of "orthodoxy" to employ it*.[22] But once the nature of "biblical teachings" becomes the item of dispute, what good will it do to monotonously urge students today to continue with their appeals to them? This is why a more preliminary question has come to the fore: where *did* the "doctrine" which "the sacred writers and men of their generation" entertained come from and whence *their* notion of "teachings"?

For his part, J. Woodbridge continues to press the case that "biblical inerrancy has been a church doctrine or Augustininian central teaching of the Western Christian churches . . . a widespread shared belief of Christian churches that have had a historical existence in the West" over against what he calls the "Rogers-McKim proposal" and in direct

---

22. Both C. Hodge and A. A. Hodge (along with Warfield) seem to indicate that there may be little *practical* difference. See, for example, Hodge, *ST* 1.140–41, and A. A. Hodge and Warfield, "Inspiration," *Presbyterian Review* 6 (1881): 225–60. Harris suggests that Warfield's appeal to evidence made it "less easy for Warfield than it had been for Charles Hodge to dismiss inconsistencies and minor factual discrepancies as insignificant." See Harris, *Fundamentalism and Evangelicalism*, 138. C. Hodge makes his famous declaration: "The errors in matters of fact which skeptics search out bear no proportion to the whole. No sane man would deny that the Parthenon was built of marble, even if here and there a speck of sandstone should be detected in its structure," while A. A. Hodge and Warfield concede: "[The Scriptures] are written in human languages, whose words, inflections, constructions, and idioms bear everywhere indelible traces of human error. The record itself furnishes evidence that the writers were in large measure dependent for their knowledge upon sources and methods in themselves fallible; and that their personal knowledge and judgments were in many matters hesitating and defective, or even wrong." "Nevertheless," Hodge and Warfield continue, "the historical faith of the Church has always been, that all affirmations of all kinds . . . are without error." The caveat, of course, is that "[e]very statement accurately corresponds to truth *just as far forth as affirmed* [my italics]." Whatever error should be found in scripture can be presumed as not being taught in scripture, which seems to resonate somewhat with C. Hodge's own conclusion of the "Parthenon" section (*ST*, 1.41). Compare Woodbridge and Balmer's clarification of the same: "In other words, Charles Hodge did not accept the possibility that the 'errors' were genuine ones." Yet Harris sees Warfield as "shifting the emphasis away from a recognition of insignificant errors towards an expectation that seeming errors in time will be proved true" (140). See Woodbridge and Balmer, "Princetonians," 267.

opposition to E. Sandeen's work.[23] Even if one were to grant Woodbridge his vision of a maximal continuity between historic Christianity and evangelical self-identity—specifically, his insistence on the centrality of inerrancy—it would still have to be noted that not all inerrancies are created equally. How did churches of old distinguish between what a biblical writer happened to believe and what they actually taught in any given time period? Is it by first determining whether what the Bible says is in error or not *and then* rendering (a negative) judgment as to whether it is being taught? Does it turn out that any time scriptural "teaching" proves at variance with established tenets accepted by educated people of the time, a *different way* of reading scripture is introduced ad hoc for the express purpose of avoiding "error" at all cost?

J. Sanders observes that "by importing numerology, tropology, allegory and other such hermeneutic techniques to the Bible one can often make a text say what one wants it to say. So-called literalists and fundamentalists are especially good at this."[24] If this is what helped churches throughout history adapt scripture to their times, it would seem that Woodbridge's expectation that scripture be accurate when it touches upon history and science differs in significant ways from the kind of "inerrancy" advocated by our Christian forebears.[25] Agreement with Woodbridge, therefore, can only be partial since what Holmes says about Origen can be said mutatis mutandis for any number of pre-Enlightenment theologians: "Did Origen [for example] . . . believe in the 'inerrancy' of Scripture? Yes. Does this mean that he may be cited as evidence in support of the thesis that 'the Church throughout its history has always held to the inerrancy of the literal sense of the text'? No."[26]

Furthermore, I do not think most "inerrantists" from Christianity's past can count as inerrantist in Woodbridge's modern usage unless they happened to participate in an actual, historical culture that is in key

23. See Woodbridge, "Evangelical Self-Identity."

24. Sanders, "Response," 124.

25. Compare Kermode, "Institutional Control," 76: "[The first Christians] instituted a new way of reading [the OT], as a repertory of types prefiguring Christianity. In so doing they virtually destroyed its value as history or as law; it became a set of scattered indications of events it did not itself report." For an attempt to integrate the first Christians' view of the OT with inerrancy, see Enns, "Apostolic."

26. Holmes, "Origen," 221. Compare Allert, "Issues," 273–78. This is an important consideration for deciding what kind of "inerrancy" representatives of the churches from a given time period operated with, understandings, I might add, that appear quite different in substance than the variety Woodbridge upholds.

respects more exactly like ours, that is, a culture that "affirms histori-cal-critical research, the evolutionary view of nature, and the need to examine moral norms."[27] Without these three presumptive outlooks per-meating the culture-at-large, any inerrantist witness Woodbridge finds in the Christian tradition *will not be inerrantist in the same way that fun-damentalists and evangelicals are today.* In other words, the inerrantists of the past, by virtue of their historical location, would not culturally qualify as inerrantist in the modern sense. For as F. Manuel was fond of pointing out: "Even when men of successive generations repeat each other verbatim, their words have markedly different tonal qualities and connotations. There is a certain core of meaning that remains the same over the centuries, but only a certain core."[28] That the core of Christianity includes "inerrancy" is certainly debatable, but more to the point, that the core of "inerrancy" itself should be identified with Woodbridge's full-blown version of it seems unthinkable, at least not without a paral-lel continuity also being established with respect to three distinctively modern cultural pressures: 1) the historical criticism of sacred texts, 2) evolutionary models of religion, and 3) pluralistic societal dynamics that make morality and religion out to be historically contingent.

It seems to me that the bibliological core Woodbridge mistakes for inerrancy involves a more basic inference from the general belief in *di-vine inspiration*: Since God inspired scripture, there will always be some-thing to be gained from reading and re-reading every part of scripture. While studying the hermeneutics of the gospel writers, for example, J. Doeve came to recognize this. Because of their belief in the inspiration of Holy Scripture, ancient readers took it for granted that "there is noth-ing, absolutely nothing in Scripture without a *meaning* [my italics]."[29] Or as J. Kugel observes in his discussion of the "independent life" sacred texts took on as their role in enabling the God-Israel dialogue increased:

27. Theissen's description of three, often overlooked, although absolutely crucial, features of Protestant fundamentalism. They may "all [be] values upheld in most Protestant churches," but inerrantist fundamentalists tend to uphold with them with a peculiar, inordinate vigilance. See Theissen, *Bible*, xvi, xvii.

28. Manuel, *Shapes*, 4

29. See Doeve, *Jewish Hermeneutics*, 89. Compare Longenecker's observation that because scriptures were thought to be inspired, "the transmitted texts for the Jew of the first century" were "extremely rich in content and pregnant with many mean-ings." See Longenecker, *Biblical Exegesis*, 6. See also Fishbane, *Exegetical Imagination*, 2: "Everything depends on creative readings of [scripture's] inherent God-given possibilities."

"Yet one aspect of biblical exegesis did remain constant, and it should already be apparent in these brief remarks about Judea in the Persian period. It is precisely the belief that sacred texts have a bearing on the present."[30] Thus how readers of scripture understand their present times is what suggests to them how to best take meaning away from holy scripture, which means if during the Enlightenment, an objective account of how things really are is what would prove most meaningful, then that is precisely what divine inspiration will guarantee. Similarly, when ancient Jews were first exposed to "all the sciences of the Greeks" they could not help but conclude that "God was interested in educating his children in all the sciences of the Greeks," and that on account of divine inspiration *"such learning is available to a diligent student of Scripture* [my italics]." But even so, interestingly enough, these early developments could never have been accomplished without the allegorization and re-application of scripture by interpreters.[31]

In my view, then, these two considerations—1) an ahistorical overemphasis on the literal meaning of biblical texts and 2) the observation that contemporary inerrancy is a "phenomenon of modernity"—militate against Woodbridge's main thesis. Inerrantist arguments positing overwhelming continuities between contemporary evangelical identity and that of premodern churches may not be grappling self-critically enough with modernity's so-called "uncoupling" effects, which includes the "impoverishment and colonization" of the "life-world" at the hands of a rationality of expert culture. In other words, modern developments effectively rob the life-world of any substantial "shared meaning." F. Schüssler Fiorenza identifies these very considerations as essential to "fundamentalist" thought generally. Interestingly enough, he further claims *that fundamentalists have introduced innovations to Christian theology*:

30. See Kugel, "Early Interpretation," 38. Compare Detweiler who identifies the first two traits of a sacred text as 1) "considered to be divinely inspired" and 2) "bring[ing] a message from a deity or deities in the form of a disclosure": "This is what the believer can return to, repeatedly, to study, to interpret toward her redemption or ethical instruction." Detweiler mentions that inspiration guarantees the truth of the message conveyed by the sacred text over against claims made by rival groups. In the present discussion, the suggestion is that with the rise of historical criticism and evolutionary descriptions of religion, inerrantists were (too) quick to interpret biblical truth claims in a way that made them conflict directly with specific developments in modern thinking. See chapters 3 and 4 above.

31. See Instone-Brewer, "Theology of Hermeneutics."

> If one views fundamentalism as having a static conception of faith
> or as wanting to preserve the pristine past, one concedes that the
> past belongs to a fundamentalist reading of scripture and one
> overlooks the extent to which a literalist interpretation of scripture
> contrasts with classical Christian interpretations. . . . The classical
> expositions of scripture with their multiplicity of senses of scrip-
> ture sought to interpret scripture in a way that related the text's
> meaning to personal, historical, and communal life. Its pluralism
> and multi-dimensionality contrasts with the one-dimensionality of
> a literalist interpretation that contemporary hermeneutical theory
> also seeks to overcome.[32]

In short, "[B]oth the circumstances to which and the means by which today's [inerrantists] respond are unprecedented."[33]

Notwithstanding, some students are losing patience with the iner-rantist habit of first determining whether scripture is in danger of saying anything erroneous and then going back to make authoritative ad hoc corrections with respect to what the biblical authors are putatively said to "teach,"[34] which raises an important meta-bibliological observation: what a biblical writer happened to believe and what scripture actually teaches is neither suggested by the phenomena nor scriptural statements after all, but rather by the expectations brought to the biblical texts by readers themselves. These expectations regard the kinds of character-istics an inspired set of scriptures should "obviously" possess. Warfield grew more aware of this as contemporary scholars became more knowl-edgeable about what *kind* of cultural artifact scripture appeared to be. Scholars were now in a position to begin a *next phase* of bibliological reflection, which involved trying to incorporate results taken from the burgeoning field of biblical studies. What was promising to become a more robust understanding of scripture as human artifact seemed to be just on the horizon. Scholars began returning to their reflections on the doctrine of scripture with the results of researches in biblical studies in the back of their minds. The conclusion to be drawn was that their newfound notions of scripture as historically contingent writings have revolutionary implications for the initial doctrinal framework they were

---

32. Schüssler Fiorenza, "Fundamentalism," 247–48. Schüssler Fiorenza has Catholic fundamentalism in mind but a similar reaction is evidenced in Protestantism.

33. Appleby, "Fundamentalism," *Struggle over the Past*, 23. I am applying Appleby's remarks on "fundamentalism" to inerrancy.

34. Walton's *Lost World* comes to mind.

working with when they first began their studies. But conservatives like Warfield (*Works*, 1.138) strongly believed that any such project had to be immediately and indefinitely halted:

> Under whatever safeguards, indeed, it may be attempted, and with whatever caution it may be prosecuted, the effort to modify the teaching of Scripture as to its own inspiration by an appeal to the observed characteristics of Scripture, is an attempt not to obtain a clearer knowledge of what the Scriptures teach, but to *correct* that teaching.

The nature of the changes being proposed to traditional understandings of biblical inspiration struck Old Princeton as fundamentally undermining scripture as a credible source of doctrine and this they could not tolerate. It flew in the face of what they took to be the Reformed, evangelical oeuvre. Warfield (*Works*, 1.51), for example, found it "amazing that any or all of such expedients can blind the eyes of any one to the stringency of this issue."

In my view, these and other developments present evangelicals with a rather interesting dilemma, one C. Hodge decides to tactfully deal with by carefully leaving specific questions open regarding what content scripture might actually be teaching (*ST*, 1.171): "If geologists finally prove that [the earth] has existed for myriads of ages, it will be found that the first chapter of Genesis is in full accord with the facts, and that the last results of science are embodied on the first page of the Bible." Hodge's cultural expectation for the Bible is clear enough: whatever the "last results of science" turn out to be, the "teachings" of the Bible, wherever they may be found, will prove compatible with them. Yet an arbitrary restriction is being placed here on inspiration qua teaching. According to Hodge, inspiration is *not* a doctrine subject to modification based on further insights from the several disciplines. The only kind of data permitted for consideration is that ultimately reconcilable with his already established doctrine of scripture. Students with no personal or institutional stake in the theological traditions of Old Princeton will likely be among the first to acknowledge that contemporary writers such as M. Erickson (who Sawyer discusses) and Helm who urge evangelicals to keep the stress on "doctrine" while making "phenomena" subordinate to it are equating pre-conceived notions of what scripture should be like with what the Bible purportedly authoritatively teaches, at least when it comes to "the nature and extent" of scripture's inspiration.

Of course, the purpose of the present chapter is neither to condemn nor vindicate Hodge, for example, but rather to explore what might be learned about inerrancy today by critically examining what Hodge, Hodge and Warfield all had to say about the nature and extent of biblical inspiration, particularly their views on the relationship between the Bible's teachings and phenomena. On the face of it, B. B. Warfield (*Works*, 1.117) himself welcomed a critical investigation of inerrantist bibliology: "it is important to keep ourselves reminded that the doctrine of inspiration which has become established in the Church, is open to all legitimate criticism, and is to continue to be held only as, and so far as, it is ever anew critically tested and approved." Historically speaking, Warfield was better positioned than Hodge the elder to formulate and address the question at hand: if inspiration is the doctrine we are interested in constructing from scratch—so that we might carefully "test and approve" it against the findings of Christians (and others) who are engaged in researches of every imaginable kind—it will help none for inerrantists to urge students in the meantime to continue invoking the doctrine. For it is the adequacy of the doctrine itself that we are in the process of faithfully (albeit critically) revisiting. As we have already seen, Warfield is clearer than Hodge on the place he reserves for the contribution of biblical "phenomena" for determining the nature and extent of biblical inspiration.

Perhaps as controversies over the inspiration and authority of scripture became more "high-stakes," Warfield began to mark out for himself a more definite, conservative position. Either way, he seems to have remained in consistent agreement with Hodge on a number of important points. A first has to do with pressing the contention that if the inspiration (and inerrancy) of scripture has the unambiguous support of the full gamut of church tradition and the biblical witness itself, not to mention the views of Christ and the apostles themselves, then any countervailing evidence presented against the doctrine would have to be great enough to overturn such weighty and trustworthy supports as those mustered by the Old Princeton bibliologists (*Works*, 1.141):

> The Biblical doctrine of inspiration, therefore, has in its favor just this whole weight and amount of evidence. It follows on the one hand that it cannot rationally be rejected save on the ground of evidence which will outweigh the whole body of evidence which goes to authenticate the Biblical writers as trustworthy witnesses to and teachers of doctrine.

Along the same lines, Charles Hodge had written (*ST*, 1.170): since the "whole doctrine of plenary inspiration [was] taught by the lips of Christ himself . . . the Christian need not renounce his faith in the plenary inspiration of the Bible, although there may be some things about it in its present state which he cannot account for." For both C. Hodge and Warfield, the Christian sureties believers have already come to trust are sure enough to perpetually keep doubts about "discrepancies" at bay.

In order to conceive the inspiration of scripture aright, the scholars at Old Princeton seem to have followed a two-tiered, bibliological prolegomena. One can glean a two-phased methodological approach from a refrain of disclaimers Warfield (*Works*, 1.142 [1.274]) makes in his writings:

> The present writer, in order to prevent all misunderstanding, desires to repeat here what he has said on every proper occasion— that he is far from contending that without inspiration there could be no Christianity. "Without any inspiration . . . we could have had Christianity; yea, and men could still have heard the truth and through it been awakened, and justified, and sanctified, and glorified. The verities of our faith would remain historically proven to us—so bountiful has God been in His fostering care— even had we no Bible; and through those verities, salvation."

However, what Warfield (*Works*, 1.141) allows with his right hand, he manages only to take back with his left:

> The Biblical doctrine of inspiration, therefore, has in its favor just this whole weight and amount of evidence. It follows on the one hand that it cannot rationally be rejected save on the ground of evidence which will outweigh the whole body of evidence which goes to authenticate the Biblical writers as trustworthy witnesses to and teachers of doctrine. *And it follows, on the other hand, that if the Biblical doctrine of inspiration is rejected, our freedom from its trammels is bought logically at the somewhat serious cost of discrediting the evidence which goes to show that the Biblical writers are trustworthy as teachers of doctrine. In this sense, the fortunes of distinctive Christianity are bound up with those of the Biblical doctrine of inspiration* [my italics].

Notice how Warfield's bibliological prolegomena works in two closely related, yet distinct, stages. The first asserts that Christianity's legitimacy is not established by the Bible. The second concludes that if the validity of the inspiration of scripture is compromised, then so is the validity of Christianity as a whole. Warfield appears to be declaring both 1) "It is not the case that scripture establishes Christianity," and 2) "It is the case that if scripture is not established then neither is Christianity." Yet these appear, at least at first glance, to be in considerable tension.

I did not find it a straightforward affair to apprehend how exactly Warfield thought that these two tenets could be simultaneously held without reasoning in a circle. For it will not do to simply state the sentences and conjoin them as if they were two propositions that could both be affirmed in the same way at the same time. In fact, an initial attempt at a diagram yielded a peculiar result. Let p be the declarative statement "The Bible is inspired and inerrant," and q be the declarative statement "Christianity is true," Warfield's position appears to translate as $\sim(p \to q)$ $\wedge (\sim p \to \sim q)$ resulting in the following truth table:

p	q	$\sim$	p	$\to$	q	$\wedge$	$\sim$	p	$\to$	$\sim$	q
T	T	F	T	T	T	F	F	T	T	F	T
T	F	T	T	F	F	T	F	T	T	T	F
F	T	F	F	T	T	F	T	F	F	F	T
F	F	F	F	T	F	F	T	F	T	T	F

Fig. 1 Truth table for the conjunct $\sim(p \to q) \wedge (\sim p \to \sim q)$

From one vantage point, at least, this cannot possibly be what Warfield is trying to say since the conjunction could only be true if p is true and q is false. To see this, simply follow the column that has the "$\wedge$" symbol at its top and go down to the second row (the top row not counting as the first row); it is the only "T" in the entire column. Next, follow that second row all the way to the left and note that the truth values that yield the "T" in the "$\wedge$" column is the combination that has p set as true and q as false. As it stands in the table, then, the Warfieldian claim is that the Bible is indeed inspired and inerrant but the whole of Christianity is false. This is clearly not what Warfield would have wanted to say![35]

The main reason the truth table does not appear to capture Warfield's essential claim is that the kind of implication invoked does not have the same sense carried by his actual sentences:

> "Without any inspiration . . . we could have had Christianity,"
> "our faith would remain historically proven to us . . . even had
>   we no Bible,"
> "the fortunes of distinctive Christianity are bound up with those
>   of the Biblical doctrine of inspiration."

35. I wonder, however, whether on another more practical level, this might be the result that an approach like Warfield's ultimately entails.

The structure seems approximate enough. Still, without the right sense of implication the table, as it stands, provides little information of use. Some other analysis will be required then of the two related approaches Warfield appeals to for the establishing of the inspiration and inerrancy of the Bible.

On one occasion, Warfield (*Works*, 1.48) lays down two ways to rationally justify the acceptance of the inspiration and inerrancy of the Bible, deeming one more important than the other:

> The account is simple enough, and capable of inclusion in a single sentence: this is the doctrine of inspiration which was held by the writers of the New Testament and by Jesus as reported in the Gospels. It is this simple fact that has commended it to the church of all ages as the true doctrine; and in it we may surely recognize an even more impressive fact than that of the existence of a stable, abiding church-doctrine standing over against the many theories of the day—the fact, namely, that this church-doctrine of inspiration was the Bible doctrine before it was the church-doctrine, and is the church-doctrine only because it is the Bible doctrine.

Thus there is an argument based on the views of the churches and a more fundamental argument based on the views of Jesus and the apostles. It is important to note that there is an overarching, even pietistic, outlook Warfield (*Works*, 1.43) is coming to the table with, which he is forthright enough to explicitly state upfront: "We know how, as Christian men, we approach this Holy Book—how unquestioningly we receive its statements of fact, bow before its enunciations of duty, tremble before its threatenings, and rest upon its promises." For each of these, Christians have traditionally approached the Bible with justified confidence. Consequently, it would be awkward in Warfield's view for a believer to begin approaching scripture expectant to rest upon God's promises without concomitantly accepting, for example, the Bible's descriptive statements of facts.

Warfield's first stage of bibliological prolegomena capitalizes on the general observation that Christian churches have historically held a special place for the Bible, particularly with regard to its being a trustworthy teacher of doctrine. From this initial observation, believers are placed in an impeccable position for establishing that inspiration (and inerrancy[36])

---

36. Warfield (*Works*, 1.256) defines "inspiration" as "that extraordinary, supernatu-

is a doctrine that the Bible teaches. Therefore, the biblical doctrine of inspiration is likewise a trustworthy doctrine (or at least more trustworthy than any of its modern alternatives). More than once, Warfield moves to bolster the case for his understanding of the inspiration of scripture by remarking that since the church has always held the Bible in high esteem as a teacher of doctrine and since inspiration is a doctrine the Bible teaches, the Bible's inspiration cannot be gainsaid as a doctrine without at the same time undermining other key doctrines also taught by the Bible. The reasoning seems cogent enough: if the Bible teaches its own inspiration and that teaching is denied as untrue, then the Bible can no longer remain as a trustworthy teacher of doctrine, which would have an obvious negative impact on the cardinal doctrines of orthodox (or what Warfield calls "distinctive") Christianity.

A second and more fundamental bibliological analysis then seems to proceed as follows. The teachings of the Lord and the testimonies of the apostles have all been deemed trustworthy by the churches. No inspiration is needed to legitimate the trustworthiness of these teachings since they can stand or fall on the Bible's established historical reliability. Still, just because inspiration is not required to validate the reliability of the Lord's teachings and the apostles' testimonies does not mean it is for that reason dispensable. To the contrary, inspiration is one of the doctrines both the Lord and the apostles happen to teach. Therefore, although it is only contingently part of the doctrines that are approved as trustworthy, by the mere fact of being taught at all by the Lord and the apostles, there is no critical warrant for our dismissing that particular doctrine without also dismissing any number of other doctrines also taught by them. "For Hodge and Warfield the final ground for the authority of Scripture lies in the claim of Scripture itself, in the acceptance of this claim by the church of all ages and in the impossibility of proving that this claim is false."[37]

The rhetorical maneuver is clever indeed, sure to resonate with the pietistic pathos of conservative Protestant America. In a quintessentially fundamentalist gesture, an incidental part of an entire doctrinal framework instantly becomes a mainstream tenet called upon to culturally

---

ral influence (or, passively, the result of it), exerted by the Holy Ghost on the writers of our Sacred Books, by which their words were rendered also the words of God, and, therefore, perfectly infallible."

37. Van den Belt, *Authority*, 195.

stand in for the whole systematic edifice, which was initially motivated *by the texture of Christian experience.*[38] A happy result is that inspiration (and inerrancy) instantly becomes indispensible to Christianity without having to be necessary. If inspiration is not necessary to Christianity, even though the *effect* of Warfield's efforts may be the construction of a closed bibliological circle, it is not the typical way circular reasoning is often committed. By all appearances, this is methodically achieved by argumentative design. By virtue of its very construction, the circle that obtains as a result of Warfield's argument is not judged to be vicious by him since it is only by virtue of a second-order self-reference, as it were, that the circle closes back on itself. One question that arises, then, is how much this ultimately matters.[39]

J. Gerstner sees Warfield's approach as being intrinsically tied to his overall apologetical concerns. Yet, somewhat inexplicably, Gerstner passes over Warfield's deductive approach in favor of what he thinks is a form of empiricism based on sense experience.[40] Harris' observation seems more to the point: "No amount of empirical investigation detracts from the fact that the doctrine of inerrancy is initially established dogmatically."[41] For Warfield (*Works*, 1.138) himself never saw reason to hesitate in remarking: "Who does not see that underlying this whole method of procedure—in its best and in its worst estate alike—there is apparent an unwillingness to commit ourselves without reserve to the *teaching* of the Bible, either because that teaching is distrusted or already disbelieved; and that it is a grave logical error to suppose that the

---

38. In an effort to sustain Barr's criticisms of fundamentalism, Hexham appeals to metonymic thinking based both on the Christian conversion experience and a new "conception of reality triggered by the Bible" and identifies it with the basic way evangelicals and fundamentalists approach their religion. See Hexham, "Trashing." Compare Zaspel who states: "For Warfield, inspiration touches at the heart of what Christianity is—a redemptive religion." See Zaspel, *Theology*, 160. And so it was that "Warfield and his supporters lumped all the opposition together as modernists. Consequently he failed to distinguish between the modernists who still accepted a supernaturalistic framework and those who wanted to begin with new presuppositions (naturalistic and idealistic)." See Coleman, "Biblical Inerrancy," 301.

39. In his ethnographic study of Creekside Baptist Church, Malley found that the circularity involved in this line of argumentation was irrelevant to believers, suggesting "that although the statement has the form of an argument, its persuasiveness derives not from the argument but from some other source." See Malley, "Biblical Authority," 307.

40. See Gerstner, "Warfield's Case," 131–32.

41. Harris, *Fundamentalism and Evangelicals*, 157.

teaching of the Bible as to inspiration can be corrected in this way any otherwise than by showing it not to be in accordance with the facts?" I believe it is fair to say that underlying Warfield's method is a bibliological pre-commitment, a profound willingness to arrive at a position as close as possible to the doctrine of inspiration already in mind. This seems to me indicative of a fundamentally deductive aspect to Warfield's approach, despite his protestations to the contrary: "Let it not be said that in speaking thus we are refusing the inductive method of establishing doctrine. We follow the inductive method."

The manner of induction he allows is peculiar on all counts, specifically prohibiting (or at the very least selectively downplaying) any "facts" that contravene the doctrine he happens to be starting with. G. Bahnsen spoke to this overall tendency among inerrantists generally in his comments on a dispute between D. Fuller and C. Pinnock over the place of induction in Warfield for the doctrine of inerrancy. What Bahnsen observed in the case of Fuller and Pinnock applies equally well to Warfield: "When we read the letters Fuller and Pinnock have exchanged, we see quite obviously that each man is committed in advance to so conducting his empirical studies that the teachings of Scripture will be vindicated."[42] For all his ingenuity, I suggest that Warfield may have ultimately been guilty of "unfairly disguising expectation as proof or argument."[43]

For his part, Warfield tries mightily to deflect such questions by presenting inspiration as a doctrine that is to be received on par with any other Christian doctrine, but this is simply not the case.[44] As Kelsey points out, "[Inspiration] differs from the other doctrines in being self-reflexive."[45] Both rounds of inquiry—the first that marvels over the constancy of church tradition as it pertains to biblical inspiration and the second that inductively culls the teaching of Jesus and the apostles regarding scripture's inspiration—come back to the central claim that inspiration is a doctrine taught by the Bible, which conveniently stream-

---

42. Bahnsen, "Inductivism," 300. Fuller says of Pinnock: "Down deep in your heart, you feel that faith has to start the knowing process." See Fuller, "Revelation," 69.

43. Bauman, "Why the Noninerrantists," 323.

44. Geisler suggests inerrancy is so different from other doctrines that it should be likened to the law of non-contradiction, having "everything in the Word depend on it" without any other doctrine being deduced from it. See Geisler, "Inerrancy," 4.

45. Similar points as some of those brought up here are found also in Kelsey, *Proving Doctrine*, 18–24.

lines the debate to considerations of how churches might fruitfully understand how and what the Bible "teaches."[46]

Warfield (*Works*, 1.138, 1.151), of course, realizes this and moves to instate rules for precisely how such an investigation can (and should) be conducted, rules which will guarantee that the doctrine of inspiration with which he begins remains intact:

> When we approach the Scriptures to ascertain their doctrine of inspiration, we proceed by collecting the whole body of relevant facts. Every claim they make to inspiration is a relevant fact; every statement they make concerning inspiration is a relevant fact; every allusion they make to the subject is a relevant fact; every fact indicative of the attitude they hold towards Scripture is a relevant fact. But the characteristics of their own writings are not facts relevant to the determination of their doctrine. . . . We are averse, however, to supposing that in such an inquiry the relevant "phenomena" of Scripture are not first of all and before all the claims of Scripture and second only to them its use of previous Scripture. And we are averse to excluding these primary "phenomena" and building our doctrine solely or mainly upon the characteristics and structure of Scripture, especially as determined by some special school of modern research by critical methods certainly not infallible and to the best of our own judgment not even reasonable. And we are certainly averse to supposing that this induction, if it reaches results not absolutely consentaneous with the teachings of Scripture itself, has done anything other than discredit those teachings, or that in discrediting them, it has escaped discrediting the doctrinal authority of Scripture.

Note how the procedure just described is contrived as an attempt to guarantee the desired bibliological results. According to Warfield, the inductive procedure is utilized to ascertain the teaching of scripture with respect to inspiration but at the same time, if the induction yields results not supporting the biblical teaching then the entire Bible is immediately called into question as having any doctrinal authority. Although the situation *could* be construed as Warfield states, this is certainly not the only way to frame the question and arguably not even the best. The matter has to do once again (see chapter five above) with how theology is being brought ahead of time to Warfield's exegesis, necessitating the presump-

---

46. Compare Stonehouse, "Authority," 139–40.

tion that other results delivered by alternate exegeses of the passages in question cannot possibly be permitted without jeopardizing the Bible as an authority on doctrine. Warfield (*Works*, 1.139) states that "it is one thing to correct our exegetical processes and so modify our exegetical conclusions in the new light obtained by a study of the facts, and quite another to modify, by the facts of the structure of Scripture, the Scriptural teaching itself, as exegetically ascertained." J. Dunn is right to question Warfield's suggestion, particularly his definitive assessment of his own exegesis. Sure, Warfield's bibliological ploy might work to the advantage of those who are already happy with the "full inerrancy position":

> On the other hand, those less happy with the inerrancy line are less happy not because they wish to resist a clearly stated teaching of scripture, but because they do not think this in fact is what scripture teaches. They do not find the teaching passages pointing to such a thoroughgoing conclusion. To clarify what precisely they do teach about scripture's inspiration and authority, it is necessary to listen to the fuller testimony of scripture: necessary, that is, to observe not only what scripture teaches about scripture, but also how scripture uses scripture.[47]

This brings us to the considerations with which the present chapter opened. Scripture's teaching passages, to be recognized as such, must first be incorporated among the various "phenomena." Furthermore, once identified, if the teaching passages are judged not to lead to an explicit doctrine of scripture, then the phenomena of scripture can be legitimately called upon for help in better understanding what the nature and extent of inspiration might happen to be *without setting teachings against the phenomena or vice versa*. Warfield's crusade to establish the notion that "it is indisputable that the Bible does, in fact, claim for itself divine inspiration"[48] does nothing but reiterate what all evangelical parties already believe. Most Christians believe the Bible is inspired. It is the *nature and extent* of such inspiration that both inerrantists and post-inerrantists alike continue to tease out both via what the Bible appears to teach as well as by its phenomena.[49] Thus Warfield (*Works*, 1.151) claims too much when he surmises:

47. Dunn, *Living Word* (2e), 74–75.

48. Zaspel, *Theology*, 172.

49. Compare Beegle, *Inspiration*, 60: "The evidence can be viewed from three possible points of view: 1) Scripture teaches the doctrine of inerrancy, but the phenomena

> If we start from the Scripture doctrine of inspiration, we approach the phenomena with the question whether they will negative this doctrine, and we find none able to stand against it, commended to us as true, as it is, by the vast mass of evidence available to prove the trustworthiness of the Scriptural writers as teachers of doctrine. But if we start simply with a collection of the phenomena, classifying and reasoning from them, whether alone or in conjunction with the Scriptural statements, it may easily happen with us, as it happened with certain of old, that meeting with some things hard to be understood, we may be ignorant and unstable enough to wrest them to our own intellectual destruction, and so approach the Biblical doctrine of inspiration set upon explaining it away.

Quite the contrary, the phenomena of scripture are not being called upon to explain away anything much less biblical doctrine. Much rather they are called upon to help fill out what the nature and extent of inspiration may happen to be. Along the way, they have helpfully suggested that "the proponents of Princeton theology," particularly in light of their opinion that their arguments be practically granted the status of demonstration, "have read their inerrancy dogma into the teaching of Jesus and the New Testament."[50]

In this chapter, I have sought to both problematize the teaching-phenomenon dichotomy and especially criticize the use to which it was put by scholars at Old Princeton. It is simply not true that students who question inerrancy are led to do so because of their method. By Old Princeton's own standards, it is genuinely legitimate to call upon phenomena for help with discerning the nature and extent of the Bible's inspiration.

---

of Scripture disprove this claim; 2) Scripture teaches the doctrine of inerrancy, therefore any contradictions or errors are in appearance only; and 3) Scripture does not teach the doctrine of inerrancy, therefore the phenomena of Scripture are to be accepted as an important factor in determining a Biblical view of inspiration."

50. Dunn, *Living Word* (2e), 106. Following in Warfield's footsteps, contemporary inerrantists seem convinced that whether one accepts inerrancy or not depends largely on one's approach to the Bible. They teach that if students would simply submit to the exegetical results of the inerrantist tradition, they will come to see that there is such a high probability associated with its arguments ("exegeses") that the strength of demonstration might as well be assigned to them. In practice they go further, requiring that any opposing view *must* be a demonstration: "No doubt this presumption may be overcome by clear demonstration. But clear demonstration is requisite" (*Works*, 1.118).

Conclusion

R EFLECTING ON SOME OF the ground covered in the last two chapters raises an interesting dialogical thought: it is all too easy in disputes in bibliology to accuse everyone else of reading their views into scripture all the while maintaining that one's own in-group is *not* guilty of doing so. As a point of fact, Warfield (*Works*, 1.138) objected more than once that it should be obvious to impartial onlookers that his opponents were the ones who approached scripture with their minds already made up. And yet repeatedly in this work I have suggested that *inerrantists* are coming to the scriptures already having worked out on dogmatic grounds the properties scripture perforce exhibits. Only *after* carrying out dogmatic deductions would they be properly motivated to insist in their exegeses that scripture *must* look and act in conformity with modernist inerrantist expectations.

But there is nothing new in this pattern of accusation and counter-accusation in the history of theology, particularly regarding what a priori bibliological assumptions are being invoked. Warfield (*Works*, 1.118), to continue with his example, complained that his contemporaries held "the even deeper error of the assertion latterly becoming much too common that, the doctrine of verbal inspiration, as a recent writer puts it, 'is based wholly upon an *a priori* assumption of what inspiration *must be* [italics in original], and not upon the Bible as it actually exists.'" It should come as no surprise then that some students today have begun to reason that if such a stalwart tradition as Old Princeton managed to convince a whole generation of conservative believers to bind up "the cause of distinctive Christianity . . . with the cause of the Biblical doctrine of inspiration"—all the while basing their case on pro-inerrantist eisegeses and having them pass for "demonstrative" induction—then does this not raise the possibility (or even the likelihood) that *all* believers, inerrantist and non-inerrantist alike, are guilty of doing much the same thing in support of their favorite position?

Such considerations seem to me worth pursuing, although it would involve a complicated line of inquiry into the dense thickets of philosophical hermeneutical theory. Obviously, this kind of study cannot be taken up here. In the literature, however, students will find that some more adventurous evangelicals have not hesitated to initiate the discussion, but I am not sure that an inerrantist understanding of scripture can emerge from a full-blown investigation into "hermeneutics" unscathed. Although in chapter two I advocated the establishing of hermeneutical distance between believers and the Bible, students should also make note of the following observation:

> . . . all [evangelicals] perceive biblical authority to be threatened by either subjective or autonomous interpretive procedures. . . . [E]vangelicals continue to resist the suggestion that human consciousness is any way constitutive of truth or meaning. Since phenomenological hermeneutics are rooted in precisely this suggestion, evangelicals seem to be misguided or to be acting in bad faith when they claim to take hermeneutics on board.[1]

In my view, a conversation that entertains subjectivity as co-constitutive of biblical truth is one that students should begin to take up with more seriousness.

Fortunately for us, as I suggested in chapter five it is not necessary for students to cease feeding on scripture until they are in a position to articulate a plausible bibliology, as if spirituality requires theoretical "warrant" or epistemic justification in order for it to be legitimated or become operative. I think what will prove crucial for students at this point is what they decide to do theologically *in the meantime*. I believe that it is the interim period that will to a great extent determine what further developments students will be able to achieve in bibliology. In a culture of fear, of course, nothing can *officially* happen "in the meantime" save political reaffirmations of traditional statements of faith that confess inerrancy. Under such conditions, it would not be surprising for students to end up so stagnant in spirit that they give up on faith outright. In chapter one above, I mentioned that there are some unhealthy dynamics at work within inerrantism. In chapter two, I made the suggestion that a key component to spiritual progress will likely include deliberate attempts on the student's part to establish some kind of hermeneutical

---

1. Harris, *Fundamentalism and Evangelicals*, 311–12.

distance between oneself and the Bible with an eye toward being able to read the Bible again with "new" eyes.

Interestingly enough, this suggestion dovetails with a piece of advice given by N. T. Wright to the effect that believers should consider reading fresh, contemporary translations of scripture in place of their older, customary versions.[2] By doing so, he suggests, believers would be more likely to see just how provocative and radical the Christian gospel truly is. In fact, he became so convicted about this—that believers could further their own spiritual development by reading the Bible afresh— that he ended up publishing a new translation of the New Testament for devotional reading.[3]

J. Dunn, too, has commented on the progress inerrantists stand to make in bibliology by "relaxing" and "subordinating" their insistence upon inerrancy to a trained sensitivity regarding the intentions of biblical texts. According to Dunn, if this were to happen with more frequency, it would become easier for inerrantists not merely to admit but also genuinely appreciate that the road from translation to exposition and from exposition to interpretation is fraught with exegetical and hermeneutical uncertainty, to the point that "the same uncertainty affects even the most central elements in New Testament teaching."[4] Perhaps biblical "teachings" only provide a general doctrinal sketch, just enough to motivate churches to embark upon their mission of Spirit-led, faith-based Kingdom building. Perhaps the fact of the matter is that God is in the historical process of making a polysemous, communicative gesture to humankind—a gesture not limited to the provision of holy scripture, nor only mediated to believers via scripture—in which believers are free to participate in any number of fruitful ways. For our purposes, we might say that bibliology, being theology, "is the tradition discriminating between itself and the Word of God, acknowledging the contingency and, therefore, openness to revision of the ways in which it has sought to represent the gospel."[5]

---

2. Wright, *Following Jesus*, xi.

3. Wright, *Kingdom New Testament*.

4. Dunn, *Living Word* (2e), 81. A point absolutely lost on G. Bray who adduces Dunn as an example of how "the charismatic reader is left exposed to the most radical forms of liberal thought which he may piece together in a quite disorganized way." See Bray, "Unity," 78–79.

5. Webster, "Reading Theology," 60.

As I came to the end of writing my first book, *Inerrancy and the Spiritual Formation of Younger Evangelicals*, I discovered that its main contention had been voiced twenty-five years earlier by a Roman Catholic biblical scholar, Raymond Brown.[6] Now as I come to the completion of the present work, I have found once again that its central points were outlined almost thirty years before by another Roman Catholic, this time a theologian, Avery Dulles. As I read through each of Dulles' objections to a "propositional" model of revelation, it occurred to me that he had concisely summarized a number of similar points I was seeking to make in the present work.

The first objection Dulles mentions is that "the church Fathers and their medieval followers, by and large, were open to a great variety of allegorical and spiritual interpretations that went well beyond the literal meaning of isolated propositions, and sometimes even bypassed the literal sense."[7] Although Dulles is inveighing against a propositional view of revelation with this objection, I had occasion to bring this consideration to mind in chapters five and six while discussing the widespread evangelical understanding that inerrancy is a central doctrine for historic Christianity.

A second objection Dulles discusses involves developments in critical scholarship which have established that "even passages that profess to be historical are shot through with poetic, legendary, and mythical elements . . . Modern advances in science and historiography make it well-nigh impossible to use the Bible any longer as an authoritative source of scientific and historical information, as was done in the pre-critical era." In chapters two through four, I more or less conceded the substance of this observation while trying not to embrace a triumphalist attitude with respect to "modern advances" in the various disciplines. The Chicago Statement, in my view, simply presumes too much in terms of *how* students should understand that scripture's narratives are "true." Contemporary metaphysics entertains a wider array of positions than the Chicago Statement allows for. Perhaps these other metaphysical considerations can be fruitfully put to the service of re-conceptualizing "truth" in the case of biblical narratives.

A third point raised by Dulles is the recognition that "in communications, propositions play a rather modest part." In chapters three and

---

6. Brown, *Critical Meaning*.

7. Dulles, *Models of Revelation*, 48. Dulles' criticisms appear on pp 48–52.

four, I explored the idea that the illocutionary and perlocutionary acts of biblical communication are what turn out to be "true" for biblical narratives. If this gets things even partly right, then the notion that narratives in scripture must be true by corresponding to events in actual history is called into sufficient question for students to begin considering whether an alternate view to the Chicago Statement might now be profitably constructed and whether appeals to speech act theory can genuinely contribute to that discussion.

In chapter five, I touched upon yet another objection Dulles mentions. This one has to do with how a propositional model of revelation is "a highly authoritarian one, requiring submission to concepts and statements that have come out of situations radically different from those of contemporary believers." The observation Dulles makes that resonates most with what I ventured to say in chapter five is that within inerrantism there is little to no regard for "whether [revelation] actually illuminates the believer's own situation," particularly how "little allowance is made for the kind of faith that probes and questions." To help on this score, I suggested that students might consider looking more to philosophy than theology in order to find some ideational room to breathe.

Dulles' last objection has to do with how a "doctrinal understanding of revelation" is not generally conducive to constructive dialogue with others. "Convinced of possessing the pure and complete deposit, the theologian looks on members of other groups as heretics or infidels," writes Dulles. In chapter one, I described this pattern at length within both inerrantist fundamentalism and evangelicalism. In chapter six, I analyzed an "inerrancy circle" as instantiated at Old Princeton and noticed how inerrantist exegesis works to close itself off from critique by tying the fortune of Christianity to the fate of inerrancy. Thus, anyone who begins thinking about criticizing inerrancy is metonymically interpreted as a heretic or infidel, as it were.

The main reason Catholic writers went to great lengths in the early 1980s to address these kinds of topics is because, according to R. Brown, ultraconservatives within Catholicism had begun to set their minds on "duplicating in a decade the mistakes that Protestants took centuries to make."[8] I submit that inerrancy—understood as the claim that the Bible makes propositional truth-claims and that wherever these truth-claims are made in the Bible, these claims must turn out to be true—*is* a mistake

8. Brown, "And the Lord Said?," 15.

that conservative Protestantism has made. Be that as it may, I do not think I am quite ready to completely give up on the doctrine—at least not yet. Perhaps there is an outside chance of rehabilitating inerrancy, but if so, it will have to look much different than the way inerrantists presently conceive it. In a culture of fear, however, not much of this can happen openly. In fact, given the present climate it would not surprise me if somewhere along the way students resigned themselves to the judgment that the inerrantist program cannot be rehabilitated: it is simply destined to fail. Either way, students must be encouraged to exercise their imaginations and contribute toward the construction of a more versatile bibliology that will be better equipped to engage the unforeseen challenges of the twenty-first century.

Bibliography

Abraham, William. "Foreword." In *Interdisciplinary Perspectives on the Authority of Scripture: Historical, Biblical and Theoretical Perspectives*, edited by Carlos Bovell, ix–xvi. Eugene, OR: Pickwick Publications, 2011.

Akenson, Donald. *Surpassing Wonder: The Invention of the Bible and the Talmuds*. Chicago: The University of Chicago Press, 2001.

Alexander, Loveday. "This Is That." *Princeton Seminary Bulletin* 25 (2004): 189–204.

Alexander, Philip. "The Bible in Qumran and Early Judaism." In *Text in Context: Essays by Members of the Society for Old Testament Study*, edited by A. D. H. Mayes, 35–62. New York: Oxford University Press, 2000.

Allert, Craig. *A High View of Scripture? The Authority of the Bible and the Formation of the New Testament Canon*. Grand Rapids: Baker, 2007.

———. "Issues in Forming a Doctrine of Inspiration." In *Interdisciplinary Perspectives on the Authority of Scripture: Historical, Biblical and Theoretical Perspectives*, edited by Carlos Bovell, 259–88. Eugene, OR: Pickwick Publications, 2011.

———. "What Are We Trying to Conserve?: Evangelicalism and *Sola Scriptura*." *Evangelical Quarterly* 76 (2004): 327–48.

Allison, Dale. *The Historical Christ and the Theological Jesus*. Grand Rapids: Eerdmans, 2009.

Alves, Rubem. *Protestantism and Repression: A Brazilian Case Study*. Translated by John Drury. Maryknoll, NY: Orbis Books, 1985.

Ammerman, Nancy. "Accounting for Christian Fundamentalisms: Social Dynamics and Rhetorical Strategies." In *Accounting for Fundamentalisms: The Dynamic Character of Movements*. The Fundamentalist Project Volume 4. Edited by Martin Marty and R. Scott Appleby, 149–70. Chicago: University of Chicago Press, 1994.

Ankerberg John, and Dillon Burroughs. *Taking a Stand for the Bible: Today's Leading Experts Answer Critical questions about God's Word*. Eugene, OR: Harvest House Publishers, 2009.

Antoun, Richard. *Understanding Fundamentalism: Christian, Islamic and Jewish Movements*. 2nd ed. New York: Rowman and Littlefield, 2008.

Appleby, R. Scott. "Fundamentalism as a Global Phenomenon." In *The Struggle over the Past: Fundamentalism in the Modern World*, edited by William Shea, 3–30. Lanham, MD: University Press of America, 1993.

Arnold, Bill. "Pentateuchal Criticism, History of." In *Dictionary of the Old Testament: Pentateuch*, edited by T. Desmond Alexander and David Baker, 622–31. Downers Grove, IL: InterVarsity Press, 2003.

Avalos, Hector. *¿Se puede saber si Dios existe?* Amherst, NY: Prometheus, 2003.

Bahnsen, Greg. "Inductivism, Inerrancy, and Presuppositionalism." *Journal of the Evangelical Theological Society* 20 (1977): 289–305.

Bailey, Lloyd. "Biblical Math as *Heilsgeschichte?*" In *A Gift of God in Due Season: Essays on Scripture and Community in Honor of James A. Sanders*, edited by Richard Weis, 84–102. Sheffield: Sheffield Academic Press, 1996.

Barr, James. *Escaping from Fundamentalism*. London: SCM Press, 1984.

———. *Fundamentalism*. 2nd ed. London: SCM Press Ltd., 1981.

Bauckham, Richard. "The Relevance of Extracanonical Jewish Texts to New Testament Study." In *Hearing the New Testament: Strategies for Interpretation*, edited by Joel Green, 90–108. Grand Rapids: Eerdmans, 1995.

Bauman, Michael. "Why the Noninerrantists Are Not Listening: Six Tactical Errors Evangelicals Commit." *Journal of the Evangelical Theological Society* 29 (1986): 317–24.

Beal, Timothy. *The Rise and Fall of the Bible: The Unexpected History of an Accidental Book*. New York: Houghton Mifflin Harcourt, 2011.

Beale, Gregory. "Can the Bible Be Completely Inspired by God and Yet Still Contain Errors? A Response to Some Recent 'Evangelical' Proposals." *Westminster Theological Journal* 73 (2011): 1–22.

———. *The Erosion of Inerrancy in Evangelicalism: Responding to New Challenges to Biblical Authority*. Wheaton, IL: Crossway, 2008.

Beegle, Dewey. *The Inspiration of Scripture*. Philadelphia: Westminster Press, 1963.

Benin, Stephen. *The Footprints of God: Divine Accommodation in Jewish and Christian Thought*. Albany, NY: State University of New York Press, 1993.

Bergen, Robert. "Authorial Intent and the Spoken Word: A Discourse-critical Analysis of Speech Acts in Accounts of Israel's United Monarchy (1 Sam 1—1 Kings (*sic*) 11)." In *Giving the Sense: Understanding an Using Old Testament Historical Texts*, edited by David Howard and Michael Grisanti, 360–79. Grand Rapids: Kregel, 2003.

Berkhof, Louis. *Systematic Theology*. Phillipsburg, NJ: Presbyterian and Reformed Publishing, 1996.

Bloesch, Donald. *Holy Scripture: Revelation, Inspiration and Interpretation*. Grand Rapids: InterVarsity Press, 1994.

———. "The Sword of the Spirit: The Meaning of Inspiration." *Themelios* 5 (1980): 14–19.

Boone, Kathleen. *The Bible Tells Them So: The Discourse of Protestant Fundamentalism*. Albany, NY: State University of New York Press, 1989.

Bovell, Carlos. *By Good and Necessary Consequence: A Preliminary Genealogy of Biblicist Foundationalism*. Eugene, OR: Wipf and Stock, 2009.

———. "Inerrancy, a Paradigm in Crisis." In *Interdisciplinary Perspectives on the Authority of Scripture: Historical, Biblical and Theoretical Perspectives*, edited by Carlos Bovell, 91–106. Eugene, OR: Pickwick Publications, 2011.

———. *Inerrancy and the Spiritual Formation of Younger Evangelicals*. Eugene, OR: Wipf and Stock, 2007.

———. "Integrating the History of Philosophy and Apologetics: Understanding Anselm's *Proslogion* Argument as Contemplative Ascent." *Canadian Theological Review* (forthcoming).

———. "Pragmatism as a Potential Bridge for Interacting with Analytical Philosophy of Religion." *Heythrop Journal* (forthcoming).

———. "Two Examples of How the History of Mathematics Can Inform Theology." *Theology and Science* 8 (2010): 69–84.

Bovell, Carlos, editor. *Interdisciplinary Perspectives on the Authority of Scripture: Historical, Biblical and Theoretical Perspectives.* Eugene, OR: Pickwick Publications, 2011.

Bow, Charles. "Samuel Stanhope Smith and Common Sense Philosophy at Princeton." *Journal of Scottish Philosophy* 8 (2010): 189–209.

Bray, Gerald. "Unity and Diversity in Christian Theology." In *The Challenge of Evangelical Theology: Essays in Approach and Method,* edited by Nigel M. de S. Cameron, 58–81. Edinburgh: Rutherford House, 1987.

Briggs, Richard. "The Bible before Us: Evangelical Possibilities for Taking Scripture Seriously." In *New Perspectives for Evangelical Theology: Engaging with God, Scripture and the World,* edited by Tom Greggs, 14–28. New York: Routledge, 2010.

———. *Reading the Bible Wisely.* Grand Rapids: Baker, 2003.

———. "What Does Hermeneutics Have to Do with Biblical Interpretation?" *Heythrop Journal* 47 (2006): 55–74.

Bronowski, Jacob. *The Origins of Knowledge and Imagination.* New Haven: Yale University Press, 1978.

Brown, Raymond. "'And the Lord Said?' Biblical Reflections on Scripture as the Word of God." *Theological Studies* 42 (1981): 3–19.

———. *The Critical Meaning of the Bible: How a Modern Reading of the Bible Challenges Christians, the Church, and the Churches.* Mahwah, NJ: Paulist Press, 1981.

Bubner, Rüdiger. "On the Ground of Understanding." In *Hermeneutics and Truth,* edited by Brice Wachterhauser, 68–82. Evanston, IL: Northwestern University Press, 1994.

Bullock, C. Hassell. "History and Theology: The Tale of Two Histories." In *Giving the Sense: Understanding and Using Old Testament Historical Texts,* edited by Michael Grisanti and David Howard, 97–111. Grand Rapids: Kregel, 2003.

Burgess, Alexis, and John Burgess. *Truth.* Princeton, NJ: Princeton University Press, 2011.

Campbell, James. *A Thoughtful Profession: The Early Years of the American Philosophical Association.* Chicago: Open Court, 2006.

de S. Cameron, Nigel M. "The Logic of Biblical Authority." In *The Challenge of Evangelical Theology: Essays in Approach and Method,* edited by Nigel M. de S. Cameron, 1–16. Edinburgh: Rutherford House, 1987.

Carr, David. *Writing on the Tablet of the Heart: Origins of Scripture and Literature.* New York: Oxford University Press, 2005.

Carroll, Robert. *Wolf in the Sheepfold: The Bible as Problematic for Theology.* London: SCM Press, 1997.

Carson, Donald. *Collected Writings on Scripture.* Wheaton, IL: Crossway, 2010.

———. *The Gagging of God: Christianity Confronts Pluralism.* Grand Rapids: Zondervan, 1996.

———. "The Role of Exegesis in Systematic Theology." In *Doing Theology in Today's World: Essays in Honor of Kenneth S. Kantzer,* edited by John Woodbridge and Thomas McComiskey, 39–76. Grand Rapids: Zondervan, 1991.

Cavell, Stanley. *Must We Mean What We Say? A Book of Essays.* New York: Cambridge University Press, 2002.

———. *The Claim of Reason: Wittgenstein, Skepticism, Morality, and Tragedy.* New York: Oxford University Press, 1979.

Childs, Brevard. *The Book of Exodus: A Critical, Theological Commentary*. Philadelphia: Westminster, 1974.

Churchouse, Matthew. "Defining and Refining Inerrancy: Revisiting the Doctrine for the 21st Century." M. A. thesis, University of Birmingham, 2009. Online: <http://etheses.bham.ac.uk/311/1/churchouse09MPhil.pdf.>

Cohen, Edmund. *The Mind of a Bible-Believer*. Updated ed. Amherst, NY: Prometheus Books, 1988.

Coleman, Richard. "Biblical Inerrancy: Are We Going Anywhere?" *Theology Today* 31 (1975): 295–303.

Coleman, Simon. "Global Consciousness and the Conservative Protestant Imagination." In *Fundamentalism: Church and Society*, edited by Martyn Percy and Ian Jones, 97–109. London: SPCK, 2002.

Craig, William. "Review of Michael J. Murray, ed., *Reason for the Hope Within*." *Philosophia Christi* 1 (1999): 129–33.

Crapanzano, Vincent. *Serving the Word: Literalism in America from the Pulpit to the Bench*. New York: The New Press, 2000.

Daley, Brian. "Foreword." In *Retrieving Nicaea: The Development and Meaning of Trinitarian Doctrine* by Khaled Anatalios, ix–xiv. Grand Rapids: Baker, 2011.

Dash, Darryl. "Evangelicalism's Uneasy Conscience." Online: <http://www.christianweek.org/stories.php?id=29&cat=guest>.

David, Marian. "Truth-making and Correspondence." In *Truth and Truth-making*, edited by E. J. Lowe and A. Rami, 137-57. Ithaca: McGill-Queen's University Press, 2009.

Davies, Philip. *Memories of Ancient Israel: An Introduction to Biblical History—Ancient and Modern*. Louisville, KY: Westminster John Knox, 2008.

Davies, Paul, and Julian Brown. *The Ghost in the Atom: A Discussion of the Mysteries of Quantum Physics*. New York: Cambridge University Press, 1986.

Davis, Stephen. "What Do We Mean When We Say, 'The Bible Is True?'" In *But Is It All True? The Bible and the Question of Truth*, edited by Alan Padgett and Patrick Keifert, 86–103. Grand Rapids: Eerdmans, 2006.

Dayton, Donald. "Evangelicalism without Fundamentalism," *Christian Century* (July 19–26, 1978): 710–13. Online: <http://www.religion-online.org/showarticle.asp>.

Dembski, William. *The End of Christianity: Finding a Good God in an Evil World*. Nashville, TN: Broadman and Holman, 2009.

Detweiler, Robert. "What Is a Sacred Text?" *Semeia* 31 (1985): 213–30.

DeYoung, Curtiss. *Living Faith: How Faith Inspires Social Justice*. Minneapolis: Fortress Press, 2007.

Doeve, Jan Willem. *Jewish Hermeneutics in the Synoptic Gospels and Acts*. Assen: Van Gorcum and Company, 1953.

Dorrien, Gary. *The Remaking of Evangelical Theology*. Louisville: Westminster John Knox, 1998.

Ducasse, Curt. "Facts, Truth, and Knowledge." *Philosophy and Phenomenological Research* 5 (1945): 320–32.

Dulles, Avery. *Models of Revelation*. Garden City, NY: Doubleday and Company, Inc., 1983.

Dummett, Michael. "Theology and Reason." *New Blackfriars* 69 (1988): 237–45.

Dunn, James. *The Living Word*. Philadelphia: Fortress Press, 1987.

———. *The Living Word*. 2nd ed. Minneapolis: Fortress Press, 2009.

Edgar, William, and K. Scott Oliphint. *Christian Apologetics Past and Present: A Prima: ,
Source Reader*. Wheaton, IL: Crossway, 2009.

Ehrlich, Carl. "Philistines." In *Dictionary of the Old Testament: Historical Books*, edited
by Bill Arnold and H. G. M. Williamson, 782–92. Grand Rapids: InterVarsity Press,
2005.

Ehrman, Bart. *Misquoting Jesus: The Story Behind Who Changed the Bible and Why*. New
York: HarperCollins, 2005.

Elledge, Casey. *The Bible and the Dead Sea Scrolls*. Atlanta: Society of Biblical Literature,
2005.

Ellis, Earle. *The Making of the New Testament Documents*. Leiden: Brill, 1999.

Engel, Pascal. *Truth*. McGill-Queens University Press, 2002.

Enns, Peter. "Apostolic Hermeneutics and an Evangelical Doctrine of Scripture: Moving
beyond a Modernist Impasse." *Westminster Theological Journal* 65 (2003): 263–88.

———. *Inspiration and Incarnation: Evangelicals and the Problem of the Old Testament*.
Grand Rapids: Baker, 2005.

———. "Interaction with Bruce Waltke." *Westminster Theological Journal* 71 (2009):
97–114.

———. *The NIV Application Commentary: Exodus*. Grand Rapids: Zondervan, 2000.

———. "William Henry Green and the Authorship of the Pentateuch: Some Historical
Considerations." *Journal of the Evangelical Theological Society* 45 (2002): 385–403.

Erickson, Millard. "Biblical Inerrancy: The Last Twenty-Five Years." *Journal of the
Evangelical Theological Society* 25 (1982): 387–94.

Feinberg, John. *No One Like Him: The Doctrine of God*. Wheaton, IL: Crossway, 2001.

Feinberg, Paul. "The Meaning of Inerrancy." In *Inerrancy*, edited by Norman Geisler,
267–306. Grand Rapids: Zondervan, 1980.

———. "Truth, Meaning and Inerrancy in Contemporary Evangelical Thought." *Journal
of the Evangelical Theological Society* 26 (1983): 17–30.

———. "Truth: Relationship of Theories of Truth to Hermeneutics." In *Hernemeneutics,
Inerrancy and the Bible*, edited by Earl Radmacher and Robert Preus, 1–50. Grand
Rapids: Zondervan, 1984.

Fishbane, Michael. *Biblical Interpretation in Ancient Israel*. New York: Oxford University
Press, 1985.

———. *The Exegetical Imagination: On Jewish Thought and Theology*. Cambridge, MA:
Harvard University Press, 1998.

———. *The Garments of Torah: Essay in Biblical Hermeneutics*. Indianapolis: Indiana
University Press, 1989.

Fitch, David. *The End of Evangelicalism? Discerning a New Faithfulness for Mission:
Towards an Evangelical Political Theology*. Eugene, OR: Cascade Books, 2011.

Flusser, David. *The Sage from Galilee: Rediscovering Jesus' Genius*. Grand Rapids:
Eerdmans, 2007.

Fowler, James. *Stages of Faith: The Psychology of Human Development and the Quest for
Meaning*. New York: HarperCollins, 1985.

Frame, John. "Covenant and the Unity of Scripture." Online: <http://www.frame-
poythress.org/frame_articles/1999Covenant.htm>.

———. *The Doctrine of God*. Phillipsburg, NJ: Presbyterian and Reformed Publishing,
2002.

Franke, John. *Manifold Witness: The Plurality of Truth*. Nashville, TN: Abingdon, 2009.

Fuller, Daniel. "On Revelation and Biblical Authority." *Journal of the Evangelical Theological Society* 16 (1973): 67–69.

Geisler, Norman. "Beware of Philosophy: A Warning to Biblical Scholars." *Journal of the Evangelical Theological Society* 42 (1999): 3–19.

———. "Inerrancy and Foundationalism." *Bulletin of the Evangelical Philosophical Society* 3 (1980): 1–5.

———. "The Concept of Truth in the Inerrancy Debate." *Bibliotheca Sacra* 137 (1980): 327–36.

Geisler, Norman, and William Nix. *A General Introduction to the Bible.* Rev. and exp. Chicago: Moody Press, 1986.

Gerstner, John. "Warfield's Case for Biblical Inerrancy." In *God's Inerrant Word: An International Symposium on the Trustworthiness of Scripture*, edited by John Montgomery, 115–42. Minneapolis: Bethany Fellowship, 1974.

Gill, Jerry. *Mediated Transcendence: A Postmodern Reflection.* Macon, GA: Mercer University Press, 1989.

———. *Metaphilosophy: An Introduction.* Washington, D. C.: University of America Press, 1982.

Goodrick, Edward. "Let's Put 2 Timothy 3: 16 Back in the Bible." *Journal of the Evangelical Theological Society* 25 (1982): 479–87.

Gracia, Jorge. "Suárez and the Doctrine of the Transcendentals." *Topoi* 11 (1992): 121–33.

Greidanus, Sidney. *Preaching Christ from Genesis: Foundations for Expository Sermons.* Grand Rapids: Eerdmans, 2007.

Grenz, Stanley, and John Franke. *Beyond Foundationalism: Shaping Theology in a Postmodern Context.* Louisville, KY: Westminster/John Knox, 2001.

Groothius, Douglas. "Review of *Uneasy Conscience of Modern Fundamentalism*." Online: http://www.denverseminary.edu/article/the-uneasy-conscience-of-modern-fundamentalism/

Grudem, Wayne. *Bible Doctrine: Essential Teachings of the Christian Faith.* Grand Rapids: Zondervan, 1999.

———. "Scripture's Self-Attestation and the Problem of Formulating a Doctrine of Scripture." In *Scripture and Truth*, edited by Donald Carson and John Woodbridge, 19–64. Grand Rapids: Zondervan, 1983.

Habermas, Gary. "Jesus and the Inspiration of Scripture." *Areopagus Journal* (January 2002): <http://digitalcommons.liberty.edu/cgi/viewcontent.cgi?article=1093&context=lts_fac_pubs&sei-redir=1#search=%22jesus%20inspiration%20scripture%22>.

Hackett, Stuart. *The Reconstruction of the Christian Revelation Claim: A Philosophical and Critical Apologetic.* Grand Rapids: Baker, 1984.

Harlow, Daniel. "After Adam: Reading Genesis in an Age of Evolutionary Science." *Perspectives on Science and Christian Faith* 62 (2010): 179–95.

———. "Creation According to Genesis: Literary Genre, Cultural Context, Theological Truth." *Christian Scholar's Review* 37 (2008): 163-98.

Harries, Karsten. "Philosophy in Search for Itself." In *What Is Philosophy?*, edited by C. P. Ragland and Sarah Heidt, 47–73. New Haven, CT: Yale University Press, 2001.

Harris, Harriet. *Fundamentalism and Evangelicals.* New York: Oxford University Press, 1998.

———. "Fundamentalism in a Protestant Context." In *Fundamentalism: Church and Society*, edited by Martyn Percy and Ian Jones, 7–24. London: SPCK, 2002.

———. "Scripture and Prayer: Participating in God." In *Interdisciplinary Perspectives on the Authority of Scripture: Historical, Biblical and Theoretical Perspectives*, edited by Carlos Bovell, 344–53. Eugene, OR: Wipf and Stock, 2011.

Harrison, Everett. "The Phenomena of Scripture." In *Revelation and the Bible: Contemporary Evangelical Thought*, edited by Carl Henry, 237–50. Grand Rapids: Baker, 1958.

Harrisville, Roy, and Walter Sundberg. *The Bible in Modern Culture: Baruch Spinoza to Brevard Childs*. 2nd ed. Grand Rapids: Eerdmans, 2002.

Helm, Paul. "Analysis Extra: 'The Phenomena.'" Online: <http://paulhelmsdeep.blogspot.com/2008/07/analysis-extra-phenomena.html>.

———. "B. B. Warfield's Path to Inerrancy: An Attempt to Correct Some Serious Misunderstandings." *Westminster Theological Journal* 72 (2010): 23–42.

———. "Charles Hodge and the Method of Systematic Theology." Online: <http://paulhelmsdeep.blogspot.com/2007/09/charles-hodge-method-of-systematic.html>.

———. *The Divine Revelation: The Basic Issues*. Vancouver: Regent College Publishing, 1982.

Helseth, Paul. "B. B. Warfield's Apologetical Appeal to 'Right Reason': Evidence of a 'Rather Bald Rationalism'?" *Scottish Bulletin of Evangelical Theology* 16 (1998): 156–77.

———. "'Re-Imagining' the Princeton Mind: Postconservative Evangelicalism, Old Princeton, and the Rise of Neo-fundamentalism." *Journal of the Evangelical Theological Society* 45 (2002): 427–50.

Henze, Matthias, editor. *A Companion to Biblical Interpretation in Second Temple Judaism*. Grand Rapids: Eerdmans, 2011.

Hesse, Mary. "How to Be a Postmodernist and Remain a Christian." In *After Pentecost: Language and Biblical Interpretation*, edited by Craig Bartholomew, Colin Greene, and Karl Möller, 91–96. Grand Rapids: Zondervan, 2001.

Hexham, Irving. "Trashing Evangelical Christians." In *Tough-Minded Christianity: Honoring the Legacy of John Warwick Montgomery*, edited by William Dembski and Thomas Schirrmacher, 69–91. Nashville, TN: Broadman and Hollman, 2008.

Hicks, Peter. *Evangelicals and Truth: A Creative Proposal for a Postmodern Age*. Leicester: Apollos, 1998.

Hill, Samuel. "The Spirit of Fundamentalism." In *The Struggle over the Past: Fundamentalism in the Modern World*, edited by William Shea, 209–16. Lanham, MD: University Press of America, 1993.

Holmes, Michael. "Origen and the Inerrancy of Scripture." *Journal of the Evangelical Theological Society* 24 (1981): 221–31.

Holmes, Stephen. "Kings, Professors, and Ploughboys: On the Accessibility of Scripture." *International Journal of Systematic Theology* 13 (2011): 403–15

Hunt, Stephen. "The Devil's Advocates: The Function of Demonology in the World View of Fundamentalist Christianity." In *Fundamentalism: Church and Society*, edited by Martyn Percy and Ian Jones, 66–91. London: SPCK, 2002.

Instone-Brewer, David. "Theology of Hermeneutics." In *Encyclopedia of Midrash: Biblical Interpretation in Formative Judaism*, edited by Jacob Neusner and Alan Avery-Peck, 292–316. Leiden: Brill, 2005.

Jensen, Robert. "On the Authorities of Scripture." In *Engaging Biblical Authority: Perspectives on the Bible as Scripture*, edited by William Brown, 53–61. Louisville, KY: Westminster John Knox, 2007.

Johnston, Mark. *Surviving Death*. Princeton, NJ: Princeton University Press, 2010.

Katongole, Emmanuel, and Chris Rice. *Reconciling All Things: A Christian Vision for Justice, Peace and Healing*. Downers Grove, IL: InterVarsity Press, 2008.

Kelsey, David. "Appeals to Scripture in Theology." *The Journal of Religion* 48 (1968): 1–21.

———. *Proving Doctrine: The Uses of Scripture in Modern Theology*. Harrisburg, PA: Trinity International Press, 1989.

Kermode, Frank. "Institutional Control of Interpretation." *Salmagundi* 43 (1979): 72–86.

Kinnaman, David. *Unchristian: What a New Generation Really Thinks about Christianity . . . and Why It Matters*. Grand Rapids: Baker, 2007.

Kirkham, Richard. *Theories of Truth: A Critical Introduction*. Cambridge, MA: The MIT Press, 1992.

Kivy, Peter. *The Performance of Reading: An Essay in the Philosophy of Literature*. Malden, MA; Blackwell, 2009.

Knight, Henry, III. *A Future for Truth: Evangelical Theology in a Postmodern World*. Nashville, TN: Abingdon, 1997.

Knuuttilla, Simo. "Biblical Authority and Philosophy." In *Biblical Concepts in Our World*, edited by Dewi Phillips and Mario von de Ruhr, 113–27. New York: Palgrave Macmillan, 2004.

Koch, Klaus. *The Growth of the Biblical Tradition: The Form-Critical Method*. Translated by S. M. Cupitt. New York: Charles Scribner's Sons, 1969.

Kugel, James. "Appendix 1: Apologetics and Biblical Criticism Lite." Online: <http://www.jameskugel.com/apologetics.pdf>.

———. "Early Interpretation: The Common Background of Late Forms of Biblical Exegesis." In *Early Biblical Interpretation* by James Kugel and Rowan Greer, 9–106. Philadelphia: Westminster Press, 1986.

———. *How to Read the Bible*. New York: Free Press, 2007.

———. "On the Bible and Literary Criticism." *Prooftexts* 1 (1981): 217–36.

Kunne, Wolfgang. *Conceptions of Truth*. New York: Oxford University Press, 2003.

Kuyper, Abraham. *Sacred Theology*. Lafayette, IN: Sovereign Grace Publishers, 2001.

Lamarque, Peter, and Stein Olsen. *Truth, Fiction and Literature*. New York: Oxford University Press, 1994.

Larkin, Jr., William. *Culture and Biblical Hermeneutics: Interpreting and Applying the Authoritative Word in a Relativistic Age*. Grand Rapids: Baker, 1988.

Lehmann, David. "Fundamentalism and Globalism." In *Fundamentalism: Church and Society*, edited by Martyn Percy and Ian Jones, 110–44. London: SPCK, 2002.

Lewis, Gordon. *Testing Christianity's Truth Claims: Approaches to Christian Apologetics*. Lanham, MD: University Press of America, 1990.

Lindars, Barnabas. "Elijah, Elisha and the Gospel Miracles." In *Miracles: Cambridge Studies in Their Philosophy and History*, edited by Charles Moule, 63–79. New York: A. R. Mowbray, 1965.

———. *New Testament Apologetic: The Doctrinal Significance of the Old Testament Quotations*. Philadelphia: Westminster, 1961.

Long, V. P. *Art of Biblical History*. In *Foundations of Contemporary Interpretation: Six Volumes in One*, edited by Moisés Silva. Grand Rapids: Zondervan, 1996.

Longenecker, Richard. *Biblical Exegesis in the Apostolic Period*. 2nd ed. Grand Rapids, Eerdmans, 1999.

Longman, Tremper. "Storytellers and Poets in the Bible: Can Literary Artifice Be True?" In *Inerrancy and Hermeneutic: A Tradition, a Challenge, a Debate*, edited by H. Conn, 137–49. Grand Rapids: Baker, 1988.

Lynch, Michael. *Truth in Context: An Essay on Pluralism and Objectivity*. Cambridge, MA: MIT Press, 1998.

MacDonald, Nathan. *Karl Barth and the Strange New World within the Bible: Barth, Wittgenstein, and the Metadilemmas of the Enlightenment*. Revised edition. Colorado Springs, CO: Paternoster, 2001.

Machen, J. G. *Christianity and Liberalism*. Grand Rapids: Eerdmans, 1923.

Malley, Brian. "Biblical Authority: A Social Scientist's Perspective." In *Interdisciplinary Perspectives on the Authority of Scripture: Historical, Biblical and Theoretical Perspectives*, edited by C. Bovell, 303–22. Eugene, OR: Pickwick Publications, 2011.

———. *How the Bible Works: An Anthropological Study of Evangelical Biblicism*. New York: Altamira Press, 2004.

Manuel, Frank. *Shapes of Philosophical History*. Stanford, CA: Stanford University Press, 1965.

Marcu, Daniel. "Perlocutions: The Achilles' Heel of Speech Act Theory." *Journal of Pragmatics* 32 (2000): 1719–41.

Marsden, George. *Fundamentalism and American Culture*. 2nd ed. New York: Oxford University Press, 2006.

Marshall, I. H. "Are Evangelicals Fundamentalist?" *Vox Evangelica* 22 (1992): 7–24.

———. *Biblical Inspiration*. London, 1982; repr. Carlisle: Paternoster Press, 1995.

Martin, William. "Special Revelation as Objective." In *Revelation and the Bible: Contemporary Evangelical Thought*, edited by Carl Henry, 61–72. Grand Rapids: Baker, 1958.

Martinich, Aloysius, and Avrum Stroll. *Much Ado about Nonexistence: Fiction and Reference*. Rowman and Littlefield, 2007.

Mason, Steve. "Encountering the Past through the Works of Flavius Josephus." In *Historical Knowledge in Biblical Antiquity*, edited by Jacob Neusner, Bruce Chilton, and William Green, 105–38. Dorset: Deo Publishing, 2007.

Mazar, Amihai. "The Patriarchs, Exodus, and Conquest Narratives in Light of Archaeology." In *The Quest for the Historical Israel: Debating Archaeology and the History of Early History* by Israel Finkelstein, Amihai Mazar, and Brian Schmidt, 57–65. Atlanta: Society of Biblical Literature, 2007.

McConnel, Tim. "The Old Princeton Apologetics: Common Sense or Reformed?" *Journal of the Evangelical Theological Society* 46 (2003): 647–72.

McGowan, Andrew. *The Divine Authenticity of Scripture: Retrieving an Evangelical Heritage*. Downers Grove, IL: InterVarsity, 2007.

McKenzie, Steven. *How to Read the Bible: History, Prophecy, Literature—Why Modern Readers Need to Know the Difference and What It Means for Faith Today*. New York: Oxford University Press, 2005.

Mercer, Calvin. *Slaves to Faith: A Therapist Looks Inside the Fundamentalist Mind*. Westport, CN: Praeger, 2009.

Milavec, Donald. "The Bible, the Holy Spirit, and Human Powers." *Scottish Journal of Theology* 29 (1976): 215–35.

Miller, James. *The Old Testament and the Historian*. Philadelphia: Fortress, 1976.

Möller, Karl. "Words of (In-)evitable Certitude? Reflections on the Interpretation of Prophetic Oracles of Judgement." In *After Pentecost: Language and Biblical Interpretation*, edited by Craig Bartholomew, Colin Greene, and Karl Möller, 352–86. Grand Rapids: Zondervan, 2001.

Montgomery, John Warwick. "Inspiration and Inerrancy: A New Departure." *Bulletin of the Evangelical Theological Society* 8 (1965): 45–75.

Moore, A. W. *Points of View*. New York: Oxford University Press, 1997.

————. *The Infinite*. 2nd ed. New York: Routledge, 2001.

Moreland, J. P. "How Evangelicals Became Over-committed to the Bible and What Can Be Done about It." In *Interdisciplinary Perspectives on the Authority of Scripture: Historical, Biblical and Theoretical Perspectives*, edited by C. Bovell, 289–302. Eugene, OR: Pickwick Publications, 2011.

————. *Love Your God with All Your Mind: The Role of Reason in the Life of the Soul*. Colorado Springs, CO: NavPress, 1997.

————. *Kingdom Triangle: Recover the Mind, Renovate the Soul, Restore the Spirit's Power*. Grand Rapids: Zondervan, 2007.

————. *Scaling the Secular City: A Defense of Christianity*. Grand Rapids: Baker, 1987.

————. "The Rationality of Belief in Inerrancy." *Trinity Journal* 7 (1986): 75–86.

————. "Truth, Contemporary Philosophy, and the Postmodern Turn." *Journal of the Evangelical Theological Society* 48 (2005): 77–88.

Moreland J. P., and William Craig. *Philosophical Foundations for a Christian Worldview*. Downers Grove, IL: InterVarsity Press, 2003.

Morrison, John. *Has God Said? Scripture, the Word of God, and the Crisis of Theological Authority*. Eugene, OR: Pickwick Publications, 2006.

Murray, Michael. "Reason for Hope (in the Postmodern World)." In *Reason for the Hope Within*, edited by Michael Murray, 1–19. Grand Rapids: Eerdmans, 1999.

Nienhuis, David. *Not by Paul Alone: The Formation of the Catholic Epistle Collection and the Christian Canon*. Waco, TX: Baylor University Press, 2007.

Nicole, Roger. "The Biblical Concept of Truth." In *Scripture and Truth*, edited by Donald Carson and John Woodbridge, 287–98. Grand Rapids: Zondervan, 1983.

Nichols, Stephen, and Eric Brandt. *Ancient Word, Changing Worlds: The Doctrine of Scripture in a Modern Age*. Wheaton, IL: Crossway Books, 2009.

Nikulun, Dmitri. *Dialectic and Dialogue*. Stanford, CA: Stanford University Press, 2010.

Noll, Mark. *The Scandal of the Evangelical Mind*. Grand Rapids: Eerdmans, 1994.

————. *Jesus Christ and the Life of the Mind*. Grand Rapids: Eerdmans, 2011.

Oegema, Gerbern. *Early Judaism and Modern Culture: Literature and Theology*. Grand Rapids: Eerdmans, 2011.

Olson, Roger E. *Reformed and Always Reforming: The Postconservative Approach to Evangelical Theology*. Grand Rapids: Baker, 2007.

Omnès, Roland. *Converging Realities: Toward a Common Philosophy of Physics and Mathematics*. Princeton, NJ: Princeton University Press, 2005.

Organ, Barbara. *Is the Bible Fact or Fiction? An Introduction to Biblical Historiography*. New York: Paulist Press, 2004.

Orr, James. *Revelation and Inspiration*. London, 1910; repr., Vancouver: Regent College Publishing, 2002.

Osborne, Grant. "Historical Narrative and Truth in the Bible," *Journal of the Ev.* *Theological Society* 48 (2005): 673–88.

———. *The Hermeneutical Spiral*. 2nd ed. Grand Rapids: Zondervan, 2006.

Oswalt, John. *The Bible among the Myths: Unique Revelation or Just Ancient Liter*. Grand Rapids: Zondervan, 2009.

Packer, James. *"Fundamentalism" and the Word of God*. Grand Rapids: Eerdmans, 1958.

Paddison, Angus. "The Authority of Scripture and the Triune God." *International Journal of Systematic Theology* 13 (2011): 448–62.

Pakaluk, Michael. "A Defense of Common Sense Realism." *Philosophical Quarterly* 52 (2002): 564–81.

Parris, David. *Reception Theory and Biblical Hermeneutics*. Eugene, OR: Pickwick Publications, 2009.

Pavel, Thomas. *Fictional Worlds*. Cambridge, MA: Harvard University Press, 1986.

Payne, J. Barton. "Hermeneutics as a Cloak for the Denial of Scripture." *Bulletin of the Evangelical Theological Society* 3 (1960): 93–100.

———. "Higher Criticism and Biblical Inerrancy." In *Inerrancy*, edited by N. Geisler, 85–116. Grand Rapids: Zondervan, 1980.

———. "Paper from the 1957 Mid-Western Section: 'The Uneasy Conscience of Modern Liberal Exegesis.'" *Bulletin of the Evangelical Theological Society* 1 (1958): 14–18.

Peckham, John. "Intrinsic Canonicity and the Inadequacy of the Community Approach to Canon-Determination." *Themelios* 36 (2011): 203–215.

Percy, Martyn. "Fundamentalism: The End of Terms?" In *Fundamentalism: Church and Society*, edited by Martyn Percy and Ian Jones, 185–89. London: SPCK, 2002.

Phillips, Dewi. *Religion and Friendly Fire: Examining Assumptions in Contemporary Philosophy of Religion*. Burlington, VT: Ashgate Publishing, 2004.

Pickup, Martin. "New Testament Interpretation of the Old Testament: The Theological Rationale of Midrashic Exegesis." *Journal of the Evangelical Theological Society* 51 (2008): 353–81.

Pinnock, Clark. *The Scripture Principle: Reclaiming the Full Authority of the Bible*. 2nd ed. Grand Rapids: Baker, 2006.

Plantinga, Alvin. "Comment on Knuuttila's 'Biblical Authority and Philosophy.'" In *Biblical Concepts in Our World*, edited by Dewi Phillips and Mario von de Ruhr, 128–34. New York: Palgrave Macmillan, 2004.

Porter, J. R. "Folklore and the Old Testament." The 1979 Ethel M. Wood Lecture. Online: <http://www.biblicalstudies.org.uk/pdf/emwl/folklore_porter.pdf>.

Powell, Mark Allan. *What is Narrative Criticism?* Minneapolis: Fortress Press, 1990.

Powell, Mark E. "Canonical Theism and the Challenge of Epistemic Certainty: Papal Infallibility as a Case Study." In *Canonical Theism: A Proposal for Theology and the Church*, edited by William Abraham, Jason Vickers, and Natalie van Kirk, 195–209. Grand Rapids: Eerdmans, 2008.

Poythress, Vern. "Kinds of Biblical Theology." *Westminster Theological Journal* 70 (2008): 129–42.

———. "Problems for Limited Inerrancy." *Journal of the Evangelical Theological Society* 18 (1975): 93–102.

Ramm, Bernard. *Special Revelation and the Word of God*. Grand Rapids: Eerdmans, 1961.

Rhees, Rush. "The Fundamental Problems of Philosophy." *Philosophical Investigations* 174 (1994): 573–86.

Richter, Sandra. *The Epic of Eden: A Christian Entry into the Old Testament*. Downers Grove, IL: InterVarsity Press, 2008.

Roach, David. "How Old? Age of Earth Debated among SBC Scholars." *Florida Baptist Witness*, October 20, 2010; Online: <http://www.gofbw.com/news.asp?ID=12220&fp=Y>.

Rohrbaugh, Richard. *The Biblical Interpreter: An Agrarian Bible in an Industrial Age*. Philadelphia: Fortress Press, 1978.

———. *The New Testament in Cross-Cultural Perspective*. Eugene, OR: Cascade, 2007.

Rorty, Richard. *Consequences of Pragmatism*. Minneapolis: University of Minnesota Press, 1982.

Sandeen, Ernest. *Roots of Fundamentalism: British and American Millenarianism, 1800–1930*. Chicago: University of Chicago Press, 1970.

Sanders, James. "Biblical Criticism and the Bible as Canon." *Union Seminary Quarterly Review* 43 (1977): 157–65.

———. "Hermeneutics of Text Criticism." *Textus* 18 (1995): 1–26.

———. "Response to Lemcio." *Biblical Theology Bulletin* 11 (1981): 122–24.

———. "The Challenge of Fundamentalism: One God and World Peace." *Impact* 19 (1987): 12–30.

———. *Torah and Canon*. 2nd ed. Eugene, OR: Cascade Books, 2005.

Sawyer, M. James. *The Survivor's Guide to Theology*. Grand Rapids: Zondervan, 2006.

Schimmel, Solomon. *The Tenacity of Unreasonable Beliefs: Fundamentalism and the Fear of Truth*. New York: Oxford University Press, 2008.

Schindler, D. C. *Hans Urs von Balthasar and the Dramatic Structure of Truth: A Philosophical Investigation*. New York: Fordham University Press, 2004.

Schreiner, Susan. *Are You Alone Wise? The Search for Certainty in the Early Modern Era*. New York: Oxford University Press, 2011.

Searle, John. *Expression and Meaning: Studies in the Theory of Speech Acts*. New York: Cambridge University Press, 1979.

———. "Illocutionary Acts and the Concept of Truth." In *Truth and Speech Acts: Studies in the Philosophy of Language*, edited by Dirk Greimann and Geo Siegwart, 31–40. New York: Routledge, 2007.

Seely, Paul. "The Subordination of Scripture to Human Reason at Old Princeton." In *Interdisciplinary Perspectives on the Authority of Scripture: Historical, Biblical and Theoretical Perspectives*, edited by Carlos Bovell, 28–45. Eugene, OR: Pickwick Publications, 2011.

Sexton, Jason. "How Far Beyond Chicago? Assessing Recent Attempts to Reframe the Inerrancy Debate." *Themelios* 34 (2009): 26–49.

Sheppard, Gerald. "Biblical Hermeneutics: The Academic Language of Evangelical Identity." *Union Seminary Quarterly Review* 32 (1977): 81–94.

Shults, F. Leron. *Christology and Science*. Burlington, VT: Ashgate, 2008.

Shults F. Leron, and Steven Sandage. *Transforming Spirituality: Integrating Theology and Psychology*. Grand Rapids: Baker, 2006.

Shüssler Fiorenza, Francis. "Roman Catholic Fundamentalism: A Challenge to Theology." In *The Struggle over the Past: Fundamentalism in the Modern World*, edited by William Shea, 231–54. Lanham, MD: University Press of America, 1993.

Slob, Wouter. *Dialogical Rhetoric: An Essay on Truth and Normativity after Postmodernism*. Boston: Kluwer Academic Publishers, 2002.

Smith, Christian. *The Bible Made Impossible: Why Biblicism Is Not a Truly Evangelical Reading of Scripture*. Grand Rapids: Brazos, 2011.

Smith, James K. A. "Who's Afraid of Postmodernism? A Response to the 'Biola S In *Christianity and the Postmodern Turn: Six Views*, edited by Myron Penn 28. Grand Rapids: Brazos Press, 2005.

Smith, Mark. *The Priestly Vision of Genesis 1*. Minneapolis: Fortress Press, 2010.

Smith Peter, and Robert Tuttle. "Biblical Literalism and Constitutional Originalism." *GWU Legal Studies Research Paper No. 502* (March 1, 2010). Online: <http://papers.ssrn.com/sol3/papers.cfm?abstract_id=1561933>.

Sparks, Kenton. *God's Word in Human Words: An Evangelical Appropriation of Critical Biblical Scholarship*. Grand Rapids: Baker, 2008.

Spina, Frank. "Canonical Criticism: Childs Versus Sanders." In *Interpreting God's Word Today: An Inquiry into Hermeneutics from a Biblical Theological Perspective*, edited by Wayne McCown and James Massey, 165–94. Anderson, IN: Warner Press, 1982.

Springsted, Eric. "Theology and Spirituality or, Why Theology Is Not Critical Reflection on Religious Experience." In *Spirituality and Theology: Essays in Honor of Diogenes Allen*, edited by Eric Springsted, 49–62. Louisville, KY: Westminster John Knox, 1998.

Stark, Thom. *The Human Faces of God: What Scripture Reveals When It Gets God Wrong (and Why Inerrancy Tries to Hide It)*. Eugene, OR: Wipf and Stock, 2011.

Steinmetz, David. "Uncovering a Second Narrative: Detective Fiction and the Construction of Historical Method." In *The Art of Reading Scripture*, edited by Ellen Davis and Richard Hays, 54–65. Grand Rapids: Eerdmans, 2003.

Sternberg, Meir. *The Poetics of Biblical Narrative: Ideological Literature and the Drama of Reading*. Bloomington, IN: Indiana University Press, 1987.

Stiver, Dan. "Ricoeur, Speech-act Theory, and the Gospels of History." In *After Pentecost: Language and Biblical Interpretation*, edited by Craig Bartholomew, Colin Greene, and Karl Möller, 50–72. Grand Rapids: Zondervan, 2001.

———. "Theological Method." In *The Cambridge Companion to Postmodern Theology*, edited by Kevin Vanhoozer, 170–85. New York: Cambridge University Press, 2003.

Stonehouse, Ned. "The Authority of the New Testament." In *The Infallible Word: A Symposium*, edited by Ned Stonehouse and Paul Wooley, 92–140. Philadelphia: Presbyterian and Reformed Publishing, 1946.

Sullivan, Clayton. *Toward a Mature Faith: Does Biblical Inerrancy Make Sense?* Decatur, GA: SBC Today, 1990.

Sundholm, Göran. "Existence, Proof and Truth-Making: A Perspective on the Intuitionistic Conception of Truth." *Topoi* 13 (1994): 117–26.

Theissen, Gerd. *The Bible and Contemporary Culture*. Translated by David Green. Minneapolis: Fortress, 2007.

Thiselton, Anthony. "Can 'Authority' Remain Viable in a Postmodern Climate? Biblical Authority in the Light of Contemporary Philosophical Hermeneutics." In *Thiselton on Hermeneutics*, 625–42.

———. "Communicative Action and Promise in Interdisciplinary, Biblical and Theological Hermeneutics." In *The Promise of Hermeneutics* by Roger Lundin, Clarence Walhout, and Anthony Thiselton, 133–239. Grand Rapids: Eerdmans, 1999.

———. "'Faith,' 'Flesh,' and 'Truth' as Context-Dependent Concepts: 'Language-Games and Polymorphous Concepts.'" In *Thiselton on Hermeneutics*, 183–90.

———. *Hermeneutics: An Introduction*. Grand Rapids: Eerdmans, 2009.

———. "Does Lexicographical Research Yield 'Hebrew' and 'Greek' Concepts of Truth? (1978), and How Does This Research Relate to Notions of Truth Today?" In *Thiselton on Hermeneutics*, 267–87.

———. *The Hermeneutics of Doctrine*. Grand Rapids: Eerdmans, 2007.

———. *Thiselton on Hermeneutics*. Grand Rapids: Eerdmans 2006.

Tilghman, Benjamin. *An Introduction to the Philosophy of Religion*. Cambridge, MA: Blackwell Publishers, 1994.

Torrance, Alan. "Can the Truth Be Learned? Redressing the 'Theologistic Fallacy' in Modern Biblical Scholarship." In *Scripture's Doctrine and Theology's Bible: How the New Testament Shapes Christian Dogmatics*, edited by Markus Bockmuehl and Alan Torrance, 143–64. Grand Rapids: Baker, 2008.

Trembath, Kern. *Evangelical Theories of Biblical Inspiration: A Review and Proposal*. New York: Oxford University Press, 1987.

van den Belt, Henk. "Scripture as the Voice of God: The Continuing Importance of *Autopistia*." *International Journal of Systematic Theology* 13 (2011): 434–47.

———. *The Authority of Scripture in Reformed Theology: Truth and Trust*. Leiden: Brill, 2008.

Vanderveken Daniel, and Susumu Kubo. "Introduction." In *Essays in Speech Act Theory*, edited by Daniel Vanderveken and Susumu Kubo, 1–22. Philadelphia: John Benjamins, 2002.

Vanhoozer, Kevin. "Lost in Translation? Truth, Scripture, and Hermeneutics." *Journal of the Evangelical Theological Society* 48 (2005): 89–114.

———. "On the Very Idea of a Theological System." In *Always Reforming: Explorations in Systematic Theology*, edited by Andrew McGowan, 125–82. Downers Grove, IL: InterVarsity Press, 2006.

———. *The Drama of Doctrine: A Canonical Linguistic Approach to Christian Theology*. Louisville, KY: Westminster John Knox, 2005.

———. "The Semantics of Biblical Literature: Truth and Scripture's Diverse Literary Forms." In *Scripture and Truth*, edited by Donald Carson and John Woodbridge, 53–104. Grand Rapids: Zondervan, 1986.

———. "Triune Discourse: Theological Reflections on the Claim that God Speaks (Part 1)." In *Trinitarian Theology for the Church: Scripture, Community, Worship*, edited by Daniel Treier and David Lauber, 25–49. Downers Grove, IL: InterVarsity Press, 2009.

———. "Triune Discourse: Theological Reflections on the Claim that God Speaks (Part 2)." In *Trinitarian Theology for the Church: Scripture, Community, Worship*, edited by Daniel Treier and David Lauber, 50–78. Downers Grove, IL: InterVarsity Press, 2009.

Vision, Gerald. *Veritas: The Correspondence Theory of Truth and Its Critics*. Cambridge, MA: MIT Press, 2009.

Volf, Miroslav. "The Challenge of Protestant Fundamentalism." In *Fundamentalism as an Ecumenical Challenge*, edited by Hans Küng and Jürgen Moltmann, 97–106. London: SCM Press, 1992.

Walhout, Clarence. "Narrative Hermeneutics." In *The Promise of Hermeneutics* by R. Lundin, C. Walhout, and A. Thiselton, 65–132. Grand Rapids: Eerdmans, 1999.

Waltke, Bruce. "Interaction with Peter Enns." *Westminster Theological Journal* 71 (2009): 115–28.

———. "Revisiting *Inspiration and Incarnation*." *Westminster Theological Journal* 71 (2009): 83–95.

Walton, John. *The Lost World of Genesis One: Ancient Cosmology and the Origins Debate.* Grand Rapids: InterVarsity, 2009.

Wang, Hao. *Beyond Analytic Philosophy: Doing Justice to What We Know.* Cambridge, MA: The MIT Press, 1986.

Ward, Timothy. *Word and Supplement: Speech Acts, Biblical Texts, and the Sufficiency of Scripture.* New York: Oxford, 2002.

———. *Words of Life: Scripture as the Living and Active Word of God.* Downers Grove, IL: InterVarsity Press, 2009.

Watson, Francis. "Hermeneutics and the Doctrine of Scripture: Why They Need Each Other." *International Journal of Systematic Theology* 12 (2010): 118–43.

Webb, William. *Slaves, Women and Homosexuals: Exploring the Hermeneutics of Cultural Analysis.* Downers Grove, IL: InterVarsity Press, 2001.

Webster, John. "The Dogmatic Location of the Canon." *Neue Zeitschrift für Systematische Theologie und Religionsphilosophie* 43 (2001): 17–43.

———. "Hermeneutics in Modern Theology: Some Doctrinal Reflections." *Scottish Journal of Theology* 51 (1998): 307–41.

———. "Locality and Catholicity: Reflections on Theology and the Church." *Scottish Journal of Theology* 45 (1992): 1–18.

———. "Reading Theology." *Toronto Journal of Theology* 13 (1997): 53–63.

———. "Resurrection and Scripture." In *Christology and Scripture: Interdisciplinary Perspectives*, edited by Andrew Lincoln and Angus Paddison, 138–55. New York: T & T Clark, 2008.

Welsch, Wolfgang. "Richard Rorty: Philosophy beyond Argument and Truth?" In *The Pragmatic Turn in Philosophy: Contemporary Engagements between Analytic and Continental Thought*, edited by W. Egginton and M. Sandbothe, 163–86. Albany, NY: State University of New York Press, 2004.

Westphal, Merold. *Whose Community? Which Interpretation? Philosophical Hermeneutics for the Church.* Grand Rapids: Baker, 2009.

Wheeler, Samuel. *Deconstruction as Analytic Philosophy.* Stanford: Stanford University Press, 2000.

Wilkens, Steve, and Don Thorsen. *Everything You Know about Evangelicals Is Wrong (Well, Almost Everything): An Insider's Look at Myths and Realities.* Grand Rapids: Baker, 2010.

Williams, A. N. "Tradition." In *The Oxford Handbook of Systematic Theology*, edited by John Webster, Kathryn Tanner and Iain Torrance, 362–77. New York: Oxford University Press, 2007.

Williams, Bernard. *Truth and Truthfulness: An Essay on Genealogy.* Princeton, NJ: Princeton University Press, 2002.

Williams, David. "Scripture, Truth and Our Postmodern Context." In *Evangelicals and Scripture: Tradition, Authority and Hermeneutics*, edited by Vincent Bacote, Laura Miguélez, and Dennis Okholm, 229–43. Grand Rapids: InterVarsity, 2004.

Williams, Ritva. *Stewards, Prophets, Keepers of the Word: Leadership in the Early Church.* Peabody, MA: Hendrickson Publishers, 2006.

Wimbush, Vincent. "And the Students Shall Teach Them . . . : The Study of the Bible and the Study of Meaning Construction." In *The Bible and the American Myth: A*

Symposium on the Bible and Constructions of Meaning, edited by Vincent Wimbush, 1–12. Macon, GA: Mercer University Press, 1999.

Witherington, Ben. *The Living Word of God: Rethinking the Theology of the Bible*. Waco, TX: Baylor University Press, 2007.

Wittgenstein, Ludwig. *Philosophical Investigations*. Translated by G. E. M. Anscombe. Malden, MA: Blackwell, 1997.

Wolterstorff, Nicholas. *Divine Discourse: Philosophical Reflections on the Claim that God Speaks*. New York: Cambridge University Press, 1995.

———. "Postscript: A Life in Philosophy." In *Practices of Belief: Selected Essays*. New York: Cambridge University Press, 2009.

———. "The Importance of Hermeneutics for a Christian World View." In *Disciplining Hermeneutics: Interpretation in Christian Perspective*, edited by Roger Lundin, 25–48. Grand Rapids: Eerdmans, 1997.

———. "The Promise of Speech Act Theory for Biblical Interpretation." In *After Pentecost: Language and Biblical Interpretation*, edited by Craig Bartholomew, Colin Greene, and Karl Möller, 73–96. Grand Rapids: Zondervan, 2001.

Woodbridge, John. *Biblical Authority: A Critique of the Rogers/McKim Proposal*. Grand Rapids: Zondervan, 1982.

———. "Evangelical Self-Identity and the Doctrine of Inerrancy." In *Understanding the Times: New Testament Studies in the 21st Century: Essays in Honor of D. A. Carson on the Occasion of His 65th Birthday*, edited by Andreas Köstenberger and Robert Yarbrough, 105–38. Wheaton, IL: Crossway, 2011.

Woodbridge, John, and Randall Balmer. "The Princetonians and Biblical Authority." In *Scripture and Truth*, edited by Donald Carson and John Woodbridge, 251–86. Grand Rapids: Zondervan, 1983.

Work, Telford. *Living and Active: Scripture in the Economy of Salvation*. Grand Rapids: Eerdmans, 2002.

Wright, Edmond. *Narrative, Perception, Language and Faith*. New York: Palgrave Macmillan, 2005.

Wright, N. T. *Following Jesus: Biblical Reflections on Discipleship*. Grand Rapids: Eerdmans, 1994.

———. *Kingdom New Testament: A Contemporary Translation*. New York: HarperCollins, 2011.

Wright, Terry. *Providence Made Flesh: Divine Presence as a Framework for a Theology of Providence*. Eugene, OR: Pickwick Publications, 2009.

Wuthnow, Robert, and Matthew Lawson, "Sources of Christian Fundamentalism in the United States." In *Accounting for Fundamentalisms: The Dynamic Character of Movements*. The Fundamentalist Project Volume 4. Edited by. M. Marty and R. S. Appleby, 18–56. Chicago: University of Chicago Press, 1994.

Wylie, Alison. "Arguments for Scientific Realism: The Ascending Spiral." *American Philosophical Quarterly* 23 (1986): 287–97.

Wyrick, Jed. *The Ascension of Authorship: Attribution and Canon Formation in Jewish, Hellenistic, and Christian Traditions*. Cambridge, MA: Harvard University Press, 2004.

Yarbrough, Robert. "The Embattled Bible: Four More Books." *Themelios* 34 (2009): 6–25.

Young, D. "A Mathematical Approach to Certain Dynastic Spans in the Sumerian King List." *Journal of Near Eastern Studies* 47 (1988): 123–29.

Young, Davis A. *The Biblical Flood: A Case Study of the Church's Response to Extrabiblical Evidence*. Grand Rapids: Eerdmans, 1995.

Young, Francis M. *Virtuoso Theology: The Bible and Interpretation*. Pilgrim Press, 1992; repr. Wipf and Stock, 2002.

Young, S. "Inerrantist Scholarship on Daniel: A Valid Historical Enterprise?" In *Interdisciplinary Perspectives on the Authority of Scripture: Historical, Biblical and Theoretical Perspectives*, edited by C. Bovell, 204–35. Eugene, OR: Pickwick Publications, 2011.

Zaspel, Fred G. *The Theology of B. B. Warfield: A Systematic Summary*. Wheaton, IL: Crossway, 2010.

Made in the USA
Lexington, KY
19 July 2012